Abraham Lincoln:
God's Humble Instrument

Millennial Mind Publishing
An imprint of American Book Publishing
5442 So. 900 East, #146
Salt Lake City, UT 84117-7204
www.american-book.com
Printed in the United States of America on acid-free paper.

Abraham Lincoln: God's Humble Instrument

Designed by Ahmad Shadman, design@american-book.com

ISBN-13: 978-1-58982-518-5
ISBN-10: 1-58982-518-7

Library of Congress Cataloging-in-Publication Data available by request. E-mail info@american-book.com.

Special Sales

These books are available at special discounts for bulk purchases. Special editions, including personalized covers, excerpts of existing books, and corporate imprints, can be created in large quantities for special needs. For more information e-mail info@american-book.com.

Abraham Lincoln: God's Humble Instrument

Ron L. Andersen

Dedication

This book is gratefully dedicated to the Almighty God, the author of this nation's "new birth of freedom" that was superintended by His humble instrument, Abraham Lincoln.

Table of Contents

Introduction

On the eve of the Civil War, America found itself in a state quite different from that envisioned by our Founding Fathers. This nation had drifted far from the hoped-for state of all men being treated with respect and equality. America was not a nation that embraced law, order, or racial equality, nor did it honor the freedom of speech and of religion guaranteed in the Constitution.

Instead, in the 1850s, quite arguably America's darkest decade, the United States Congress passed, and the president of the United States signed into law, the Kansas-Nebraska Act—making the enslavement of black Americans a legal right for white Americans, as well as a choice through the ballot box, for newly created territories to the West. Three years later in 1857, the United States Supreme Court ruled in the Dred Scott case that the Negro is a "being of an inferior order" and thereby unfit to receive all of the inalienable rights guaranteed by the Constitution.

It was during this same decade that the Declaration of Independence was assailed for its "foolish" statement that "all men are created equal." This was repeatedly declared in the halls of Congress and in newspapers throughout the country. This self-evident truth was decried as a self-evident lie by many Americans.

And from the pulpits of Christian churches North and South, preachers gave thanks to God for His gift of the black man and woman, who were to be enslaved by white Christian Americans for the purpose of amassing their wealth and prosperity, thus giving white Americans the promise of a life of ease and sophisticated aristocracy. President Lincoln responded to this in his second inaugural address near the close of the Civil War, saying, "It may seem strange that any men should dare to ask a just God's assistance in wringing their bread from the sweat of other men's faces…"[1]

Lawless mobs and vigilante groups repeatedly took the law into their own hands to burn and plunder, and to expel from their homes and farms fellow American citizens with differing opinions regarding slavery or religion. Moreover, a movement was rapidly arising to ensure that foreign immigrants be denied access to elected public office or public positions.

And if all this were not enough, Southern radicals had launched a plan for rebellion against the United States with the purpose of forming their own Confederacy of states in which the above-mentioned white Protestant superiority could prosper, unchallenged by a growing number of abolitionists in the North and by a backwoods country lawyer named Abraham Lincoln.

It was at the nadir of these moral and political declines that Lincoln told a friend, just days before his unlikely election as president and the first shots of the Civil War, "I see the storm coming and I know [God's] hand is in it…"[2]

---

[1] *The Eloquent President,* Ronald C. White, 290.
[2] *Abraham Lincoln: Man of God,* John Wesley Hill, 230.

Chapter One

"Thar's Suthin' Peculiarsome about Abe"

By the mid 1800s there were an estimated four million African slaves in America. Numerous times Abraham Lincoln expressed his fear that God was angry at the sad mistreatment of these men, women, and children by slave owners and by the state and federal governments that passed a bushel of grossly discriminatory laws to preserve the slaves' subjugation. He believed that God did not approve of wealthy merchants and slave owners—driven by greed—who had taken it upon themselves to carve up and weaken this "almost chosen" [3] nation, as Lincoln called it, by seceding from the Union for their own personal gain. There are those who believe, as did Lincoln himself, that it was by divine design that we find at the helm of this nation, at its most critical hour of civil war, an awkward, self-educated backwoodsman who possessed a singularly remarkable humility and intellect: a man whom, from his early years, God appeared to mold into the most powerful and influential president to ever lead this land. As president, Lincoln relied on the Judeo-Christian God of the Bible to a remarkable degree, and he repeatedly addressed the people of this nation with messages

---

[3] *Collected Works of Abraham Lincoln, IV*, Roy Basler, 236.

that one would expect to hear from the mouth of a prophet, not from a politician. Referring to God, on whom Lincoln so completely relied, he said:

> I have had so many evidences of His direction, so many instances when I have been controlled by some other power than my own will, that I cannot doubt that this power comes from above. I frequently see my way clear to a decision when I am conscious that I have not sufficient facts upon which to found it. But I cannot recall one instance in which I have followed my own judgment founded upon such a decision, where the results were unsatisfactory; whereas, in almost every instance where I have yielded to the views of others I have had occasion to regret it. [4]

Lincoln had a consuming sense and conviction that God created this nation for some higher purpose and that the political events and social trends of this nation culminating in the mid 1800s had, for some time, been diverging from that destiny. He believed that this political and moral drift from the original intentions of the Founding Fathers had angered the Living God, as Lincoln referred to Him who authored its inception, and that the Civil War was the Almighty's judgment for the nation's sins. Of the Founding Fathers, Lincoln said:

> I recollect thinking then, boy even though I was, that there must have been something more than common that those men struggled for. I am exceedingly anxious that that thing which they struggled for; that something even

---

[4] *Abraham Lincoln: Man of God*, John Wesley Hill, 124.

more than National Independence; that something that held great promise to all the people of the world to all time to come; I am exceedingly anxious that this Union, the Constitution, and the liberties of the people shall be perpetuated in accordance with the original idea for which the struggle was made, and I shall be most happy indeed if I shall be an humble instrument in the hands of the Almighty, and of this, his almost chosen people, for perpetuating the object of that great struggle.[5]

As president, Lincoln frequently referred to his resolve to do the will of God. On one occasion, he said, "It is my earnest desire to know the will of Providence in this matter. And when I can learn what it is, I will do it!"[6] William J. Wolf, author of *The Almost Chosen People*, said,

In this sense Lincoln is one of the greatest theologians of America—not in the technical meaning of producing a system of doctrine, certainly not as the defender of some one denomination, but in the sense of seeing the hand of God intimately in the affairs of nations. Just so the prophets of Israel criticized the events of their day from the perspective of the God Who is concerned for history and Who reveals His will within it. Lincoln stands among God's latter-day prophets.[7]

---

[5] *Collected Works of Abraham Lincoln, IV*, Roy Basler, 23.
[6] *The Almost Chosen People*, William J. Wolf, 22.
[7] *The Almost Chosen People*, William J. Wolf, 24.

On another occasion during the raging Civil War, Lincoln said,

> We are indeed going through a trial—a fiery trial. In the very responsible position in which I happen to be placed, being a humble instrument in the hands of our heavenly Father, as I am, and as we all are, to work out His great purposes, I have desired that all my works and acts may be according to His will; and that it might be so, I have sought his aid—but if after endeavoring to do my best in the light which He affords me, I find my efforts fail, I must believe that for some purpose unknown to me, He wills it otherwise.[8]

In the remarkable line of successes that contributed to this nation's establishment and survival, slavery was already an insidious threat to these freedoms and government. The human rights and dignity of millions of African men, women, and children, whose only differences from the white Americans were the color of their skin and their restricted opportunities for education and self-development. A web of deceit developed that was fueled by unparalleled wealth on the part of the slave owners and proslavery politicians, a wealth that would move men and women to accept and then embrace every conceivable measure, including the creation of laws and judicial rulings to protect the abominable practice of enslavement for the purpose of protecting their river of free-flowing wealth and self-aggrandizement. This unbridled avarice would lead to a dangerously destructive blow to this strongest nation on earth with the Southern slave states' secession. With the states' rights zeal thus

---

[8] *Abraham Lincoln's Daily Treasure*, edited by Thomas Freiling, 253.

4

reinforced, as well as the extreme depth of division on the institution of slavery and other political issues, the end result—had the Southern states been successful—could easily have been an American continent dotted from coast to coast with individual nation-states, many polluted with the continued inhumanity of slavery. And instead of remaining the strongest nation on the earth, it would have been a grouping of self-interested, intensely divided, and weakened nation-states, leaving the Constitution vulnerable to those whose aim was to change it.

Lincoln reflected his awareness of the impending danger when he used a Biblical phrase to describe the tenuous situation in America: a "house divided against itself shall not stand."[9] He believed that the divisive nature of the slavery issue threatened the very existence of this nation. Sensing "something more than common"[10] for which our Founding Fathers strove, Lincoln carried the deepest conviction that this nation was formed for a wise purpose known to God, and he believed that its preservation was of the utmost importance not just to the nation, but also to the world and future generations of the world. Prior to his election to the Presidency he said, "Our political problem now is 'Can we, as a nation, continue together *permanently—forever*—half slave, and half free?' The problem is too mighty for me. May God, in his mercy, superintend the solution."[11] Moreover, in the four months between his election as president in November 1860 and his inauguration in March of 1861, the nation to the North passively watched, and many encouraged the dramatic division of this nation through the secession of the Southern states. Abraham Lincoln would take his oath of office to protect the nation and would stand resolute in preserving the Union of states, frequently expressing his conviction that God

---

[9] *Holy Bible, Matthew* 12:25.
[10] *Collected Works of Abraham Lincoln , IV,* Roy Basler, 23.
[11] *Collected Works of Abraham Lincoln , IV,* Roy Basler, 23.

willed that this nation remain whole, that the freedoms proffered in the Constitution be preserved, and that the slaves be set free. The eventual abolishment of slavery and the preservation of both the Union and the Constitution came at a ghastly price of death and destruction that would be unleashed upon the citizens of the United States in the form of civil war—a maelstrom that the promoters of secession and slavery never imagined.

There is an ocean of recorded firsthand experiences of Lincoln's character, his sense of purpose, and his leadership. Of the thousands of books that are written on Lincoln, a handful of them have focused on his faith. One of those was a book written in 1920 by William Barton entitled *The Soul of Lincoln*. Barton interviewed hundreds of those who knew Lincoln, and collected thousands of letters, manuscripts, and documents about his life. "Barton's inquiry ultimately brought him to this conclusion: Abraham Lincoln believed and professed faith in the Christian God. He read the Bible, he believed the New Testament message, and believed God both listened to and answered his prayers"[12] "I talk to God," President Lincoln once told General Daniel Sickles, "because my mind is relieved when I do."[13] He added, "When I could not see any other resort, I would place my whole reliance in God, knowing that all would be well, and that He would decide for the right."[14]

Abraham Lincoln was born in Kentucky, on February 12, 1809, in the midst of an enormous religious revival in America, referred to as the Second Great Awakening. Western Kentucky was regarded to be the epicenter of this revival. It is recorded that on one summer Sunday young Abraham and his family attended a sermon where the preacher "yelled, shrieked, wrung his hands in sobs of hysterics, until a row of women were laid out to rest and recover in the shade of an oak tree, after they

---

[12] *Abraham Lincoln's Daily Treasures*, edited by Thomas Freiling, 8.

[13] *Abraham Lincoln's Daily Treasures*, edited by Thomas Freiling, 11.

[14] *Abraham Lincoln's Daily Treasures*, edited by Thomas Freiling, 11.

had moaned, shaken, danced up and down, worn themselves out with 'the jerks' and fainted."[15] Young Abraham was noted to have looked on soberly, being left more troubled than inspired by the spectacle. During this era one often paid a price for expressing doubts about the contents of a preacher's delivery. William J. Wolf observes, "The tactic of backwoods religion in meeting skeptical criticism was to shout it down as a work of the devil."[16]

Abraham's father, Thomas, a man of faith and an itinerate, and mostly unsuccessful, farmer and carpenter, was caught up in the spirited revival of conflicting doctrines that broiled in Western Kentucky where Methodists, Baptists, and Presbyterian preachers competed for converts. In 1816 the Lincolns moved a few miles north to southern Indiana. Here Thomas was chosen by the local church committee to direct the building of the Little Pigeon log meetinghouse. Thomas built the pulpit, window casings, and cabinets for the tiny chapel, and it is very likely that his only son Abraham assisted with the project. Thomas Lincoln, his wife, and his daughter Sarah joined the Pigeon Creek Baptist Church in Illinois, but fourteen-year-old Abraham made no move to join. This was not due to a lack of religious interest on Abraham's part, for his mother, a woman of deep faith in God who had a profound influence on him, read from the Bible to Abraham and his sister from the time they could understand. By this period in Abraham's young life he himself was an avid reader of the Bible and he continued to willingly attend the sermons with his family. There are a number of accounts by Lincoln's acquaintances that confirm a deep faith in God and also some doubts regarding certain widely accepted doctrinal tenets espoused by the Protestant religions. We do, however, have record of his

---

[15] *Abraham Lincoln The Prairie Years*, Carl Sandburg, 37.
[16] *Almost Chosen People*, William J. Wolf, 40.

7

speaking and writing often, as an adult, of his love of the Bible teachings and his determination to follow them.

Lincoln knew little about the family of his mother, Nancy Hanks. They came to Kentucky from Virginia in 1780. Most of them were illiterate but respectable farmers. Lincoln's law partner in Springfield claims that on a one-horse-buggy ride from Springfield to Petersburg in the early 1850s, Lincoln told him that he believed his mother to be the illegitimate daughter of Lucy Hanks and a "well bred Virginia farmer or planter."[17]

On Abraham's father's side, Samuel Lincoln, a weaver in the County of Norfolk England, immigrated to Massachusetts in 1637 where he became prosperous as a businessman and respected as a pillar in his church. Seven generations later Thomas Lincoln and Nancy Hanks were married. Thomas Lincoln built a one-room log cabin, measuring sixteen feet by eighteen feet. It had no glass windows and a dirt floor; a typical cabin for the region and time. It was in this cabin, on a cold February 12, 1809, near Hogdonville, Kentucky, that the second child of Thomas and Nancy Hanks Lincoln—a son—was born. He was named after Thomas' father, Abraham.

Thomas often told young Abraham and his older sister, Sarah, the story of their grandfather Abraham, who, after hearing of the fertile land in Kentucky from their distant relative Daniel Boone, sold his farm in Virginia and moved his wife and five children to Kentucky, where he eventually owned 5,544 acres of the richest land in Kentucky. One day in 1786, the senior Abraham and his three sons Mordecai, Josiah, and eight-year-old Thomas were planting a cornfield when they were suddenly attacked by Indians. Abraham was killed instantly. Fifteen-year-old Mordecai ran to the cabin and sent Josiah to the settlement for help. Peering through the logs in the cabin, he saw young

---

[17] *Lincoln,* David Herbert Donald, 20.

Thomas sitting in the field by his father's body while an Indian quietly crept out of the forest toward Thomas. Mordecai picked up a rifle and "aimed at the silver pendant on the Indian's chest,"[18] and killed him before he could reach his brother. Lincoln later in life said that "the legend more strongly than all others imprinted upon my mind and memory."[19]

Unbeknownst to young Thomas at the time, this tragedy would abruptly end his prospects of prosperity as an heir to his father's estate. The law, following the ancient rule of primogeniture, was still in effect, making the oldest son, Mordecai, the only heir to his father's wealth. Mordecai became the only Lincoln relative whom Abraham ever knew, of whom Lincoln once said, "Uncle Mord had run off with all of the talent of the family."[20] While Mordecai became a respected citizen, horse breeder, and a man of considerable property, Josiah and Thomas were left with nothing and had to fend for themselves. Mordecai later moved north to Hancock County, Illinois.

Abraham has no recollection of his birthplace, his family having moved, when he was just two years old ten miles northeast to a small farm and another one-room cabin on Knob Creek. Here, Lincoln had memories of working a big field with his father and of the beautiful setting of the farm, nestled between two small hills and the crystal clear Knob Creek. It was at this place that his mother gave birth to a third child, Thomas, who died in infancy, no doubt leaving young Abraham, Sarah, and their parents to grieve the loss.

Land title problems arose in Kentucky, prompting Thomas to move the young family again in 1816. Abraham was seven years old when the family tearfully said their last goodbye to baby Thomas, lying in his solitary grave in Redmon Cemetery, and then rumbled away in their wagon filled with their belong-

---

[18] *Lincoln,* David Herbert Donald, 21.
[19] *Lincoln,* David Herbert Donald, 21.
[20] *The Story Life of Abraham Lincoln,* Wayne Whipple, 18.

ings to the north, across the Ohio River into southern Indiana. Lincoln later said that this move to another state was also "partly on account of slavery."[21] Thomas Lincoln did not agree with slavery and quite likely taught the same thinking to his children. In 1864 Lincoln referred to himself as "naturally anti-slavery," further stating, "I cannot remember when I did not so think and feel."[22] The new homestead was on Little Pigeon Creek in Spencer County, and was so remote in an unbroken forest that part of the trek was made with neither road nor trail, with Thomas and Abraham hacking out a path so the family could arrive at their new homestead. Here Thomas built a "half-faced camp,"[23] a shelter with three walls, a roof, no floor, and the fourth side open to the elements. A fire was kept night and day at the open side of the shelter. In this they lived until Thomas and neighboring farmers could build a cabin. It was a wild and lonely region with the nearest neighbors living one and two miles away. Many years later Lincoln revisited the place and remembered it with this verse:

> When first my father settled here,
> 'Twas then the frontier line:
> The panther's scream, filled night with fear
> And bears preyed on the swine.[24]

Their first year's "backbreaking toil and...desperate loneliness for all the family"[25] was much relieved when Nancy's aunt and uncle, Elizabeth (Hanks) and Tom Sparrow, moved nearby. They brought with them, much to the delight of Sarah and Abraham, the fun loving eighteen-year-old Dennis Hanks, the

---

[21] *Lincoln,* David Herbert Donald, 23.

[22] *Lincoln,* David Herbert Donald, p 24

[23] *Lincoln,* David Herbert Donald, p 25

[24] *Lincoln,* David Herbert Donald, p 24

[25] *Lincoln,* David Herbert Donald, p 24

illegitimate nephew of Elizabeth, whom they had known earlier in Kentucky.

Their delight was short lived. Soon after the Sparrows' arrival, Abraham was kicked in the forehead by a horse, leaving him bleeding and unconscious for nearly a day. Some believed that he was dead; however, he did revive, save for being unable to speak for several hours.

At about that same time a devastating sickness passed through the region bringing dizziness, nausea, and stomach pain. These conditions progressed to irregular respiration and pulse, and then coma, resulting in death six or seven days later. The settlers correctly surmised that the sickness was connected with the cow's milk they drank, although it wasn't until years later that scientists discovered that it came from a poisonous white snakeroot plant that the cows ate as they grazed loose in the forest. Tom and Elizabeth Sparrow were the first afflicted and they both succumbed. As Thomas was building their coffins, his wife, Nancy, fell ill with the milk-sick, as they called it. She languished for several days suffering the same symptoms as the Sparrows; Dennis Hanks remembered, "She knew she was going to die and she called the children to her dying side and told them to be good and kind to their father, to one another, and to the world, expressing hope that they might live as they had been taught by her to love men, love reverence, and worship God."[26] He continued,

> Here in this rude house, of the milk sickness, died one of the very best women in the whole race, known for kindness, tenderness, charity, and love to the world. Mrs. Lincoln always taught Abe goodness, kindness, read

[26] *Lincoln, An Illustrated Biography*, Philip B. Kunhardt Jr.,Philip Kunhardt III,Peter W. Kunhardt p 38

the good Bible to him, taught him to read and
to spell, taught him sweetness and benevo-
lence as well...[27]

She died on October 5, 1818, and was buried on a wooded
knoll next to the Sparrows. Burials were usually done within a
day of death and Nancy's was done without a formal funeral
service. This was common on the frontier because there was
often no preacher in the area. Settlers relied on itinerate preachers, who passed through the region to hold services and provided the sought-after closure. Because of this, funeral services
were often held weeks or even months after the burial when a
preacher became available. Stories vary on nine-year-old Abraham's role in his mother's funeral. One states that he wrote a
letter to a preacher asking him to conduct the service. Another
version, by Rose Strunsky, avers,

> The boy Abraham had his standards of
> life. There were things of too much meaning
> to let pass without some gesture. And the un-
> ceremonious burial in the forest haunted him.
> When he heard that a wandering preacher had
> reached the neighborhood he tramped many
> miles through the snow to bring him to the
> spot where the dead body lay, so that a funer-
> al sermon might be delivered over the now
> white grave.[28]

Dennis Hanks moved in with the Lincolns and helped with
the hunting and farming; he also helped to raise the spirits of
the remaining Lincolns as they grieved the loss of their wife

---

[27] *Lincoln, An Illustrated Biography,* Philip B. Kunhardt Jr.,Philip Kunhardt
III,Peter W. Kunhardt p 38
[28] *The Soul of Lincoln,* William E. Barton, p 40

and mother. Twelve-year-old Sarah felt so lonesome at times that she would sit by the fire and cry. In their efforts to console her, Dennis later recalled, "me 'n' Abe got 'er a baby coon an' a turtle, an' tried to get a fawn but we couldn't ketch any."[29] We have no written record of Lincoln's sadness at his mother's passing but in later years he wrote a letter to a bereaved child in which he said, "In this sad world of ours, sorrow comes to all; and to the young, it comes with bitterest agony, because it takes them unawares...I have had experience enough to know what I say."[30] By age nine, Abraham Lincoln personally knew the "bitterest agony" of losing an infant brother, his aunt and uncle, and then his beloved mother. He would later in life also know the unspeakable grief of losing his only sister and two adored sons.

It has been suggested by some historians that the death of Lincoln's mother and her charge to be "good and kind...to the world"[31] influenced his superior level of kindness, humility, and charity. Her loving deathbed charge coupled with his lifelong search for divine truth in the Bible, by which he must certainly have been influenced by reading of the kindness and righteousness of Jesus, were probably catalysts for Abraham Lincoln's becoming one of the more singular examples of a Christ-like life in all of history.

An early example of his compassionate nature was an account by Lincoln himself in 1817. Just prior to his eighth birthday he spotted a flock of wild turkeys outside the new and unfinished cabin. Knowing that their very survival depended on successful hunting, he took the gun and, through an open chink of the logs, "shot through a crack, and killed one of them." It hurt him so deeply to have killed the animal that he said, "I

---

[29] *Lincoln,* David Herbert Donald, p 26

[30] *Lincoln,* David Herbert Donald, p 27

[31] *Lincoln, An Illustrated Biography,* Philip B. Kunhardt Jr.,Philip Kunhardt III,Peter W. Kunhardt p 38

never since pulled a trigger on any larger animal."[32] After his
mother's death, he was known to reprove other children for
senseless cruelty to animals. He was remembered to have scold-
ed them when he observed that they would catch terrapins and
place hot coals on their backs to force them from their shells.
He told them "that an ant's life was to it as sweet as ours was to
us."[33]

The grief of the Lincoln family at the passing of their mother and wife was soon tempered by the arrival of Thomas' new
wife, Sarah Bush Johnston. Thomas could see that his family
was faring poorly in the absence of their wife and mother, so
thirteen months after Nancy's death, on a cold November day,
he struck out for Kentucky with Sarah on his mind. He traveled
on lonely roads, crossing the Ohio River to Elizabethtown with
the hope of returning home with a wife. Arriving at the door of
young widowed Sarah, with her three small children, he "argued
straight-out: 'I have no wife and you have no husband. I came
a-purpose to marry you. I knowed you from a gal and you
knowed me from a boy. I've no time to lose; and if you're
willin' let it be done straight off.'" Her answer: "I got a few little
debts."[34] She made him a list; he paid them, and they were married December 2, 1819.

Sarah Bush Lincoln's arrival marked a turning point in the
life of the young and grieving Abraham. David Herbert Donald
describes her remarkable entry into the Lincoln's life:

> She brought with her, first, her collection of
> domestic possessions—comfortable bedding, a
> walnut bureau that had cost her forty-five dol-
> lars, a table and chairs, a spinning wheel, knives,

---

[32] *Lincoln*, David Herbert Donald p 27

[33] *Lincoln*, David Herbert Donald p 27

[34] *Lincoln, An Illustrated Biography*, Philip B. Kunhardt Jr.,Philip Kunhardt
III,Peter W. Kunhardt p 12

forks, and spoons—so that the Lincoln children felt they were joining a world of unbelievable luxury. Her children—Elizabeth, John D., and Matilda, who ranged from thirteen to eight years in age—brought life and excitement to the depressed Lincoln family. But most of all she brought with her the gift of love. Sarah Bush Lincoln must have been touched to see the dirty, ill-clad, hungry Lincoln children, and she set to work at once, as she said, to make them look "more human. She soaped—rubbed and washed the children clean," Dennis Hanks remembered, "so that they look[ed] pretty neat—well and clean."[35]

At her suggestion, the whole household was reorganized. Thomas Lincoln and Dennis Hanks had to give up hunting for a while to split logs and make a floor for the cabin, and they finished the roof, constructed a proper door, and cut a hole for a window, which they covered with greased paper. The cabin was high enough to install a loft, reached by climbing pegs driven into the wall, and here she installed beds for the three boys Dennis Hanks, Abraham, and John D. Downstairs she had the whole cabin cleaned, a decent bedstead was built, and Thomas used his skill as a carpenter to make another table and stools. Remarkably, these reforms were brought about with a minimum of friction.[36]

---

[35] *Lincoln,* David Herbert Donald, p 27
[36] *Lincoln,* David Herbert Donald, p 27

What was even more extraordinary was that Sarah Bush Lincoln was able to blend the two families harmoniously and without jealousy. She treated her own children and the Lincoln children with absolute impartiality. She grew especially fond of Abraham. "I never gave him a cross word in all my life…His mind and mine—what little I had—seemed to move together—move in the same channel."[37] Many years later, when asked to compare her son and her stepson, she told an interviewer, "Both were good boys, but I must say—both now being dead that Abe was the best boy I ever saw or ever expect to see."[38]

Starved for a mother's affection, Abraham returned her love. He called her "Mama," and he never spoke of her except in the most affectionate terms. After he had been elected president, he recalled the sorry condition of Thomas Lincoln's household before Sarah Bush Johnston arrived, and told of the encouragement she had given him as a boy. "She had been his best friend in this world," a relative reported him as saying, "and…no man could love a mother more than he loved her."[39] After the death of Nancy Hanks and the arrival of his new mother, Lincoln always referred to Nancy, endearingly, as his "angel mother" to distinguish between the two.

Even though Sarah and Thomas were themselves illiterate, they did what they could to educate their children. Abraham attended school at different periods throughout his youth, the aggregate of which amounted to about one year. Sarah described Abraham as being driven to master all that he read and heard. "He must understand everything—even to the smallest thing—minutely and exactly. He would repeat it over and over to himself again and again…and when it was fixed in his mind to suit him he…never lost that fact or his understanding of

---

[37] *Team of Rivals*, Doris Kearns Goodwin, p. 49

[38] *The intimate World of Abraham Lincoln*, C. A. Tripp, p. 29

[39] *Lincoln*, David Herbert Donald, p 28

it."[40] Referring to his mind, he later recalled, "It was very hard to scratch anything on it and almost impossible after you get it there to rub it out."[41]

Before long, adult neighbors in the area were approaching him to write letters for them. Dennis Hanks remembered, "Abe was getting hungry for book[s], reading everything he could get his hands on."[42] He took books with him to the fields to read during rest periods. John Hanks recalls Abraham's routine upon returning from the work of the day: "He would go to the cupboard, snatch a piece of cornbread, take down a book, sit down in a chair, cock his legs up as high as his head, and read."[43] The other possession of great import that Sarah Bush brought to the Lincolns was her books. Although there were only a few, Abraham devoured them. They included the Bible, *Aesop's Fables*, and *The Pilgrims' Pride*. John Hanks remembered, "He kept the Bible and *Aesop's Fables* always within reach, and read them over and over again."[44] Sarah remembered, "When he came across a passage that struck him, he would write it down on boards if he had no paper and keep it there till he did get paper—then he would re-write it—look at it and repeat it."[45]

He had a deep fascination with writing. He would scrawl words with charcoal, and shape them in dirt, in sand and in snow. This embryonic fascination would eventually develop into, arguably, one of the greatest writing faculties possessed by the greatest communicator this nation would ever know, and upon whom this same nation, some forty years hence, would so desperately rely.

---

[40] *Lincoln,* David Herbert Donald, p 29

[41] *Lincoln, An Illustrated Biography,* Philip B. Kunhardt Jr.,Philip Kunhardt III,Peter W. Kunhardt p 39

[42] *Lincoln,* David Herbert Donald, p 30

[43] *Lincoln,* David Herbert Donald, p 30

[44] *The Soul of Abraham Lincoln*, William E. Barton, p 47

[45] *Lincoln,* David Herbert Donald, p 30

Dennis would make Abe homemade ink from blackberry briar root and copperas, an "ornery ink,"[46] and Abe would fashion pens from a turkey buzzard feathers. Dennis remembered, "He would write his name and say, 'Denny look at that, will you?' *Abraham Lincoln!* That stands fur me. Don't look a blamed bit like me!"[47] "And," Dennis said, "He'd stand and study it a spell. 'Peared to mean a heap to Abe.'"[48] "Aunt Sairy's never let the children pester him. She always said Abe was goin' to be a great man some day. An' she wasn't goin' to have him hindered."[49]

Sarah Bush Lincoln remembered,

> He was the best boy I ever saw. He never told me a lie in his life, never evaded, never quarreled, never dodged nor turned a corner to avoid any chastisement or other responsibility. He never swore or used profane language in my presence nor in others' that I remember of…He loved children well, very well.[50]

He was fascinated by history and biographies. He enjoyed the autobiography of Benjamin Franklin—a poor boy who raised himself to greatness on principles of integrity and faith—and most especially the *Life of George Washington*, the singular and God-fearing leader of this nation's independence and democracy. Lincoln's admiration of the Founding Fathers was expressed later with "I recollect thinking then, boy even though I was, that

---

[46] *Abraham Lincoln*, Carl Sandburg, p 13
[47] *Abraham Lincoln*, Carl Sandburg, p 13
[48] *Abraham Lincoln*, Carl Sandberg, p 13
[49] *Abraham Lincoln*, Carl Sandberg, p 13
[50] *Lincoln, An Illustrated Biography*, Philip B. Kunhardt Jr.,Philip Kunhardt III,Peter W. Kunhardt p 39

there must have been something more than common that those men struggled for."[51]

Abraham was always taller than other children his age. To school he wore a coonskin cap, buckskin breeches, and moccasins. "The way we all dressed them days,"[52] Dennis recalled. For winter snow they had "birch bark, with hickory bark soles, stropped on over yarn socks."[53] Most school sessions were held during winter months, so in this fashion the Lincoln children would walk for up to four miles to attend. One classmate remembered, "There was bare and naked six or more inches of Abe Lincoln's shin bone."[54] David Donald describes his young life in *Lincoln* this way: "Unconscious of his peculiar appearance, he would rapidly gather the other students around him, cracking jokes, telling stories, making plans. Almost from the beginning he took his place as leader. His classmates admired his ability to tell stories and make rhymes, and they enjoyed his public speaking pranks. In their eyes he was clearly exceptional and he carried away from his brief schooling the self-confidence of a man who has never met his intellectual equal."[55] Yet through it all, it was frequently noted that Abraham, in sharp contrast to other men and boys on the frontier, did not swear, smoke, chew, drink, or despise Negroes or Indians.

In the evenings, farm boys would gather at the Gentryville store and talk about how Abraham "was always diggin' into books, picking a piece of charcoal to write on a shovel, shaving off what he wrote, and then write some more." Dennis Hanks said, "Thar's suthin' peculiarsome about Abe"[56] Dennis contin-

---

[51] *The Almost Chosen People*, William J. Wolf p 24

[52] *The Boyhood of Lincoln*, Elenor Atkinson, p 12

[53] *The Boyhood of Lincoln*, Elenor Atkinson, p 12

[54] *Lincoln*, David Herbert Donald, p 32

[55] *Lincoln*, David Herbert Donald, p 32

[56] *Abraham Lincoln*, Carl Sandburg, p 13

ued, "It seemed that Abe made books tell him more than they told other people."[57] The other farm boys had gone to school and read *The Kentucky Preceptor*, but Abe picked out such a question as "Who has the most right to complain, the Indian or the Negroes?" and would talk about it, up and down in the cornfields.[58] Once hearing that court would be in session in nearby Boonville, Indiana, Abe walked the fifteen miles to watch the proceedings. He observed every detail with rapt interest as the lawyers methodically worked their cases to the juries. Captivated and intrigued by the spectacle, he was also perplexed at the unlikely prospect of doing anything with his life outside of working the land on the frontier.

By age sixteen, Abraham was a skinny but strong six feet two inches, and his family depended upon him more and more for his share of the farm work, in which he had but little interest. Most neighbors agreed that while Abe wasn't lazy, his mind was often on his books to the neglect of the daily chores. John Romine remarked, "Abe Lincoln worked for me...didn't love work half as much as his pay. He said to me one day that his father taught him to work, but he never taught him to love it."[59] Abraham's father, Thomas, was an easygoing man who according to Dennis Hanks was the only one who "could beat his son telling stories—cracking a joke."[60] Above all, Abraham was remembered by fellow settlers "for his kindliness, his sense of fair play, his helpfulness to others, his love of...animals, his ambition to excel."[61]

Abraham Lincoln was remarkably strong and would not back away from a friendly challenge of strength. At eighteen, Abe could "take an ax at the end of the handle and hold it out

---

[57] *Abraham Lincoln*, Carl Sandburg, p13
[58] *Abraham Lincoln*, Carl Sandburg, p13
[59] *Abraham Lincoln*, Carl Sandburg, p 51
[60] *Lincoln,* David Herbert Donald, p 32
[61] *Abraham Lincoln*, Benjamin P. Thomas, p 14

from his shoulders in a straight horizontal line, easy and steady."[62] Many years later, while president in his fifties, after vigorously chopping some wood while visiting some soldiers, he repeated this feat of holding steady the ax parallel to the ground, to the amazement of the much younger men who could not duplicate the show of strength. Another neighbor remembered, "He could sink an ax deeper into wood than any man I ever saw."[63] One day, the toughest brothers in the county, the Grigsbys, challenged Abraham's stepbrother John D. and him to a tag-team type of wrestling match. John D. was being beaten handily by William Grigsby, when Abraham stepped through the rowdy crowd, tagged his partner, and in short order took hold of Grigsby and tossed him from the center of the ring. At which time, it is said that Abe Lincoln called out in youthful exuberance, "I'm the big buck of this lick."[64] There is no record of anyone stepping forward to challenge his declaration.

By this time, it was becoming clear in his mind that he had to make a break from the generations of Lincoln landowners and farmers, but he had no idea what he would do or become, given the scarcity of opportunities in that region of frontier America. A year later changes occurred in Lincoln's adolescent life. His sister Sarah married and moved away. Eighteen months later she would die in childbirth, leaving Abe deeply saddened at her passing. His stepsister Matilda, who was very fond of Abraham, also married and moved away. He and Dennis Hanks got the idea of selling firewood to the steamers on the Ohio River to put a few coins in their penniless pockets, only to find that demand was slack and money was scarce. But it was the lure of the river that gave Abraham his first glimpse of opportunity for income and escape from the confinement of frontier Pigeon

---

[62] *Abraham Lincoln*, Carl Sandburg, p 14

[63] *Abraham Lincoln*, Carl Sandburg, p 14

[64] *Abraham Lincoln*, Carl Sandburg, p 15

Creek. He jumped at an offer to take a flatboat of goods to New Orleans for $8 a month. New Orleans, with its forty thousand residents, was the first city Abraham had ever visited. The large buildings, the markets, the ships at port, and the other features of a bustling city undoubtedly enthralled him. Here French was spoken as much as English, and it was in New Orleans that he first encountered slaves in large numbers and the harsh reality of slavery's inhumanity. While in New Orleans he would have undoubtedly seen advertisements such as:

> I will at all times pay the highest cash price for Negroes of every description, will also attend to the sale of Negroes on commission, having a jail and yard fitted up expressly for boarding them.[65]

Another one read:

> For sale—several likely girls from 10 to 18 years old, a woman 24, a very valuable woman 25, with three very likely children.[66]

It was here that he saw his first slave market and the haunting image of human beings in chains being sold and purchased like livestock: husbands, wives, and children separated out to different buyers, never to see each other again. He told his companion, "Boy, let's get away from this. If ever I get a chance to hit that thing [slavery] I'll hit it hard."[67] Later, to friends he said of the experience, "Slavery ran the iron into me then and

---

[65] *Abraham Lincoln the Boy, the Man*, Lloyd Ostendorf, p 55
[66] *Abraham Lincoln the Boy, the Man*, Lloyd Ostendorf, p 55
[67] *Abraham Lincoln the Boy, the Man*, Lloyd Ostendorf, p 55

there."[68] Upon his return to his family in Illinois, he dutifully handed his earned salary over to his father.

---

[68] *Abraham Lincoln the Boy, the Man*, Lloyd Ostendorf, p 55

Chapter Two

Honest Abe, the Young Bachelor

In March of 1830, Abraham was helping his father move the family to Macon County in central Illinois. Another outbreak of the "milk-sick" surfaced again in Pigeon Creek and Thomas wasn't about to have any more of that. He sold the place and headed north and west. By this time, at age twenty-one, Abraham had "reached his majority," meaning he was old enough to strike out on his own and to vote in elections. He could not be happier for the opportunity to establish a new life in Illinois, the state in which he would live the next thirty years of his life. It was a "slow and tiresome" journey slogging through mud, on poor roads, fording creeks and rivers, often breaking their way through ice. At one icy fording, Lincoln records, "My little dog jumped out of the wagon and the ice being thin he broke through and was struggling for life. I could not bear to lose my dog, and I jumped out of the wagon and waded waist deep in the ice and water, got hold of him and helped him out and saved him."[69]

That summer, after years of delivering speeches to trees, stumps, and corn stalks, Abraham Lincoln jumped at his first opportunity to deliver one to real people. He had heard that

---

[69] *Abraham Lincoln*, Carl Sandburg, p 21

two state legislative candidates were to speak at the Renshaw store in Decatur, so Lincoln made the journey and when the opportunity presented itself, he stepped forward and advocated improvement of the nearby Sangamon River for better navigation.

Their first winter in Illinois was disastrous, with snow falling to several feet deep, below-zero temperatures, and dying livestock, followed by a devastating run-off in spring that ultimately convinced Thomas to make yet another move, this time one hundred miles southeast to Coles County. This move did not include his son; Abraham had other plans and was ready to build his own life with only one thing certain in his mind: his future would not include farming.

Like a "piece of floating driftwood,"[70] as he referred to himself at that time, he headed to New Salem—an Illinois hamlet of about one hundred residents and approximately the size of Chicago in 1831. It was however the largest community in which Lincoln had ever resided. New Salem was located about fifteen miles northwest of Springfield. He hired on with hard-drinking Denton Offutt, for $12 a month, to cut down trees for the local sawmill. Offutt, observing Abe's intellect, honesty, and sobriety, would later hire him to clerk in his store. He would tell his tavern friends that Abe "knows more than anyone else in the United States."[71] Offutt also boasted of Abe's uncommon strength and prowess as a wrestler, prompting bets that Lincoln could throw Jack Armstrong, the Clary's Grove champion. Men came from miles around to view the match at Offutt's store. "They pawed and clutched in many holds and twists till Lincoln threw Armstrong and had both shoulders to the grass," at which time Armstrong's gang started toward Lincoln with shouts and threats. Abe stepped to the store wall and defiantly told the an-

---

[70] *Lincoln*, David Herbert Donald, p 38
[71] *Abraham Lincoln*, Carl Sandburg, p 24

gry gang that he would "fight, race, or wrestle any who wanted to try him."[72] Jack Armstrong suddenly broke through the crowd and gripped Abe's hand, silenced them, and said that Lincoln was "fair" and "the best feller that ever broke into this settlement."[73] The two became best of friends.

Some days after the match, the Clary's Grove boys wanted to "see what stuff Abe Lincoln had in him."[74] So they rode into New Salem, sought out their target, and issued him a series of challenges. First, he was to wrestle a man from Little Grove. "All right," Abe nodded.[75] Second, he was to run a footrace against a running champion from the nearby community of Wolf. Abe coolly responded, "Trot him out."[76] And finally they demanded that he fight a man from Sand Ridge. "Nothing wrong about that," Abe replied.[77] Abe ran faster than the champion from Wolf. In the match with the man from Little Grove, the man, "short and heavy, stripped for action, ran at Abe like a battering ram. Abe stepped aside, caught his man by the nape of the neck, threw him heels over head, and gave him a fall that nearly broke the bones."[78] Following this match a committee from the gang approached him and said, "You have sand in your craw and we will take you into our crowd."[79]

Even with this acceptance into their gang, there is no record of Abe participating in the mischief and drinking of the rowdy Clary's Grove boys, as he was never known to have indulged in either vice throughout his life. But he would, when asked, judge their horse races and cockfights, umpire their wrestling matches, and settle their disputes. A story circulated that Abe was pre-

---

[72] *Abraham Lincoln*, Carl Sandburg, p 25

[73] *Abraham Lincoln*, Carl Sandburg, p 25

[74] *Abraham Lincoln*, Carl Sandburg, p 25

[75] *Abraham Lincoln*, Carl Sandburg, p 25

[76] *Abraham Lincoln*, Carl Sandburg, p 25

[77] *Abraham Lincoln*, Carl Sandburg, p 25

[78] *Abraham Lincoln*, Carl Sandburg, p 25

[79] *Abraham Lincoln*, Carl Sandburg, p 25

sent when the gang offered a gallon jug of whiskey to an old man if he would crawl into a barrel and allow them to roll him down a hill. The old man was game for this but it is said that Abe, feared that the old man could be injured with the prank, talked and laughed them out of doing it.

Everyone in this tiny settlement soon grew fond of this awkward yet hard-working and accommodating young man who was always willing to do any kind of labor. He established himself with the men of the town, who would daily gather at the store to exchange news and gossip. Young Abraham became a favorite with his inexhaustible stream of stories and good-natured jokes. He would live the next six years in this hamlet that would grow to about three hundred residents and then just as rapidly die away; or as Lincoln said, it "winked out"[80] as people, seeing no future, moved on. He changed his boarding to the local tavern, whose owner, Henry Onstott, said of Abe, "Lincoln never drank liquor of any kind and never chewed or smoked. We never heard him swear, though Judge Weldon said…that once in his life when he was excited he said, By Jing!"[81]

During his New Salem years Lincoln would work as a store clerk, soldier, postmaster, and surveyor. He was always looking to do a kindness or watching out for the underdog. He was strong but not a bully—apparently free from bad habits of all kinds—and was known to be generous and sympathetic. It was widely told in the settlement of the time Abe had mistakenly overcharged a woman a few pennies and, upon discovering his error, walked six miles to her home to return the overpaid change. Another time he used the wrong measure to weigh an order of tea, and again upon realization of his mistake, he walked the miles to the woman's home to deliver the rest of her order. The schoolmaster recorded, "He was among the best

---

[80] *Abraham Lincoln, Autobiography 1858-1860*
[81] *Lincoln and Salem*, Henry Onstott, p 73

clerks I ever saw, he was attentive to his business—was kind and considerate to his customers and friends and always treated them with great tenderness—kindness and honesty." [82]

Business was slow at the store, leaving time for Abe to quench his thirst for books. "My best friend," he once said, "is the man who'll get me a book I ain't read."[83] Nonfiction was of only small interest to him but he loved poetry, history and biographies, although he had grown suspicious of some of these books that he felt were untrustworthy in their factual content. He was deeply in search of anything that was truth. He also possessed a profound interest in writing and grammar. When he heard that a farmer six miles away had Samuel Kirkham's *English Grammar,* he walked to his place to borrow the book, studied it cover to cover, and returned it.

With what little money he had, he purchased his first law book, *Commentaries on the Laws of England* by William Blackstone, and studied between waiting on the few customers that traded at the store. A local resident recalled,

> His favorite place to study was a wooded knoll near New Salem, where he threw himself under a wide-spreading oak, and expansively made a reading desk of the hillside. Here he would pour over *Blackstone* day after day, shifting his position as the sun rose and sank, so as to keep in the shade, and utterly unconscious of everything but principles of common law. People went by, and he took no account of them; the salutations of acquaintances were returned with silence, or a vacant stare; and alto-

---

[82] *Lincoln*, David Herbert Donald, p 41

[83] *Lincoln, An Illustrated Biography*, Philip B. Kunhardt Jr.,Philip Kunhardt III,Peter W. Kunhardt p 38

gether the manner of the absorbed student was
not unlike that of one distraught.[84]

    Squire Bowling Green took an interest in young Lincoln and
would talk with him about Illinois law, and eventually allowed
Abe to try small cases without a fee, examine witnesses, and
make arguments. Abe once walked thirty miles to hear lawyers
in court, to scrutinize their arguments and interactions with
judges and juries.

    Abe Lincoln was very much a part of the small community:
mourning with friends at funerals, joking at social gatherings,
pitching in at house-raisings, attending Sunday services and fully
engaged with any serious conversation he could find. One cold
winter day Abe passed young Ab Trent, chopping wood in the
snow with rags covering his feet. Abe stopped to talk with him
and was told that he was chopping the wood for a dollar with
which he could buy shoes. Abe told him to run to the store to
warm his feet. After a while Abe appeared at the store, handed
Ab the ax, and told him to collect his dollar for the shoes; the
chopping was done. There were those in New Salem who
would say that Abe Lincoln would go far, maybe become a senator or even governor.

    One April morning in 1832, a breathless rider on a mud-
splattered horse raced into New Salem with news that the Illinois governor had called for four hundred volunteers from
Sangamon County to report on April 24th. The Sauk and Fox
tribes, for centuries occupants of the Illinois area now occupied
by the white settlers, had been forced across the Mississippi by
an earlier signing of treaties by firewater-filled tribal elders.
They, led by their chief Black Hawk, wanted their land back,

---

[84] *Abraham Lincoln*, Carl Sandburg, p 33

and so numbering nearly 1,900, including 450 war-painted and eagle-feathered warriors, they had crossed back over the Mississippi into Illinois. Before long, reports of burned cabins and murdered settlers filled all with fear. Offutt's store where Abe was clerk was struggling to make good, so Abe readily signed up with many of his friends and acquaintances for three months of essentially uneventful service; no Indians were fought or even seen by his militia. Years later, in 1848, in a speech he joked about his only stint of military service when asked about the Democratic presidential candidate Lewis Cass, a veteran of the War of 1812 who was purported to have broken his sword in anger when Detroit was needlessly surrendered to the British. Lincoln told the crowd,

> Yes sir in the days of the Black Hawk war, I fought, bled and came away. It is quite certain that I didn't break my sword for I had no sword to break; but I bent a musket pretty badly on one occasion. If he saw any live, fighting Indians it was more than I did, but I had a good many bloody struggles with the mosquitoes; and, although I never fainted from loss of blood, I can truly say I was often very hungry.[85]

Though he sometimes made light of this brief military experience, there was some significance to it for young Lincoln. It was customary for local militias to elect their captain. As was expected, William Kirkpatrick, a respected member of the settlement, stepped forward as the candidate. Young Abraham stood silent until someone called his name to be considered as well; he nervously stepped forward. Then the men were in-

---

[85] *Lincoln*, David Herbert Donald, p 45

structed to simply stand behind the man they felt should be their captain. To Abe's surprise, three-fourths of the men took their place behind him. Then slowly most of those behind Kirkpatrick moved over to Lincoln's side. He would be their captain. This became the twenty-three-year-old's first tangible realization of his fellow men's regard for him as a leader and it touched him deeply. He later wrote that this selection to be militia captain was "a success which gave me more pleasure than any I have had since."[86]

The regular army was in the area as well, directing the offensive on the "invading" Sauks and Fox tribesmen. But as often happened, militias were relegated to the least agreeable assignments, they were poorly equipped, and the militiamen were lacking in discipline. These conditions created an arduous leadership internship for the young captain. The men spent days sitting idle, other days they marched through insect-infested swamps and slept in the cold and rain with few provisions. There was often a shortage of food, leaving them at times very hungry. This generated an abundance of complaints and dissatisfaction among Lincoln's militia. On one occasion, an elderly Indian with a safe-conduct pass from a general rambled into their camp and the men rushed to kill him. Lincoln jumped to his side and said sternly, "Men this should not be done."[87] Someone in the mob called him a coward and Lincoln shot back his response, "Choose your weapons,"[88] challenging any one of them to deal with him in a duel rather than kill the innocent stranger. The men, sensing his resolve, quietly backed away and the Indian was set free.

Lincoln was new at leading military drills and recalled having to pass his two platoons through a gate during one of them, but the new captain could not remember the order to organize

---

[86] *Lincoln*, David Herbert Donald, p 45
[87] *Abraham Lincoln*, Carl Sandburg, p 30
[88] *Abraham Lincoln*, Carl Sandburg, p 30

the platoons endwise, two by two, to allow an orderly pass through. After marching them for a time in circles while he searched his mind for the correct command, he finally called out, "This Company is dismissed for two minutes, when it will fall in again on the other side of the gate."[89]

On two occasions Lincoln's militia had the unpleasant task of burying the bodies of dead, scalped, and mangled soldiers and settlers. Young Abraham's experience as a volunteer soldier would leave a deep impression on him in later years as president as to why "men go to war, march in mud, sleep in rain, on cold ground, eat pork raw when it can't be boiled."[90] Sometime later an observer recalled seeing Lincoln's eyes grow misty in his mention of the American volunteer soldier. As commander in chief, he would no doubt draw on the memory of his own privations while he observed those experienced by the hundreds of thousands of Union and Confederate soldiers. He was honorably discharged on July 10th. On the same day someone stole his horse and he was forced to walk from Wisconsin to his home, leaving him but two weeks to address his first political campaign.

Shortly before his enlistment in the militia, a number of prominent local citizens—having confidence in young Lincoln's integrity and promise—suggested that he make a run for office in the state legislature. He was no doubt touched by their confidence and he likely felt a quiet resonance at their suggestion, for political representation would mark the budding realization of his unspoken promptings to, in some unknown way, be an ambassador for good to those around him. Abraham Lincoln, from his youth until the day the assassin's bullet stilled his singular heart and intellect, genuinely carried and continually expressed in word and deed a deep and sincere brotherly kindness for all men and women. Love for the world as tenderly charged

---

[89] *Abraham Lincoln, The Man of the People*, Norman Hapgood
[90] *Abraham Lincoln*, Carl Sandburg, p 32

him by his dying mother, and so frequently read of Jesus's earthly life in the Bible, became a ruling principle in his life, a life filled with love for God and for all of his fellow men, be they friend or foe. The countless solitary farmhand and wood-chopping speeches, and the playful tree-stump oratories to his amused friends, were more than youthful imagination. They were expressions of Lincoln's emerging character and his then-unknown mission. The chance at representation in the state's legislature would be the first step in his remarkable political journey to the White House.

He set about his campaign by visiting farmers with whom he pitched hay and cradled wheat to show that he was one of them. Where people gathered at crossroads he joined in crow-bar-throwing contests and wrestling matches as he campaigned for the needed votes for his election. He printed a political handbill for his campaign that concluded with this statement that reflected the humble sincerity that would be his trademark throughout his life:

> It is probable I have already been more pre-suming than becomes me. I have no other [ambition] so great as that of being truly es-teemed of my fellow men, by rendering myself worthy of their esteem. How far I shall suc-ceed in gratifying this ambition is yet to be de-veloped. I am young and unknown to many of you. I was born and have ever remained in the humblest walks of life. I have no wealthy or popular relations to recommend me. My case is thrown exclusively upon the independent voters of this county, and if elected they will have conferred a favor upon me, for which I shall be unremitting in my labors to compen-sate. But if the good people in their wisdom

shall see fit to keep me in the background, I have been too familiar with disappointments to be very much chagrined.[91]

His platform was focused primarily on local issues like improving the Sangamon River for better navigation and commerce. He would say, "My politics are short and sweet, like the old woman's dance."[92] He ended his campaign with a speech in the county courthouse at Springfield.

In August the votes were tallied, with the top four vote-getters out of the thirteen candidates winning election. Lincoln was fifth in the voting, experiencing the first of several election defeats intermixed with the victories throughout his political life. But of the 300 voters in the New Salem precinct, 277 went for young Abraham. The seed was now planted; Lincoln had discovered his passion in political leadership.

With his unremarkable endeavors at soldiering and politicking behind him, he stated in his autobiography, "He was now without means and out of business, but anxious to remain with his friends who had treated him with so much generosity, especially as he had nothing elsewhere to go to."[93] William F. Berry, who had been a corporal in Lincoln's company, approached him about together buying a store that was for sale in New Salem. Unlike Berry, Lincoln had no money to invest in the purchase but the seller, Rowan Herndon, accepted a promissory note from Lincoln for his share. Herndon recorded, "I believed he was thoroughly honest and that impression was so strong in me I accepted his note in payment of the whole."[94]

---

[91] *Lincoln,* David Herbert Donald, p 42
[92] *Lincoln,* David Herbert Donald, p 46
[93] *Abraham Lincoln's Autobiography*
[94] *Lincoln,* David Herbert Donald, p 47

Herndon and a few other savvy merchants could probably see what Lincoln and Berry could not, that New Salem was a dying community. Even though it had grown by nearly two hundred residents in the previous two years, that number was to decline dramatically. The Sangamon River, upon which the small community had pinned its hopes, was not to be improved for navigation. Lincoln and Berry's business struggled for survival and when Berry unexpectedly died, Lincoln was left with Berry's debt added to his own, having purchased on credit goods for sale in the store. Lincoln referred to his new burden as "The National Debt."[95] He eventually closed the business and sold what he could; the store lot, once valued at $100, was auctioned off for $10.

He took a part-time job as postmaster and did odd jobs when he could to pay down the debt. The postmaster job, at which he would work for the next three years and which required only a few hours of work each week, was a delight to him, for it gave him contact with the settlers and, more importantly, it gave him time to read anything he could get his hands on, especially newspapers that would pass through the post office. He was intensely interested in current and political affairs. Again, Abe would be seen slipping a letter in his hat and going out of his way to deliver it miles away, just because he thought the addressee might appreciate receiving the letter without delay. It was also at this time that he accepted a job opportunity to be a surveyor to add to his income. This new job became a means of growing acquainted with the people in surrounding communities who would be, like all others, impressed with this honest and promising young man. Many of these people would become supporters in his upcoming second run for the state legislature two years after his defeat in 1832.

---

[95] *Abraham Lincoln, An Illustrated Biography,* Philip B. Kunhardt Jr.,Philip Kunhardt III,Peter W. Kunhardt p 47

He was eager to run again in 1834 and his friends were ready to support him. He had added motivation to run in that the $258 salary earned by legislators would be the largest sum of money he would ever have earned to that point in his life, and it would make a nice dent in the store debts that he still carried. In this campaign Lincoln made fewer statements on political issues but chose rather to approach the political race by riding throughout the county to meet face to face with the residents, many more of whom knew him through his surveying jobs, for which he had gained a reputation for accuracy and fairness. On one occasion he approached a field where some thirty men were at work harvesting grain. He began speaking to the group when someone grumbled that he would cast no vote for any man that could not hold his own in the field. Lincoln replied, "Boys if that is all, I am shure [sic] of your votes."[96] He then grabbed a harvesting cradle and with perfect ease led the harvesters on a full round of the field. The farm owner recalled that "the boys were satisfied; I don't think he lost a vote in the Croud [sic]."[97] The votes were cast on August 4th and again the top four would be elected. Lincoln received 1,376 votes, second highest of the field of thirteen candidates, and was elected, at age twenty-five, to the Illinois state legislature.

Lincoln borrowed money from Coleman Smoot to purchase the first suit of clothes he had ever owned, "so as to make," as he told a friend, "a decent appearance in the legislature."[98] This was an important purchase because the long, lanky bachelor did not often impress with his appearance. One acquaintance once said Lincoln was "the most uncouth looking young man I ever saw."[99] Motivated by his first political success, Lincoln immersed himself with even greater earnestness into his study of

---

[96] *Lincoln*, David Herbert Donald, p 52
[97] *Lincoln*, David Herbert Donald, p 52
[98] *Abraham Lincoln*, Carl Sandburg, p 41
[99] *Lincoln*, David Herbert Donald, p 53

37

the law. He had observed that most practicing lawyers in Illinois were self-taught and he was now determined to do the same.

Lincoln's political leanings were toward the conservative Whig Party, like most of his constituent-friends in New Salem, but the outlying settlements in his district and most of the state of Illinois were predominantly Democratic. December 1st finally arrived and Abraham Lincoln took his seat, new suit and all, as the next to the youngest Illinois state legislator of 1834. He was exceptionally consistent with his attendance and for the most part an attentive yet quiet participant in the proceedings. During the course of the six-week legislative session, Lincoln's superior writing ability became recognized and he was asked to draw up bills for the other legislators. Of course the affable Lincoln gladly obliged. It didn't take long for them to observe that this good-natured newcomer from New Salem seemed always to be good for a laugh.

The business of the legislature consisted of a handful of local issues including the appropriation of $2.50 to Mr. Vickery for fixing the state house stoves, the passing of a bill to encourage the killing of troublesome wolves, and the approval of Clayborn Bell's request to change his name. The legislators found themselves in a quandary when faced with solving the Schuyler County problem that occurred when county officials hired a new surveyor thinking the former had died. He was however very much alive. After considerable deliberation, the young freshman from New Salem stood and introduced two elements to the floor: humor and a solution. Lincoln elicited sound laughter when he spoke of the surveyor who "persisted not to die."[100] He went on to propose that they do nothing, and if in the future "the old surveyor should hereafter conclude to die, there would be a new one ready made without troubling the legislature."[101] After the laughter subsided, Lincoln's proposal

---

[100] *Lincoln,* David Herbert Donald, p 54
[101] *Lincoln,* David Herbert Donald, p 54

was accepted and the legislature moved on to the next item of business. Again, Lincoln easily endeared himself to those around him. One lobbyist wrote the following of the young politician: "He was raw-boned, angular, features deeply furrowed, ungraceful, almost uncouth...and yet there was a magnetism and dash about the man that made him a universal favorite."[102]

It was during this legislative session that Lincoln met his future nemesis, twenty-one-year-old Stephen A. Douglas. The confident and capable Douglas was lobbying for his own appointment as the state's attorney of the First District. Lincoln and Douglas would over the next thirty years, on both the local and national level, find themselves on the opposite sides of dozens of issues, and some two decades later would engage in their highly publicized debates for the U.S. Senate and eventually the race for president in 1860.

If there ever was a young man who needed the companionship and influence of a woman, it was Abe Lincoln. For all of his ease around people in general, around young women he was painfully shy and clumsy. He would avoid waiting on young women in his store if he could, allowing his partner to attend them. A fellow store clerk, A.Y. Ellis, remembered that Lincoln avoided waiting on the ladies, preferring instead to trade with the men and boys. On one occasion, a lady and her three stylish daughters boarded at the same log tavern as Lincoln, and during their stay Lincoln, out of shyness, avoided eating at the same table when they did. Y.A. Ellis thought it was on account of his awkward appearance and his worn and ill-fitting apparel. On another occasion, a group of young girls were laughing with amusement at his gangly long legs, to which he responded that he knew that he was not much to look at. It is likely that he was painfully conscious of his appearance and did not have the

---

[102] *Abraham Lincoln, President Elect*, Larry Mansch, p 21

means or the know-how to do much about it. David Herbert Donald aptly describes Lincoln's condition: "He needed someone to cook for him and feed him…someone to clean and repair his clothing, which—except for that expensive legislative suit—seemed never to fit and always to be in tatters. In short, he needed a wife."[103]

It was in New Salem that Abraham met his first love interest, Ann Rutledge. Unfortunately for Abraham, nineteen-year-old Ann was engaged to John McNeil—a respected and successful young businessman in New Salem. After the engagement, John left for New York to arrange affairs with his family there and upon returning would marry Ann. But three years passed and John McNeil had neither returned nor corresponded with young Ann in the last two years of his disappearance, leaving her much distressed. It was also discovered just before his departure that his name was not McNeil but McNamar, causing rumors and speculation regarding his character that only deepened Ann's despair. It was toward the end of the second year of McNamar's absence that she and Abraham grew closer as friends. Little is known of their courtship and it is probable that they were not open with their feelings toward one another because of the engagement to McNamar.

The summer of 1835 was one of the hottest on record in Illinois with unusual amounts of rain that eventually contaminated the well at the Rutledge farm. This contamination was blamed for a "brain fever,"[104] probably typhoid, that struck the young and pretty Ann Rutledge in August. Though her doctor prescribed complete rest and quiet, she insisted on sending for Abraham. Upon hearing the news, Lincoln rushed the seven miles to her home to be at her side. She soon lost consciousness and a few days later, on August 25th, Ann Rutledge died. Young Abe was devastated. He was observed to have fallen into a deep

---

[103] *Lincoln,* David Herbert Donald, p 55
[104] *Lincoln,* David Herbert Donald, p 5

depression over her suffering and untimely passing. On a rainy night after the burial, he told his landlady, Mrs. Bennett Abell, that "He could not bare [sic] the idea of it raining on her Grave[sic]."[105] Years later in the White House, Lincoln was asked by an old friend from New Salem, Isaac Cogdale, who was visiting Washington, if it was true that Lincoln had fallen in love with Ann. After pausing, Lincoln responded, "It is true—true indeed I did. I loved the woman deeply and soundly: she was a handsome girl—would have made a good and loving wife…I did honestly and truly love the girl and think often—often of her now."[106] Ironically, John McNamar suddenly returned to New Salem three weeks after Ann's death.

Lincoln immersed himself again in his studies and approximately a year after Ann's death, he passed the bar exam. And on September 9, 1836, Lincoln held a license in his hands that authorized him to practice law in the Illinois courts.

Lincoln ran again for the same office in 1836 and garnered more votes than any of the seventeen candidates. His peers in the minority Whig Party elected him as floor leader. The issues in this session were of a much higher significance than in the previous. They included the building of railroads, a highly important canal that would connect the Illinois and the Chicago Rivers, and the moving of the Illinois state capital from Vandalia to Springfield.

This legislature also passed a resolution condemning abolitionist societies and affirming that slavery was guaranteed by the Constitution. Similar resolutions had been passed in Southern states where it was against the law to speak against slavery. The Southern states' three million Negro slaves were listed on the tax books as livestock and represented a value of more than a billion dollars. For some years, the Southern states had been growing increasingly angry over the rising anti-

---

[105] *Lincoln*, David Herbert Donald, p 57
[106] *Lincoln*, David Herbert Donald, p 58

slavery sentiment in the North, and strong signs of a divided nation were evident as early as the 1830s, although many in the North at this time agreed with the Southern concerns. And with most of the residents of Illinois being of Southern origins, the proslavery resolution passed seventy-seven to six. Abraham Lincoln was one of the six to oppose the measure. But Lincoln did not stop with just his dissenting vote. He and fellow opponent to the measure Dan Stone recorded the following protest in the legislature that read in part:

> Resolutions passed on the subject of domestic slavery having passed both branches of the General Assembly at its present session, the undersigned hereby protest against the passage of the same.
> They believe that the institution of slavery is founded on both injustice and bad policy; but that the promulgation of abolition doctrines tends rather to increase than abate its evils.[107]

At the conclusion of the legislative session, Lincoln returned to what was left of his beloved New Salem to say goodbye. He too would be compelled to move on.

---

[107] *Abraham Lincoln*, Condensed, Carl Sandburg, p 53

Chapter Three

"The Lawyer Who Was Never Known to Lie" [108]

At age twenty-eight, Lincoln arrived in his new home of Springfield, riding a borrowed horse and carrying all that he owned in two small saddle bags: not an impressive sight at first glance, after six years in New Salem. While other men at this stage of life had married and owned farms or businesses, he was still poor, owned nothing, and was still heavily in debt from the business failure years earlier. The debt would be paid in full as he promised, but it would take him several more years to do it. Yet his years in New Salem were not without accomplishment. His intense personal study of law resulted in his passing of the bar exam, and the respected lawyer and future U.S. senator John Todd Stuart, cousin to Lincoln's future wife Mary Todd, had invited the bachelor to be his law partner in Springfield. In addition, Lincoln had already served two sessions in the state legislature. But financially, he viewed himself with disappointment and embarrassment.

Springfield, with its fourteen hundred residents, was to Lincoln a bustling city, peppered with mansions and log cabins. It

---

[108] *Lincoln,* David Herbert Donald, p 149

was his first to have chapels for worship along with various businesses of that day. Most of its residents were proslavery Southerners who had migrated north, and slavery was a hotly contested subject in the Illinois capital near the time of Lincoln's arrival. An antislavery group of the local Presbyterian Church would break off from their own proslavery congregation.

The state of Illinois was brought to its financial knees in the midst of the economic Panic of 1837, leaving bridges, roads, and other government-sponsored projects unfinished for lack of funds. There were seventy-eight free Negroes, twenty registered indentured servants, and six slaves in the county.

Upon Lincoln's arrival in Springfield, he tied his horse at the general store where he asked the young owner Joshua Speed the price for a bed and bedding. Speed calculated the total at $17. Lincoln hesitated, then replied forlornly, "Cheap as it is I have not the money to pay. But if you will credit me until Christmas and my experiment here as a lawyer is a success, I will pay you then. If I fail in that I will probably never pay you at all."[109] Speed said of this exchange, "The tone of his voice was so melancholy that I felt for him...I thought I never saw so gloomy and melancholy face in my life."[110] To the surprise of Lincoln, Speed offered to share his small apartment above the store with the new arrival. Lincoln promptly accepted the offer, took his saddlebags upstairs, and shortly returned saying, "Well Speed, I'm moved in."[111] Another man, William Butler, invited Lincoln to take his meals at his home where there would be no mention of board bills. Lincoln was deeply grateful for the kindnesses of these men who became his lifelong friends.

---

[109] *Lincoln*, David Herbert Donald, p 66
[110] *Lincoln*, David Herbert Donald, p 66
[111] *Lincoln*, David Herbert Donald, p 66

With all the promise of a new law career ahead of him, Lincoln carried with him into Springfield a heavy despondency along with his two saddlebags. Even with frequent complimentary articles in Springfield's *Sangamo Journal* on Lincoln's political endeavors, leaving his beloved New Salem, carrying his financial burden and the crumbling of his recent engagement proposal to Mary Owens, daughter of a wealthy landowner in Kentucky, weighed heavily on him. Mary responded coolly to the engagement proposal. A few weeks after his arrival in Springfield he wrote the following excerpts to Mary:

> Springfield, May 7, 1837
> Friend Mary
>
> I have commenced two letters to send you before this, both of which displeased me before I got half done, and so I tore them up. The first I thought wasn't serious enough, and the second was on the other extreme. I shall send this, turn out as it may.
>
> This thing of living in Springfield is rather a dull business after all; at least it is to me. I am quite as lonesome here as [I] ever was anywhere in my life. I have been spoken to by but one woman since I've been here, and should not have been by her, if she could have avoided it. I've never been to church yet, nor probably shall not be soon. I stay away because I am conscious I should not know how to behave myself.
>
> I am often thinking of what we said of your coming to live at Springfield. I am afraid you would not be satisfied. There is a great deal of flourishing about in carriages here, which it would be your doom to see without sharing in it. You would have to be poor without the means of hiding your pov-

erty. Do you believe you could bear that patiently? Whatever woman may cast her lot with mine, should any ever do so, it is my intention to do all in my power to make her happy and contented; and there is nothing I can imagine, that would make me more unhappy than to fail in the effort. I must wish you would think seriously before you decide. For my part I have already decided. My opinion is that you had better not do it. You have not been accustomed to hardship, and it may be more severe than you now imagine. I know you are capable of thinking correctly on any subject; and if you deliberate maturely upon this, before you decide, then I am willing to abide your decision.

Yours, &c.
    Lincoln[112]

After the initial shock subsided, the relationship eventually dissolved, to the apparent relief of both parties. His letter to Mary Owens reflected Lincoln's concerns over his ability to provide the necessary income to raise a family. There was an abundance of lawyers in this small town and although the law firm of Stuart and Lincoln was busy with cases, only those lawyers who would extract exorbitant fees were wealthy. Most cases were smaller matters and averaged about $5 in fees, which he and Stuart divided equally. His fellow lawyers would say that Lincoln's problem of not earning a comfortable living was of his own doing because in his new role as a lawyer, he continued to place the interests of others, even strangers, above his own.

---

[112] *Abraham Lincoln*, Carl Sandburg, p 57

It was a common thing for Lincoln to discourage unnecessary lawsuits, and consequently he was continually sacrificing opportunities to make money. One man who asked him to bring suit for two dollars and a half against a debtor, who had not a cent with which to pay, would not be put off in his passion for revenge. Lincoln therefore gravely demanded ten dollars as a retainer. Half of this he gave to the poor defendant, who thereupon confessed judgment and paid the $2.50. Thus the suit was ended, to the entire satisfaction of the angry creditor.[113]

Yes, there is no reasonable doubt that I can gain [win] your case for you," Lincoln once told a potential client. "I can set a whole neighborhood at loggerheads; I can distress a widowed mother and her six fatherless children, and thereby get for you six hundred dollars which rightly belong, it appears to me, as much to them as it does to you. I shall not take your case, but I will give you a little advice for nothing. You seem a sprightly, energetic man. I would advise you to try your hand at making six hundred dollars in some other way.[114]

Once when another attorney had collected $250 for their joint services, Lincoln refused to accept his share until the fee had been reduced to what he considered fair proportions and the overcharge had been returned to the client. When his close friend Judge David Davis, the

---

[113] *The Wit and Wisdom of Abraham Lincoln*, Edited by Anthony Gross, p 24
[114] *The Wit and Wisdom of Abraham Lincoln*, Edited by Anthony Gross, p 24

presiding judge of the circuit heard of this, he indignantly exclaimed, "Lincoln, your picayune charges will impoverish the bar."[115]

Lincoln was equally ready to take up a just case without hope of pay as he was to refuse an unjust one even at the loss of a good fee. He once dragged into court a pension agent who insisted on keeping for himself half of a $400 claim, which [Lincoln] had collected for a poor widow of a revolutionary war veteran. He knew that he could not win the case on technical merit; so he appealed to the compassion of the jury, and to a reverence for the sacrifices her deceased husband bore to win freedom for this nation. There, in his own expressive phrase, he 'skinned' [the agent], moved the jury to tears by his stirring appeal for justice to the old woman, and won the verdict, all without charge to the widow.[116]

Lincoln then paid for her hotel and the cost of travel back to her home.

Lincoln often said, "Some legal rights are moral wrongs."[117] He went on for his entire legal and political career to demonstrate that he would go to great lengths to avoid a moral wrong or injury to other persons, often resulting in lost income opportunities for himself and some occasional ridicule.

Once he was prosecuting a civil suit, in the course of which evidence was introduced showing that his client was attempting fraud. Lincoln rose and walked out of the courtroom to his hotel in deep disgust. The judge sent for him; he refused to come.

---

[115] *The Wit and Wisdom of Abraham Lincoln*, Edited by Anthony Gross, p 24
[116] *The Wit and Wisdom of Abraham Lincoln*, Edited by Anthony Gross, p 24
[117] *Recollections of Abraham Lincoln 1847-1865*, Ward Hill Lamon, p 222

"Tell the judge," he said, "my hands are dirty; I came over to wash them."[118]

Leonard Swett of Chicago, for years an intimate associate of Lincoln's, and himself one of the most renown of American lawyers, said that "sometimes, after Lincoln entered upon a criminal case, the conviction that his client was guilty would affect him with a sort of panic. On one occasion he turned suddenly to me and said, 'Swett, the man is guilty; you defend him, I can't,' and so gave up his share of a large fee."[119]

When he was engaged with Judge S.C. Parks in defending a man accused of larceny, he said, "If you can say anything for the man, do it-I can't; if I attempt it, the jury will see I think he is guilty, and convict him."[120]

The son of his long-time friend Jack Armstrong, the wrestling champion of the Clary's Grove, whose loyal friendship Lincoln won by beating him in a wrestling match in New Salem, was on trial for killing a man. Jack had passed away, but Hannah Armstrong, his widow, turned to Lincoln to save her son. He gratefully remembered that the poor woman had been almost a mother to him in his friendless days and that her cabin had been his home when he had no other. He laid aside everything else and went to her aid. The defendant's guilt was extremely doubtful.

The chief witness testified that he saw the boy strike the fatal blow and that the affair had occurred about eleven o'clock at night. Lincoln inquired how he could have seen so clearly at that late hour. By the moonlight, the witness answered. Was there light enough to see every-

118 *The Wit and Wisdom of Abraham Lincoln*, Edited by Anthony Gross, p 24
119 *The Wit and Wisdom of Abraham Lincoln*, Edited by Anthony Gross, p 25
120 *The Wit and Wisdom of Abraham Lincoln*, Edited by Anthony Gross, p 24

thing that happened? Lincoln asked. The moon was about where the sun would be at ten o'clock in the morning and nearly full, the man on the stand replied. Almost instantly Lincoln held out a calendar. By this he showed that on the night in question the moon was only slightly past its first quarter, that it set within an hour after the fatal occurrence, and that it could therefore have shed little or no light on the scene of the alleged murder. The crowded courtroom was electrified by the disclosure. "Hannah," whispered Lincoln, as he turned to the mother, "Bill will be cleared before sundown."[121] And he was.

The following document, signed by Judge David Davis, who was particularly fond of Lincoln's stories, tells of an event that occurred when Davis and Lincoln practiced law in the Eighth Circuit in Central Illinois. "I was never fined but once for contempt of court,"[122] said one of the clerks of the court in Lincoln's day.

Davis fined me five dollars. Mr. Lincoln had just come in, and leaning over my desk had told me a story so irresistibly funny that I broke into a loud laugh. The judge called me to order, saying, 'This must be stopped. Mr. Lincoln, you are constantly disturbing this court with your stories.'[123] I apologized, but told the Judge the story was worth the money. In a few minutes the Judge called me to him. 'What was

---

121 *The Wit and Wisdom of Abraham Lincoln*, Edited by Anthony Gross, p 26
122 *The Wit and Wisdom of Abraham Lincoln*, Edited by Anthony Gross, p 26
123 *The Wit and Wisdom of Abraham Lincoln*, Edited by Anthony Gross, p 26

that story Lincoln told you?' he asked. I told
him and he laughed aloud in spite of himself.
'Remit your fine,' he ordered.[124]

Mary Todd was the belle of the town and captured the interest of nearly every eligible bachelor, including Abraham. The
daughter of a prosperous Kentucky banker and merchant, Mary
had grown up with the best that money could buy, attended by
family slaves and educated in the best private schools. She was
described as having light chestnut hair, beautiful soft skin, and
stunning blue eyes. She was witty, dignified, graceful, and a
charming conversationalist. She was also described as "sarcastic—haughty—aristocratic."[125] When Abraham met her at a
party at the Edwards' mansion, he told her that he wanted to
dance with her "in the worst way."[126] Mary laughed and they
danced. After the dance she teasingly told her clumsy suitor that
he had certainly danced in the worst way. The intelligent and
vivacious Mary Todd enchanted Abraham. With her, he was
completely comfortable; they could talk for hours. Interested in
politics, she admired his ambition. She was known to have said
various times that she would marry a man who would someday
be president. By Christmas of 1840, Mary and Abraham were
engaged.

Shortly after the happy announcement, again Lincoln wa-
vered. He worried about his ability to earn the living that he
believed to be required to make Mary or any wife happy. He
owned no home, had no savings, and was still encumbered by
his shrinking yet still substantial debt. Of his poverty, he wrote
his best friend Joshua Speed, "I am so poor, and make so little
headway in the world, that I drop back in a month of idleness,

---

[124] *The Wit and Wisdom of Abraham Lincoln*, Edited by Anthony Gross, p 30
[125] *Lincoln*, David Herbert Donald, p 84
[126] *Lincoln*, David Herbert Donald, p 85

as much as I gain in a year's rowing."[127] Weakening again, he told Mary that he did not love her, though he really did, to break off the engagement, and by so doing broke Mary's heart. She shortly thereafter wrote him a letter releasing him from the engagement. Instead of feeling relieved as he did with the break with Mary Owens, Lincoln was devastated. Mary's letter made him realize that he had made a terrible mistake. He was so deeply unhappy and depressed that he did not leave his room for a week. He told Joshua Speed that he was haunted by "the never-absent idea"[128] that he had made Mary unhappy. "That still kills my soul. I can not but reproach myself, for even wishing to be happy while she is otherwise."[129] He told John Todd Stuart, "I am now the most miserable man living."[130] Another contributor to Lincoln's despondency related to his growing inner impressions that his life would someday be involved with some event or events of significance for humanity and yet circumstances seemed to prove otherwise. Joshua Speed recorded about this same time that Lincoln lamented that he had done nothing "to make any human being remember that he had lived; he wished to live to connect his name with events of his day and generation and to the interest of his fellow men."[131] To this point in his life nothing appeared to indicate to Lincoln that he was on course for any significance or renown.

Several months passed when Mrs. Simeon Francis, wife of the local newspaper editor, decided to intervene. She invited both Mary and Lincoln to a social event, brought them together, and said, "Be friends again."[132] And they were. After several more months of rebuilding their tender feelings for each other,

---

[127] *Abraham Lincoln*, Carl Sandburg, p 76
[128] *Lincoln*, David Herbert Donald, p 87
[129] *Lincoln*, David Herbert Donald, p 88
[130] *Lincoln*, David Herbert Donald, p 88
[131] *Lincoln*, David Herbert Donald, p 81
[132] *Lincoln*, David Herbert Donald, p 91

Lincoln renewed his proposal for marriage and again Mary accepted. They were quietly married with only close family and friends present, on November 4, 1842, and thirty-two-year-old Lincoln placed on twenty-four-year-old Mary's finger a plain gold ring engraved with "Love is eternal."[133]

The Lincolns' first home was a rented eight-by-fourteen-foot room on the second floor of the Globe Tavern. They ate their meals in the common dining room. For Abraham this new residence was a step up, and for Mary a significant step downward. For the first time in her life she was without personal servants and a spacious and opulent home. But Mary made no complaints. She was just happy to be married to Abraham and made the best of her lot. Lincoln was equally in love. Ending a business letter to a lawyer friend some time after their wedding, Lincoln wrote, "Nothing new here, except my marrying, which to me, is a matter of profound wonder."[134]

On August 1, 1843, Robert Todd Lincoln was born to the Lincoln union. After the birth, Lincoln ran to his dentist's office nearby to excitedly announce the miracle and joked that he feared his new son would inherit one of his long legs "and one short one, like Mary's."[135] Like all parents, Lincoln and Mary adored their children. Lincoln described Robert at age five as a "rare-ripe type, brighter at five than he would ever be again."[136] The arrival of Robert set the Lincolns to looking for a new home in earnest. Lincoln's income had actually declined since he was no longer in the state legislature and was sending money to his aging parents who were now settled in Coles County. But

---

[133] *Lincoln*, David Herbert Donald, p 93

[134] *Abraham Lincoln, the Man Behind the Myths*, Stephen B. Oates, p. 44

[135] *Lincoln, an Illustrated Biography*, Philip B. Kunhardt Jr.,Philip Kunhardt III,Peter W. Kunhardt p 90

[136] *Lincoln, an Illustrated Biography*, Philip B. Kunhardt Jr.,Philip Kunhardt III,Peter W. Kunhardt p 90

they found a small three-room frame house that they could afford to rent. Lincoln set about with increased effort to bring in more income and by the next year they purchased their first, very modest home.

Lincoln's law partner John Todd Stuart was in Washington serving in the U.S. Senate. After operating alone for a time Lincoln was invited to be a partner with Stephen T. Logan, one of the foremost attorneys in the state, from whom Lincoln would learn a great deal regarding the practice of law.

He learned that a needed boost in income could result from his joining a team of lawyers and the Eighth Circuit judge twice each year, to travel from hamlet to town in east-central Illinois to conduct the legal process. A journey of five hundred miles would be undertaken to reach each of the fourteen county seats in the district. So for the next several years he would be away from Mary and his sons for weeks at a time. This they both accepted as a necessary element of the profession. These circuit rides would sometimes last three months; the first commencing in February, and then being repeated again in September. Aside from missing his family, Lincoln by and large enjoyed these journeys; he liked meeting the locals in the district and never seemed bothered with the travel, which was usually done on horseback, whether in the searing heat or cold driving rain. Roads were at times nonexistent and flimsy bridges were sometimes washed out—but on they rode, usually with Lincoln in the lead. They slept on floors in farmhouses, barns, or crowded into a small tavern room.

Lincoln was very much at home with these conditions and with the common rural folk, so much like himself. He cared little where he slept, and he willingly ate, without complaint, whatever food was put before him. With the local residents he was always talking crops, assessing livestock, admiring their children, engaging in political discussions. In addition, and to his pleasure, he was able to lay aside the "fancy manners, city dress and civilized refinements" of bustling Springfield.[137] The arrival of the itinerate judge and lawyers always seemed to create a charged atmosphere in these rural towns.

"It was almost as if a circus had come to town; work stopped and everybody crowded into the courthouse to enjoy the legal acrobatics and cheer their favorites on as the latest local disagreements were publicly aired, dissected and eventually settled."[138]

One day Lincoln and a certain judge who were close friends, bantered over the subject of horses, a favorite topic on the frontier. Finally Lincoln said: "well look here, Judge! I'll tell you what I'll do. I'll make a horse trade with you, only it must be upon these stipulations: Neither party shall see the other party's horse until it is produced here in the courtyard of the hotel and both parties must trade horses. If either backs out of the agreement, he does so under a forfeiture of twenty-five dollars." "Agreed," cried the judge, and both he and Lincoln went in quest of their respective animals. A crowd gathered, in anticipation of the fun, and when the judge returned first, the laugh was uproarious. "He led, or rather dragged, at the end of a halter the meanest, boniest, rib-staring quadruple-blind in both eyes—that ever pressed turf." But presently Lincoln came along carrying over

[137] *Lincoln,* an Illustrated Biography, Philip B. Kunhardt Jr.,Philip Kunhardt III,Peter W. Kunhardt p 90

[138] *Lincoln,* an Illustrated Biography, Philip B. Kunhardt Jr.,Philip Kunhardt III,Peter W. Kunhardt p 76

his shoulder a carpenter's sawhorse. Then the mirth of the crowd was furious. Lincoln solemnly set his horse down, and silently surveyed the judge's animal with a comical look of infinite disgust. "Well judge," he finally said, "this is the first time I ever got the worst of it in a horse trade."[139]

On one occasion a party of lawyers, among them Mr. Lincoln, were riding across the country in the central part of the state. The road took them through a grove and as they passed along, a little bird which had fallen from the nest, lay fluttering on the ground and was noticed by several of the horsemen, including Mr. Lincoln. After riding a short distance he said to his companions, "Wait a moment, I want to go back." And as they stopped for him he was seen to ride back, dismount, and pick up the little fledgling and carefully put it in the nest. When he rejoined the party, they said: "Why, Lincoln, you need not have stopped for such a trifle as that." Pausing a little while, he answered quietly, "Well, I feel better for doing it, anyhow."[140]

Lincoln, who was one of the most generous and kind-hearted of men, often said that there was no act which was not prompted by some selfish motive. He was riding in a stage from Springfield to a neighboring town and was discussing this philosophy with a fellow passen-

---

[139] *The Wit and Wisdom of Abraham Lincoln*, Edited by Anthony Gross, p 34
[140] *The Wit and Wisdom of Abraham Lincoln*, Edited by Anthony Gross, p 30

ger. As the stage rumbled past a ditch, which was filled with mud and mire, the passengers could see a small pig, caught fast in the muck, squealing and struggling to free himself. Many in the stage laughed heartily, but Mr. Lincoln, then a lawyer asked the driver to stop for a few moments. Leaping from the stage, he walked to the ditch over his shoe tops in mud and picked the little animal up, setting it on the solid road. "Now look here," said the passenger with whom he had been talking, "you cannot say that was a selfish act." "Extremely selfish," said Mr. Lincoln. "If I had left that little fellow in there the memory of his squealing would have made me uncomfortable all day. That is why I freed him."[141]

Fellow circuit lawyer Henry C. Whitney described Lincoln's as such:

> When I first knew him his attire and physical habits were on a plane with those of an ordinary farmer. He probably had as little taste about dress and attire as anybody that ever was born: he simply wore clothes because it was needful and customary: whether they fitted or looked well was entirely above, or beneath, his comprehension...He had no clerk, no stenographer, no library, no method or system of business, but carried his papers in his hat or coat pocket.[142]

---

[141] *The Wit and Wisdom of Abraham Lincoln*, Edited by Anthony Gross, p 34
[142] *Lincoln*, an Illustrated Biography, Philip B. Kunhardt Jr.,Philip Kunhardt III,Peter W. Kunhardt p 81

Lincoln possessed a rare ability to wage legal warfare in the courtroom without personally damaging a colleague, be he friend or foe. Time and again, juries and observers would witness his fairness, honesty, and wit, for which he became widely admired throughout the district. Juries and spectators came to appreciate his methodical and logical deliberations. Leonard Swett, Lincoln's friend and respected attorney, said this of Lincoln's formidable manner:

> As he entered the trial, where most lawyers would object, he would say he "reckoned" it would be fair to let this in, or that; and sometimes, when his adversary could not quite prove what Lincoln knew to be the truth, he 'reckoned' it would be fair to admit the truth to be so and so. When he did object to the court, and when he heard his objections answered, he would often say, "Well, I reckon I must be wrong." Now, about the time he had practiced this three-fourths through the case, if his adversary didn't understand him, he would wake up in a few minutes learning that he had feared the Greeks too late and find himself beaten. He was wise as a serpent in the trial of a cause, but I have had too many scars from his blows to certify that he was not harmless as a dove. When the whole thing was unraveled, the adversary would begin to see that what [Lincoln] was so blandly giving away was simply what he couldn't get and keep. By giving away six points and carrying the seventh, he

carried his case, and the whole case hanging on the seventh, he traded away everything which could give him the least aid in carrying that. Any man who took Lincoln for a simple-minded man would very soon wake up with his back in a ditch.[143]

General John H. Littlefield, who studied law with Lincoln, tells this anecdote in his recollections of Lincoln:

All clients knew that, with 'Old Abe' as their lawyer, they would win their case—if it was fair; if not, that it was a waste of time to take it to him. After listening some time one day to a would-be client's statement, with his eyes on the ceiling, he swung around on the chair and exclaimed: 'Well you have a pretty good case in technical law, but a pretty bad one in equity and justice. You'll have to get some other fellow to win this case for you. I couldn't do it. All the time while standing talking to the jury I'd be thinking, Lincoln, you're a lair, and I believe I should forget myself and say it out loud.'[144]

Lincoln revealed his unmatched ethical standards in excerpts from handwritten notes prepared for a lecture on law:

The leading rule for the lawyer, as for the man, of every other calling, is diligence. Leaving nothing for to-morrow which can be done to-day. Discourage litigation. Persuade your neighbors to compromise whenever you

---

[143] *A. Lincoln, Esquire*, Allen D. Spiegel, p 45
[144] *The Wit and Wisdom of Abraham Lincoln*, Edited by Anthony Gross, p 34

can. Point out to them how the nominal winner is often a real loser—in fees, expenses, and waste of time. As a peacemaker the lawyer has a superior opportunity [sic] of being a good man. There will still be business enough.

Never stir up litigation. A worse man can scarcely be found than…he who habitually overhauls the register of deeds in search of defects in titles, whereon to stir up strife, and put money in his pocket. A moral tone ought to be infused into the profession, which should drive such men out of it. Resolve to be honest at all events; and if in your own judgment you cannot be an honest lawyer, resolve to be honest without being a lawyer. Choose some other occupation, rather than…consent to be a knave.[145]

George Miner tells the following story:

In the spring term of Tazwell County Court, in 1847, I was detained as a witness. Lincoln was employed in several suits, and among them was one of Case vs. Snow Brothers. The Snow brothers (who were both minors) had purchased from Mr. Case what was then called a "prairie team," consisting of two or three yoke of oxen and a prairie plow, giving therefore their joint note of some two hundred dollars; but when pay-day came they

---

[145] *Lincoln*, an Illustrated Biography, Philip B. Kunhardt Jr.,Philip Kunhardt III,Peter W. Kunhardt p 81

refused to pay, pleading the minor act. The note was placed in Lincoln's hands for collection. The suit was called and a jury impaneled. The Snow Brothers did not deny the note, but pleaded through their counsel that they were minors, and that Mr. Case knew they were at the time of the contract and conveyance. All this was admitted by Mr. Lincoln, with his peculiar phrase, "Yes, gentlemen, I reckon that's so." The minor act was read and its validity admitted in the same manner: "Yes gentlemen, I reckon that's so." The counsel for the defendants was permitted without question to state all these things to the jury, and to show by the statute that these minors could not be held responsible for their contract. By this time you may well suppose that [Lincoln's] client became quite uneasy. "What!" thought I, "this good old man who confided in these boys to be wronged in this way, and even his counsel, Mr. Lincoln, to submit in silence?" I looked at Judge Treat, but could read nothing in his calm and dignified demeanor. Just then Mr. Lincoln slowly rose to his strange, half-erect attitude and in clear, quiet accents began: Gentlemen of the jury, are you willing to allow these boys to begin life with this shame and disgrace attached to their character? If you are, I am not. The best judge of human character that ever wrote has left these immortal words for us to ponder:

Good name in man and woman, dear my lord,
Is the immediate jewel of their souls:

Who steals my purse steals trash; 'tis something,
 nothing;
'Twas mine, 'tis his, and has been slave to thousands;
But he that filches from me my good name
Robs me of that which not enriches him
And makes me poor indeed.

Then rising to his full height, and looking
upon the defendants with the compassion of a
brother, his long arm extended toward the opposing counsel, he continued: "Gentlemen of
the jury, these poor innocent boys would never
have attempted this low villainy had it not been
for the advice of these lawyers." Then for a
few minutes he showed how even the noble
science of law may be prostituted. With a
scathing rebuke to those who had thus belit-
tled their profession, he concluded: "And now,
gentlemen, you have it in *your* power to set these boys right before the world." He pleaded
for the young men only; I think he did not
mention his client's name. The jury without
leaving their seats, decided that the defendants
must pay the debt; and the latter, after hearing
Lincoln, were willing to pay it as the jury were
determined they should. I think the entire argument lasted not above five minutes.[146]

In 1844, Lincoln's partner Stephen Logan wanted to partner with his son and the Logan-Lincoln law partnership was
amicably dissolved. Lincoln had felt ready for some time to
become senior partner in his own firm. He chose the unlikely
William H. Herndon, nine years his junior. Lincoln dashed up

---

[146] *The Wit and Wisdom of Abraham Lincoln*, Edited by Anthony Gross, p 23

the stairs to the office where Herndon was studying and said, "Billy, do you want to enter a partnership with me in the law business?" "Mr. Lincoln," Herndon stammered, "this is something unexpected by me—it is an undeserved honor; and yet I will gladly and thankfully accept the kind and generous offer." Lincoln responded, "Billy, I can trust you if you can trust me," and for the next sixteen years "Mr. Lincoln" and "Billy" would be partners.[147]

His selection of Herndon was puzzling to many because Lincoln by this time in his career could have had most anyone with vastly more renown and experience join with him. But Lincoln liked Billy Herndon and saw potential in the studious and thorough young lawyer. Lincoln also viewed Herndon as representing a block of young voters whose support he would look to court in his calculated future bids for the United States Congress. The state legislature had been an opportunity for him to contribute to society and to learn the law-making process, but he knew there was more to accomplish and he was looking to the future. He considered the statewide office of governor but it was too far out of reach with his affiliation in the minority Whig party. Illinois had never elected a Whig for governor, as candidate for president, or to the U.S. Senate. His best chance for success would be as congressman in the newly created Seventh District, comprising most of the communities he had come to know so well on the circuit. For the next six years, his energies would focus on his family, his law practice, and on skillful yet ethical maneuverings to satisfy his ever-stirring political yearnings.

In time, Lincoln found himself trying cases before the Illinois Supreme Court.

---

[147] *Lincoln,* David Herbert Donald, p 100

His care and thoroughness made him one
of the most successful practitioners before the
court, and by the time he left for Washington
in 1861 he had appeared before the highest
court in Illinois in at least three hundred cases.[148]

In December 1841, he argued fourteen cases in the Supreme
Court and lost only four. In the following two years, he would
argue twenty-four cases, winning all but seven.[149]

By the early 1850s, the Lincoln-Herndon law firm had become the leading law firm in Springfield, taking nearly 30 percent of all of the cases in the county court. Herndon would
handle most of the tedious research while Lincoln spent most
of his time in the courtroom representing their clients before
the judges and juries. Lincoln, from the first day, split all fees
equally with his junior partner. While many lawyers sought out
the larger, high-fee cases, Lincoln could always be counted on
to accept the smaller ones that he felt were fair and needed
representation for justice's sake.

Herndon later recorded his remembrances of partnering
with Lincoln.

When he reached the office, the first thing
he would do was to pick up a newspaper,
spread himself out on the sofa, one leg on a
chair, and read aloud, much to my discomfort.
I once asked him why he did so. This was his
explanation: 'When I read aloud two senses
catch the idea; first I see what I read; second, I
hear it, and therefore I can remember it better.'
He paid but little attention to the fees and

---

[148] *Lincoln*, David Herbert Donald, p 100
[149] *Abraham Lincoln*, Carl Sandburg, p 79

money matters of the firm—usually leaving all such to me."[150]

He would continue to avoid cases that appeared to him to be fraudulent.

> Herndon relates, as an instance of Lincoln's moral honesty and his horror of a lie, that he [Herndon] once drew up a dilatory plea for the purpose of delaying a case for another term. But when it came to Lincoln's attention he promptly repudiated it. 'Is it founded on fact?' Lincoln inquired, and when Herndon admitted it was done merely to save their clients interests, which might otherwise be endangered, Lincoln instantly replied: 'You know it is a sham, and a sham is very often but another name for a lie. Don't let it go on record. The cursed thing may come staring us in the face long after this suit is forgotten.' And the plea was withdrawn.[151]

It is quite likely that Lincoln chose young Herndon to be his partner for the very reason this incident illustrates. Although his fellow lawyers respected Lincoln's honesty, such complete integrity routinely meant missed opportunities for income. With a young and respectful partner like Herndon, Lincoln could continue to practice law under his uniquely ethical principles, unimpeded. Billy, in fact, admired his mentor-partner and rarely

---

[150] *Lincoln*, an Illustrated Biography, Philip B. Kunhardt Jr.,Philip Kunhardt III,Peter W. Kunhardt p 84

[151] *Lincoln*, an Illustrated Biography, Philip B. Kunhardt Jr.,Philip Kunhardt III,Peter W. Kunhardt p 84

challenged Lincoln's judgment. Many other lawyers would not have been so patient with Lincoln as a partner.

The circuit-court journeys held a significant advantage for Lincoln's political aspirations. Some of his strongest supporters in future political contests would be clients, jurists, court-gallery observers, and lawyers he met on the circuit. With his uncanny ability to make friends out of opponents, he became acquainted with thousands of central Illinois voters and remembered their names and circumstances. In 1847, *Boston Courier* reporter J.H. Buckingham made a stagecoach ride with Lincoln through central Illinois, and reported that Lincoln:

> knew, or appeared to know, every body we met, the name of the tenant of every farm-house, and the owner of every plat of ground. Such a shaking of hands—such a how-d'ye-do—such a greeting of different kinds, as we saw, was never seen before, it seemed as if...he had a kind word, a smile and a bow for every-body on the road, even to the horses, and the cattle, and the swine.[152]

> All [who] claim the personal acquaintance of Mr. Lincoln," wrote one newspaperman of the day, "will agree that he is the very embodiment of good temper and affability. They will all concede that he has a kind word, an encouraging smile, a humorous remark for nearly all [who seek] his presence...[153]

The making of political speeches was at times risky, for with limited or no organized law enforcement in most frontier towns, dissenting residents were accustomed to dealing out jus-

---

[152] *Lincoln*, David Herbert Donald, p 106
[153] *Lincoln on Leadership*, Donald T. Phillips, p 18

tice on their own. One day while standing in the courthouse, directly beneath Lincoln's third-story law office, Edward Baker, Lincoln's admired friend, after whom he named his second son Edward Baker Lincoln, was making an impetuous speech, and verbally attacked a local newspaper to an audience of voters. The angered brother of the newspaper editor shouted, "Pull him down" and for a moment it appeared that the crowd was about to do just that. Lincoln was listening to the commotion from the floor above and sensed danger for his friend. His long legs suddenly appeared dangling through a trap door that separated the two floors, and down he dropped onto the platform on which Baker was being threatened. Lincoln tried in vain to calm the angry crowd until he seized the stone water jug and shouted, "I'll break it over the head of the first man who lays a hand on Baker." Thus silencing the audience, he continued in a perfect calmness, "Hold on gentlemen, let us not disgrace the age and country in which we live. This is a land where freedom of speech is guaranteed. Mr. Baker has a right to speak and ought to be permitted to do so. I am here to protect him and no man shall take him from this stand if I can prevent him." Order was then restored.[154]

On another occasion, General Usher F. Linder delivered a rather spirited address amid threats of violence from the galleries. Lincoln and Baker stepped up to the platform and stationed themselves beside the speaker. When he had finished Lincoln spoke:

> Linder, Baker and I are apprehensive that you may be attacked by some of those ruffians who insulted you from the galleries, and we have come to escort you to your hotel. We both think we can do a little fighting, so

---

[154] *The Wit and Wisdom of Abraham Lincoln*, Edited by Anthony Gross, p 9

we want you to walk between us until we get you to your hotel. Your quarrel is our quarrel and that of the great Whig party of this nation; and your speech upon this occasion is the greatest one that has been made by any of us, for which we wish to honor, love, and defend you.[155]

And they walked off unmolested amid the cheers of the audience.

Upon hearing that a railroad contractor named Radford had taken possession of the nearby polling place and was preventing the Whigs from voting, Lincoln took up an ax-handle and made for the place. "Radford, he said, "you'll spoil and blow if you live much longer." Knowing the reputation of Lincoln's strength and moral resolve, Radford "discreetly retired." Lincoln disappointedly told his friend Joshua Speed that he wanted "Radford to show fight" as he "intended just to knock him down and leave him kicking."[156]

In 1843, when Lincoln's former mentor and law partner John Todd Stuart made it known that he would not run for a third term in the U.S. House of Representatives, Lincoln and two other prominent Whigs, John J. Hardin and his close friend Edward Baker, began in earnest to vie for the vacancy. To a former colleague from the legislature Lincoln wrote, "Now if you should hear any one say that Lincoln don't want to go to Congress, I wish you...would tell him...he is mistaken. The truth is, I would like to go very much."[157]

---

[155]

www.mrlincolnandfriends.org/content_inside.asp?pageID=110&subjectID=1 - 14k -

[156] *The Wit and Wisdom of Abraham Lincoln*, Edited by Anthony Gross, p 10

[157] *Lincoln*, David Herbert Donald, p 111

But it was not to be so. His marriage into Mary Todd's wealthy and elite family brought characterizations that he was a candidate of pride, wealth, and aristocracy. A look into his heart and circumstances would reveal that none of these accusations was even remotely accurate and he felt personally injured by them. Once more, Lincoln's religious convictions damaged his reputation and political hopes as well. It was whispered about that he belonged to no church and rumors were floated that he was suspected of being a follower of deism, the religious movement based on rationalism and reason practiced by the likes of Thomas Jefferson and John Adams— also inaccurate. Baker, on the other hand, gained support from voters for being a devout Campbellite—the same sect that Lincoln's father, Thomas, was believed to have joined in his later years. But when the votes were counted, it was Hardin who was the choice of the majority of delegates, and Lincoln would lose in his first bid for national office.

It would seem that Lincoln was destined to suffer for his perceptions of divine truths. Within a year of his arrival in Springfield six years earlier in 1837, Lincoln's "peculiar" religious beliefs and the fact that he was affiliated with none of the local religious sects brought accusations and murmurings. This was even noised about through editorials in the local newspaper in Springfield, written by a vindictive and dishonest plaintiff whom Lincoln set out to expose while representing one of his first clients as a young lawyer. At some time following these editorials, Lincoln concluded that he would no longer speak openly of his religious convictions because of the difficulties that they regularly aroused. But there can be little doubt that they continued to burn warm within his soul, as evidenced by the incident recorded by Captain Gilbert J. Greene, then an eighteen-year-old printer who afterwards published the following:

"Greene," said Lincoln to him one day on the streets of Springfield, "I've got to ride out into the country tomorrow to draw a will for a woman who is believed to be on her deathbed. I may want you for a witness. If you haven't anything else to do I'd like to have you go along." The invitation was promptly accepted. On the way to the farmhouse the lawyer and the printer chatted delightfully, cementing a friendship that was fast ripening into real affection. Arriving at the house, the woman was found to be near her end. With great gentleness Lincoln drew up the document disposing of the property as the woman desired. Neighbors and relatives were present making it unnecessary to call on Greene to witness the instrument. After the signing and witnessing of the will the woman turned to Lincoln and said, with a smile: "Now I have my affairs for this world arranged satisfactorily. I am thankful to say that long before this I have made preparation for the other side of life I am so soon to enter. Many years ago I sought and found Christ as my Saviour. He has been my stay and comfort through the years, and is now near to carry me over the river of death. I do not fear death, Mr. Lincoln. I am really glad that my time has come, for loved ones have gone before me and I rejoice in the hope of meeting them so soon." Instinctively the friends drew nearer the bedside. As the dying woman had addressed her words more directly to Lincoln than to the others, Lincoln, evincing sympathy in every look and gesture, bent toward her and said: "Your faith in Christ is wise and strong;

your hope of a future life is blessed. You are to be congratulated in passing through life so usefully, and into the life beyond so hopefully." "Mr. Lincoln," said she, "won't you read a few verses out of the Bible for me?" A member of the family offered him the family Bible. Instead of taking it, he began reciting from memory the twenty-third Psalm, laying emphasis upon "Though I walk through the valley of the shadow of death I will fear no evil, for thou art with me; thy rod and thy staff they shall comfort me." Still referring to the Bible, Lincoln began with the first part of the fourteenth chapter of John: "Let not your heart be troubled; ye believe in God, believe also in me. In my Father's house are many mansions; if it were not so I would have told you. I go to prepare a place for you. And if I go and prepare a place for you, I will come again, and receive you unto myself; that where I am, there ye may be also." After he had given these and other quotations from the Scriptures, he recited various familiar comforting hymns, closing with "Rock of Ages, cleft for me." Then, with a tenderness and pathos that enthralled everyone in the room, he spoke the last stanza—

> "*While I draw this fleeting breath,*
> *When mine eyes shall close in death,*
> *When I shall rise to worlds unknown,*
> *See Thee on Thy judgment throne,*
> *Rock of Ages, cleft for me,*
> *Let me hide myself in Thee.*"

While Lincoln was reciting this stanza a look of peace and resignation lit up the countenance of the dying woman. In a few minutes more, while the lawyer and the printer were there, she passed away. The journey back to Springfield was begun in silence. It was the younger man who finally said: "Mr. Lincoln, ever since what has just happened back there in the farmhouse, I have been thinking that it is very extraordinary that you should so perfectly have acted as pastor as well as attorney." When the answer to this suggestion finally was given—and it was not given at once—Lincoln said: "God, and Eternity, and Heaven were very near to me today."[158]

In March of 1846, Mary and Abraham were blessed with the birth of their second son, Edward Baker Lincoln. In that same year Lincoln embarked on his next political race: his third try at the U.S. House of Representatives. This campaign for Congress necessitated his first public disclosure of his religious position. His opponent in this election was Peter Cartwright, a tough-talking, circuit-riding preacher, respected and renowned for having baptized more than seven thousand children and converts into his Methodist faith and for causing nearly five hundred people attending one of his sermons to start "jerking" at once. These congregational responses were not uncommon in the Methodist revivals for which Cartwright was celebrated. William J. Wolf says, "Women were particularly susceptible to this revivalistic enthusiasm. As their caps and combs came loose, Onstot, a local resident, reported, 'so sudden would be the jerking of the head that their long loose hair would crack almost as loud as a waggoners whip.'"[159] Cartwright had defeat-

---

[158] *Lincoln the Comforter,* Charles T. White, pp *11-16.*
[159] *The Almost Chosen People,* William J. Wolf, p 41

ed Lincoln in his first bid for the Illinois State Legislature. In this campaign for the U.S. House of Representatives, Cartwright and his Democratic Party supporters again used Lincoln's religious beliefs to discredit him with the voters. They "labored mightily to replace 'Whig' with 'Infidel' as Lincoln's party label." Their charge that Lincoln was "an open scoffer at Christianity" in a widely distributed handbill prompted Lincoln's first known public statement on his faith to clarify the truth and to respond to the charge. "That I am not a member of any Christian denomination is true," Lincoln wrote, "but I have never denied the truth of the Scriptures and I have never spoken with any intentional disrespect of religion in general, or of any denomination of Christianity in particular."[160] "If then I was guilty of such conduct, I should blame no man who should condemn me for it; but I do blame those, whoever they may be, who falsely put such a charge in circulation against me."[161] Wolf says, referring to the revivalist movement,

> The crude emotionalism of these gatherings can hardly have commended itself to Lincoln with his strong sense of humor and of reserve in matters of the spirit. What must have disturbed him still more was the violent feuding between the jealous denominations. One form of Baptist predestinarian opinion held that its church members were created by God for heaven whereas the greater part of mankind had been destined for eternal flames.[162]

Later in the campaign, Lincoln attended a religious meeting conducted by Cartwright, who stood and said, "All who desire

---

[160] *Lincoln*, David Herbert Donald, p 49
[161] *Abraham Lincoln*, Carl Sandburg, p 84
[162] *The Almost Chosen People*, William J. Wolf, p. 41

to give their hearts to God, and go to heaven, will stand." A sprinkling of men, women and children stood up. The preacher continued, "All who do not wish to go to hell will stand." All stood up—except Lincoln. Cartwright gravely continued: "I observe that many responded to the first invitation to give their hearts to God and to go to heaven. And I further observe that all of you save one indicated that you did not desire to go to hell. The sole exception is Mr. Lincoln, who did not respond to either invitation. May I inquire of you, Mr. Lincoln, where you are going?"

Lincoln rose slowly and replied,

> I came here as a respectful listener. I did not know that I was to be singled out by Brother Cartwright. I believe in treating religious matters with due solemnity. I admit that the questions propounded by Brother Cartwright are of great importance. I did not feel called upon to answer as the rest of you did. Brother Cartwright asks me directly where I am going. I desire to reply with equal directness: I am going to Congress.[163]

How easy it would have been for Lincoln to simply relent, choose a church, and join with it to end the surprisingly persistent ridicule for his differing beliefs. His wife had been raised a Presbyterian and at the time of their marriage was a member of the Episcopal Church. But as he expressed in his public statement, he had not joined with her church or with any other even though he would frequently attend worship services with her. By this time in his life he was avoiding conversations on his beliefs to spare him the difficulties that seemed always to fol-

---

[163] *Abraham Lincoln*, Carl Sandburg, p 84

low. He went on to say, in his public statement, "The habit of arguing thus however, I have entirely left off for more than five years."[164] He had become less expressive of these personal convictions but they must surely have continued to burn within his soul for him to continue to bear the ridicule. Why would he hold so fast to his solitary beliefs and continue to endure the criticisms for them? Many clergy and friends of his day had asked this question of him, and numerous historians and clergy since his life have pondered this same quandary. A number of conclusions have been propounded, the most consistent of which is that he was, as suggested by many, an infidel, a non-believer; that he was confused in the area of religion.

But Lincoln's life of "pure religion" merits a far different perspective and interpretation. In the gospel of John 14:15, Jesus said to his disciples, "He that hath my commandments, and keepeth them, he it is that loveth me; and he that loveth me shall be loved of my Father, and I will love him, and will manifest myself to him." If keeping the Lord's commandments serves as a measure of one's love for God, perhaps few mortals surpass Abraham Lincoln in keeping God's commandments and in his love for God and for his fellow men. Few people will have had a more consistent record from childhood to the grave, of living Christ's teachings and examples of turning the other cheek, going the extra mile, judging not, condemning not, forgiving, loving one's enemies, and loving their neighbor as one loves himself, as did Abraham Lincoln.

Churchless—but with a singularly profound faith in God that was somewhat troubling to some historians—President Lincoln would guide this nation through its most harrowing trials and judgments in more of a prophet-like way than political, frequently reminding the people of their transgressions and of the righteousness of the Almighty's judgments that he be-

---

[164] *Abraham Lincoln, the Redeemer President*, Allen C. Guelzo, p 117

lieved were being inflicted on America during the Civil War for those transgressions. If Lincoln's assessment of God's judgments was accurate, then God did in fact raise up and employ Abraham Lincoln, this purest of vessels, to speak to this untoward nation that had promoted the abominable institution of slavery by profaning the sacred Constitution and establishing laws that would guarantee its perpetuation. America had also become a land filled with lawless mobocracy, with bigotry against foreigners and against people who were constitutionally guaranteed the right to worship as they chose, and with the denial of free speech in the press—many a printing press ended up in a river or destroyed by readers who did not agree with their message. The nation was fast embracing a growing white-supremacy notion that was used to justify the enslavement of those with a black skin, open discrimination against Irish and Italian Catholic immigrants, and brutal and unpunished persecution of Americans who practiced religions differing from the mainstream, as was done to the Mormons.

Cartwright's ridicule of Lincoln's religious beliefs was of little effect in this election as the voters in the district elected Lincoln to the U.S. House of Representatives by an unprecedented margin. On October 25, 1847, the Lincolns left Springfield for their new home in Washington, DC. Stephen A. Douglas would also head to Washington as newly elected United States senator for Illinois.

Chapter Four

"I Know His Hand Is in It"

"Being elected to Congress, though I am very grateful to our friends, for having done it, has not pleased me as much as I expected."[165] Lincoln wrote this to his friend and confidante, Joshua Speed, some weeks after his victory over Peter Cartwright, following two unsuccessful runs at the office. Lincoln was the only Whig representative from Illinois and the prospects for any significant establishment of his agenda appeared to be unlikely with Democrat James K. Polk as president, even with the Whigs' slim majority in the House of Representatives. During his two years in Washington Lincoln was privileged to attend the national Whig Party convention in Philadelphia, and later that year he traveled through New England on behalf of presidential candidate Zachary Taylor, making speeches and encouraging support for his election. The *Boston Atlas* reported his to be one of the best speeches ever in Worcester. Lincoln did not know then the value that this exposure would have for him, some twelve years in the future, when he would again make a series of speeches throughout New England prior to his run for president. His speeches seemed to consistently impress his audiences.

---

[165] *Lincoln*, David Herbert Donald, p 117

In the House of Representatives he would go on to establish a stellar record of attendance, missing only 13 of the 456 roll calls in the two-year term. He made great effort to ensure that his speeches were copied (more than seven thousand copies) and sent to his constituents in Illinois; all of which he did without a secretary, addressing and franking them himself. As was the case with the Illinois state legislature, Lincoln at times had the halls of Congress drowned in laughter with his wit and anecdotes. He gave a speech on the floor, again in support of the Whig's presidential candidate, Zachary Taylor, on which the *Baltimore American* reported, saying that his manner "was so good natured, and his style so peculiar, that he kept the House in a continuous roar of merriment for the last half hour…"[166]

While serving in Congress in 1847-49, his abhorrence of slavery did not diminish but rather increased. He would listen to the lawmakers from the South argue to protect current laws and promote new ones for the promulgation of property rights in the form of the Negro slave at the expense of human rights. Just seven blocks from the nation's Capitol stood the Franklin & Armfield warehouse, the largest slave market in the entire country. Observing these slave auctions did little to ease his distaste for the practice as men, women, and children were treated like droves of horses, and he denounced them as being "a sort of Negro livery-stable."[167] Foreign observers frequently pointed out to their readers back home the gross hypocrisy of a nation founded on individual freedoms buying and selling the posterity of kidnapped Africans into slavery for no other purpose than financial gain. Lincoln often said he was naturally antislavery like his father, but he did not participate with the more extreme abolitionists because of the unfortunate fact that the original Constitution allowed for slavery and past proslavery lawmakers had built up such legal walls that it was essentially

---

[166] *Lincoln*, David Herbert Donald, p 130
[167] *Lincoln*, David Herbert Donald, p 135

illegal to pursue the abolition course. But the expansion of slavery was another matter, for he would break no law in opposing slavery's westward sprawl. Therefore, Lincoln acted when and where he could to prevent its insidious spread on the continent. Ever a saint, Lincoln would silently withdraw from debates when participants would react with anger, using instead his vote for the final expression of his position. While in Congress, Lincoln introduced a bill that would outlaw slavery in the District of Columbia, but it had little support and failed.

The widespread acceptance of slavery, even by non-slave owners in the north, is illustrated by the following that occurred in Lincoln's hometown of Springfield ten years earlier:

> In October of 1837 the news that Reverend Jeremiah Porter was to speak [against] slavery generated an angry crowd of Springfield citizens some of whom threatened to mob him. Edward Baker managed to calm the crowd sufficiently for the speech to be delivered and the Reverend to survive any violence. It resulted in the organization of a citizens group chaired by Judge Thomas C. Browne that produced the following resolution: 'The doctrine of immediate emancipation...is at variance with Christianity' and 'abolishionists...are dangerous members of society, and should be shunned by all good citizens.'[168]

Mary Lincoln and the boys were with Lincoln for part of the time in Washington but she became disillusioned with the difficulty inherent with raising children and the loneliness, as only a few wives accompanied their congressmen-husbands to Wash-

[168] *Abraham Lincoln*, Carl Sandburg, p 63

ington. After some time, they concluded that she would be happier moving back with her parents in Lexington, Kentucky. Following their departure, Lincoln missed their company and wrote to Mary, regarding his sons, saying, "Don't let the blessed fellows forget father."[169]

As time went on he regretted his pledge to serve but one term, feeling that he had established a foundation from which he would have had considerable influence in a following term. But in the end, he would honor his commitment to his supporters to not seek reelection. None of Lincoln's resolutions during his term were adopted or even debated. The conclusion of his term arrived with mild disappointment on his part for lack of any significant contribution and for the continued weakening of his Whig Party in general. In the five years following his term in the U.S. House of Representatives, Lincoln would turn away from politics, focusing on his family and his law practice. During that time he was offered the governorship of Oregon, which he declined.

Shortly after Lincoln's return from Washington, their young son Eddy died on February 1, 1850; he was not quite four years old. Researchers today believe it was tuberculosis that took him from the Lincolns. Later that year, Mary Lincoln gave birth to William Wallace, who was born on December 21, 1850. The Lincolns hoped the arrival of their third son would help ease the grief caused by Edward's death but it did not. Even ten years later, Mary's eyes would fill with tears at the very mention of Eddy's name. The Lincolns cherished their remaining sons, Robert and William. Mary was the disciplinarian. William Herndon expressed his observation that Lincoln was much too lenient with his children. In that era the Biblical directive paraphrased in Samuel Butler's 1664 poem, "spare the rod and spoil the child," was widely held as the only way

---

[169] *Lincoln*, David Herbert Donald, p 130

to rear obedient and upright children. Switchings and spankings were common parental practices and very much expected; a willow switch was a standard educational tool in many schools. The fact that Lincoln would not employ such measures of discipline was likely looked down upon, as expressed by Herndon. Explaining his thoughts on childrearing, Lincoln wrote, "It is my pleasure that my children are free and happy, and unrestrained by parental tyranny. Love is the chain, whereby to bind a child to its parents."[170]

Lincoln had a fondness for children. When neighborhood boys strung a string across the path with the sole purpose of knocking off Lincoln's stovepipe hat, Lincoln retrieved the hat, rounded up the boys, and took them around the corner to buy them some cookies. He played handball with the older boys and, on his hands and knees, would school them at marbles. When the circus would come to town he would round up the boys and girls whose parents were too poor to pay the admission, and they and his sons would enjoy the wonders there. Once he noticed a small boy beating time on a pan in the alley behind his house, and when Christmas came around Lincoln made sure that a real drum was waiting for him on Christmas morning.

The return home from Washington and his seat in the U.S. House of Representatives marked a semi-retirement from public life for Lincoln. Holding no public office, he settled into this next chapter of his life, which would include focusing more attention on his sons, his wife, his home, and his career. During the next decade the small Lincoln home would experience a number of remodels and expansions, adding an upstairs for the growing family. In 1853, their fourth son Thomas was born to them, named after Lincoln's father. Lincoln nicknamed him

---

[170] *Lincoln*, An Illustrated Biography, Philip B. Kunhardt Jr.,Philip Kunhardt III,Peter W. Kunhardt p 91

Tad because when he was a baby with a large head and tiny body, Lincoln thought he looked like a tadpole.

At age forty, Abraham Lincoln was back on the circuit with the reputation for embodying two unusual companion-characteristics for a lawyer: complete honesty and skillful legal representation. He was much sought after by the honest citizenry of the district. The not-so-honest knew to avoid him, knowing that he would either refuse their case or represent them poorly. Lincoln seemed incapable of employing any degree of duplicity or deceit. Unlike the majority of the other seasoned attorneys in his circle who were by now wealthy, Lincoln still earned a modest income. His disinclination to charge high fees and his disregard for land speculation or other forms of wealth-building—a common endeavor by his moneyed colleagues—would mean a financially modest yet adequate life for the Lincolns. Even late in his career, Lincoln wrote to a man from Quincy who had sent him a check for $25 for drawing up some legal papers, saying, "You must think I am a high-priced man. You are too liberal with your money. Fifteen dollars is enough for the job."[171] He returned $10 with the letter.

For the next eleven years, Lincoln, who now found himself one of the senior lawyers on the traveling circuit, would follow Judge David Davis on the Eight Judicial District to take on as much work for his nominal fees as he could. They were quite a mismatched pair. Judge Davis was a heavy man, whose friends good-naturedly said that he had to be surveyed for a pair of trousers, though he was immaculate in his appearance and manner. Conversely, Lincoln was tall and emaciated; seeming to care not a lick for his appearance, he wore pants that rarely reached his shoe tops and in summer he wore a white linen duster that was stained and tattered. But there was a mutual regard between the two, as both were Whigs and both detested

---

[171] *Lincoln*, Donald Herbert Donald, p 149

slavery, yet they opposed the more extreme abolitionist movement as being an impractical and illegal solution to the great
dilemma. Davis wrote to his wife that he greatly admired "Mr.
Lincoln's exceeding honesty and fairness," and would often
designate Lincoln to sit as judge when called away from the
bench."[172] Another letter from Davis to his wife contained a
description of the circuit-riding life:

> There is much mud in the winter and dust
> in the summer; taverns were overrun with
> mosquitoes, fleas, and bedbugs; the dining
> rooms were dirty and typically the tables were
> greasy—table cloth greasy—floor greasy and
> everything else ditto. Worst of all the food was
> hardly fit for the stomach of a horse.[173]

Yet for Lincoln, all these hardships were met with carefree
indifference—he never uttered a complaint. Once when the
innkeeper had run out of meat and bread, Lincoln cheerfully
responded, "Well in the absence of anything to eat I will jump
into this cabbage."[174]

In all his meekness there are rare instances of Lincoln's acting in anger. One such instance was in the defense of a man
who had stabbed and killed another. Lincoln did nothing to
deny that his client had committed the stabbing; but he believed that it was done in self-defense, after repeated threats of
harm to the defendant by the victim, and thus he argued. The
judge E.Y. Rice, who had been a lifelong Democrat and political opponent of Lincoln, sided with the prosecution's argument that Lincoln's evidence of the threats was inadmissible

---

[172] *Lincoln*, David Herbert Donald, p 146
[173] *Lincoln*, David Herbert Donald, p 147
[174] *Lincoln*, David Herbert Donald, p 147

since they could not be proved. In his second line of defense, Lincoln introduced testimony by the victim's grandfather, the widely respected Reverend Peter Cartwright, Lincoln's opponent in his earlier run for Congress. Cartwright testified that the victim on his deathbed confessed to the threats and said he had brought it upon himself, and that he forgave the defendant. Again the prosecution objected, and Judge Rice agreed to exclude Cartwright's testimony.

In a righteous indignation rarely seen in Lincoln, he angrily protested both decisions. William Herndon, who was present, remembered that Lincoln spoke so forcefully and passionately in defense of his client that he barely escaped a charge of contempt. Lincoln argued less on technical law than on the principals of morality and justice, as was his common approach. In the end, the judge retracted his rulings and allowed both evidences to go to the jury, resulting in the acquittal of Lincoln's client.

The peaceful and prosperous years following Lincoln's return from Congress were laced with a melancholy that would come over him as he pondered the uncertainties of his future. He confided in Herndon, "How hard, oh how hard it is to die and leave one's Country no better than if one had never lived in it."[175] His current course in life and his unremarkable contribution in Congress did little to sustain his inner and closely guarded sense that he was born to a high purpose. Herndon observed that some days Lincoln would arrive at the office in a cheerful mood, only to fall into a quiet gloomy state, resting his chin in his palm and staring out the window for hours. It is possible that Lincoln had some level of premonition that he was destined to be involved with something of significant importance. These bouts of melancholy may have been expressions of disappointment at so many failed opportunities that would have

---

[175] *The Recollected Words of Abraham Lincoln*, Don and Virginia Fehrenbacher, p 241

placed him in position to influence the declining moral trends in America that troubled him so.

Although, with all his heart, Lincoln had always wanted to see the slaves freed, his reverence for the Constitution that allowed for slavery kept him from joining abolition groups to end it. Over the years, Southern majorities in local and national governments had also managed to pass additional laws to fortify the institution of slavery, and Lincoln was unbending in his determination to respect and obey the law—even bad law. William Lee Miller observed, "As an emerging political leader and shaper of opinion in 1854-1860, and as President of a war-torn nation in 1861-1865, he always opposed slavery strongly—but *within* the law, *under* the Constitution, *affirming* the continuing bond of the Union."[176] To the misfortune of millions, the great Constitution possessed a serious flaw that recognized slavery without naming it. However, Lincoln and the new Republican Party were unabashed in their determination to block the spreading of slavery in the new territories and future states. In this way they could at least control its insidious spread, and do so within the law.

By 1854, and during Lincoln's five-year hiatus from politics following his return from Congress in 1849, slavery was the prominent issue of the day. However, as Lincoln followed events closely, his energies remained focused on his family and his Lincoln and Herndon law practice where he found himself in high demand for his reasonable fees, his record of success and for his unyielding integrity. As a congressman, he voted for the Wilmot Proviso in 1849, written to close to slavery the newly acquired territory from Mexico. In 1850, many citizens in the North erupted with anger at the passage of the Fugitive Slave Law aimed directly at the abolitionists' successful campaigns to protect and extend freedom to escaped slaves from the South.

---

[176] *Lincoln's Virtues,* William Lee Miller, p 236

This law eventually resulted in the unscrupulous capture of a number of free African-Americans who never had been slaves, tearing them from their families, never to be seen again, as they would be "returned" to live the rest of their lives, lost in Southern slavery. Lincoln was deeply troubled by this new act but did not oppose it because of the slaveholders' constitutional right to own slaves, and because the new law "springs of necessity from the fact that the institution is among us."[177] To oppose the Fugitive Slave Law would be to oppose the Constitution, which unfortunately, yet explicitly, made provision for fugitives to be "delivered up."[178] In his Bloomington, Illinois speech of September 12, 1854, Lincoln quipped, referring to the Fugitive Slave Law, "I own if I were called upon by a Marshall, to assist in catching a fugitive, I should suggest to him that others could run a great deal faster than I could."[179]

It was Lincoln's long-time political nemesis, Stephen A. Douglas—then the U.S. Senate's chairman of the powerful Committee on Territories and arguably the most prominent politician in America—who brought Lincoln roaring back into the national political arena. While Lincoln's modest political career appeared to be ended, his frequent rival was at his pinnacle of prominence as this nation's most powerful senator. Douglas had even been a candidate for president in 1852 and had not lost his taste for the highest office. Lincoln's abrupt turn back to politics in 1854 would change his life profoundly and start him on the pathway from relative obscurity to become the greatest of American presidents. In that year, Congress had passed, and President Franklin Pierce had signed into law, Stephen A. Douglas's Kansas-Nebraska Act and the accompanying repeal of the Missouri Compromise, the passing of which caused Lincoln to say that Stephen A. Douglas "Took us by

---

[177] *Lincoln's Virtues,* William Lee Miller, p 235
[178] *Lincoln's Virtues,* William Lee Miller, p 239
[179] *Lincoln's Virtues,* William Lee Miller, p 235

surprise—astounded us...We were thunderstruck and stunned."[180]

What was it about the passage of this Act five years after his political retirement that roused him so? Why now and not by the earlier political events just cited? What Lincoln saw in the Kansas-Nebraska Act, and the accompanying repeal of the Union-protecting and peace-promoting agreement in the Missouri Compromise, was a new law in America, passed by Congress and backed by the president of the United States, that removed a protective shield that had been laboriously put in place over the country by earlier lawmakers, and replaced it with a law that actually created a dangerous threat to the nation's very existence. The Kansas-Nebraska Act allowed for "popular sovereignty," the right for these two new territories, and all others that would follow, to choose slavery or not to choose slavery in their territory and eventually their state. William Lee Miller observed that the new law was accompanied by "the most blatant abrogation of the historic Union-protecting, peace-promoting bargain, the Missouri Compromise. It did not protect the Union; it endangered it. It did not preserve the peace; it threatened it."[181] Ironically, the Missouri Compromise, with the leadership of Senator Stephen A. Douglas, was passed overwhelmingly by both parties just four years earlier in 1850 as the tool to ease the growing agitation over slavery by establishing a delicate sectional balance of slave states and free states. Lincoln would soon be heard to publicly declare that the Kansas-Nebraska Act "would obliterate the principled rejection of slavery—making the nation morally neutral as between slavery and freedom," and he saw this moral neutrality as gravely dangerous to the future survival of this nation and its culture of freedoms.[182]

---

[180] *Lincoln's Virtues,* William Lee Miller, p 232
[181] *Lincoln's Virtues,* William Lee Miller, p 238
[182] *Lincoln's Virtues,* William Lee Miller, p 238

Lincoln said, "People who go and settle there may establish slavery or exclude it, as they see fit."[183] The door was now open for citizens of the future states west of the Mississippi River all the way to the West Coast to use their newly acquired popular sovereignty, now accorded them by this Act, to *choose* to enslave black Americans in their respective territories and states. With the passage of the Kansas-Nebraska Act, slavery had essentially become legitimized in America, changing it from the moral issue it had always been to a quality-of-life choice on the menu for white Americans, a benefit they could bestow upon themselves through the ballot box. The Kansas-Nebraska Act made the enslavement of African-Americans a perk for white Americans, and no longer a horrible injustice and abomination.

Lincoln was deeply troubled at what he saw: that this government, which he believed to be created under God by the Founding Fathers, was now placed on a dangerous slope toward its own self-disintegration. While many future states would quite probably choose against slavery, Stephen A. Douglas and the contentious Fire-Eaters of the South were certain that many other states would choose to implement the peculiar institution. What the visionary Lincoln pictured, with a soul-shaking dread, was a country of intentioned *united* states from coast to coast now with the hugely divisive institution of slavery more firmly implanted in the nation than ever before. And with his long-held conviction that this nation could not survive "half slave and half free"[184] and that a "house divided against itself"[185] could not long endure, Lincoln was stirred to the depths of his soul by this monumental misstep made by Congress and the President with this new law. What troubled him as much as any-thing was his perception that the passage of this act "entailed

---

[183] *Lincoln's Virtues*, William Lee Miller, p 240
[184] Lincoln's Speech, Springfield, Ill. June 16, 1858
[185] Lincoln's Speech, Springfield, Ill. June 16, 1858

the alteration of the moral premise of the nation" regarding the "terrible moral anomaly of American slavery."[186] While this moral premise of slavery had always been a wrong tolerated only by necessity, this dramatic political offensive and victory by proslavery activists elevated slavery from a moral wrong to a condition of choice, legally afforded to all white Americans. Racism and white supremacy would now be legal and celebrated in America. Lincoln would view this destruction of a time-honored moral principle to be as dangerous as the actual, and most certain, spread of this soul-cankering practice of slavery across the American continent.

But there was another disturbing movement taking place precisely at the same time as the passing of the Kansas-Nebraska Act in the mid 1850s. It was the combination of religious and civil forces on a national level in the form of a new political party called the American Party. This new party was better known as the "Know-Nothings" because it grew from local oath-bound secret societies throughout the nation, with the heaviest concentration in the North. These American Party members were instructed to reply to any inquiry about their secret organizations with "I know nothing," hence their better known moniker. This party was made up primarily of Protestants who had grown uneasy with the rapidly increasing numbers of Catholics in America, particularly Irish Catholics, who were immigrating to the nation's major cities. The primary objective of the Know-Nothings was to dramatically limit the immigration of foreigners to the United States, particularly those from Catholic nations. They also sought to ensure that no foreign-born, non-white, non-Protestant persons be allowed to hold any political office. It was commonly held among these Protestant Know-Nothings that Pope Pius IX, who at that time ruled Rome with an iron fist, was secretly creating a network of

---

186 *Lincoln's Virtues,* William Lee Miller, p 238

Catholics in America who were controlled by him through the Catholic bishops and priests. Such ideas spawned conspiracy theories about the Pope's purported plans to subjugate the United States. Remarkably, in 1854 alone, it is estimated that the number of Know-Nothings grew from fifty thousand to over one million. They won elections in Chicago and Boston, and carried the Massachusetts legislature and governorship. They were decisively influential in Maine, Indiana, Pennsylvania, and California, where the mayor of San Francisco was a Know-Nothing. The Know-Nothing mayor of Chicago barred all immigrants from city jobs. In the coming years, two vice presidents of the United States would be former members of the American Know-Nothing Party.

Lincoln often warned of the dangers of internal mob violence toward classes of people that were reflected in this movement. To Americans today it is appalling that so many would willingly direct their animosities toward fellow Americans who differed from themselves. Today prejudices on such a grand scale are simply not allowed by law or by the strength of public opinion. But they were promoted openly and defiantly in the 1850s. Even though public sentiment against slavery was mounting rapidly in the Northern states, there was little opposition to racial prejudice toward blacks. Yes, many Northerners felt that Negroes should be freed from slavery, but black Americans were not necessarily to be treated with the same respect and dignity afforded white Americans. At that time in America racism against African-Americans was almost universal and this discrimination was now being expanded to include the Irish who were being openly despised, as well the swelling numbers of Catholics and Mormons. The alarming and mounting political movement of hatred toward the Irish and Catholics, now added to the firmly established "peculiar institution" of slavery, would now, in 1854, be graced with the legitimizing of slavery by the United States Congress and president as a white American's privilege and black American's curse through the Kansas-Nebraska Act. The attitude of derision for different classes of people, whether based on religion or ethnicity, was now legally and legitimately sewn into the American fabric.

If all of this was not enough, a capstone was placed onto this wave of white Protestant superiority by the 1857 decision of the United States Supreme Court on the Dred Scott case, which fueled this growing bonfire of racism and discrimination by ruling that the Negroes were less than human, referring to them as "beings of an inferior order,"[187] and were to be treated as such in America.

It was the legalizing of this very arrogant and blatant racial and religious discrimination on the part of white America in the form of the Know-Nothing movement, the Dred Scott Decision, and the Kansas-Nebraska Act that "took [Lincoln] by surprise," "astounded him" and left him "thunderstruck."[188]

Why had Stephen A. Douglas, a Northerner, sponsored this slavery-promoting Kansas-Nebraska Act? For one, he had always been proslavery, as had many others in the North and certainly in Illinois. At that time he was the powerful chairman of the Senate Committee on Territories, with the addition to the Union of a number of states and territories already to his credit. He desperately wanted the Nebraska and Kansas territories admitted as well but they were deadlocked in Congress over the slavery issue. Some (mostly Southern) senators insisted that they both be admitted as slave territories, and of course those opposed to the spread of slavery were equally determined to block its march westward. Douglas appeared to have an additional motive. He had narrowly missed being nominated for president in 1852 at age thirty-nine and most certainly had his eye on the 1856 presidential election. Knowing this, the Southern block of politicians placed enormous pressure on Douglas to accept their

---

[187] US Supreme Court, Dred Scott Decision of 1857
[188] *Lincoln's Virtues*, William Lee Miller, p 232

offer of support for his nomination in the next presidential election in exchange for his leadership on the Kansas-Nebraska Act, but with the caveat that there be an *explicit* statement that the Missouri Compromise be rendered "inoperative"—the very Compromise that Douglas himself had led to passage just four years earlier. To get his bill through, he reluctantly agreed, predicting "a hell of a storm."[189] President Lincoln's close aides Nicolay and Hay later wrote, in 1886, that "the storm of agitation which this measure aroused dwarfed all former ones in depth and intensity."[190] Another leading scholar, David Potter, wrote in 1976 that the debate over the Nebraska bill from January to May 1854 "was perhaps to this day America's fiercest congressional battle...a struggle of unprecedented intensity."[191] It became so heated that some of the lawmakers were known to have brought guns into the Senate and House chambers, and threats of bloodshed were made. In fact, Douglas was more accurate than he probably knew, as the conflict did have the appearance of a storm from hell.

Expansion of slavery on the continent meant expansion of the already-immense division in the Union, and the Kansas-Nebraska bill would be the legal vehicle to widen that division. With South Carolina's actual secession just six years away, it's not hard to envision this continent as a group of individualized nation-states much like Europe—all with their own individual and varied constitutions, thus creating the very weakness that the original Constitution was designed to prevent.

From the beginning, the Confederacy had little hope of survival with their new imitation Constitution, complete with even more overt legitimizing of racism against blacks and reinforcing the superiority of the whites, by the deletion of equal rights to

---

[189] *The Shattering of the Union: America in the 1850's,* Eric Walther
[190] *Lincoln's Virtues,* William Lee Miller, p 241
[191] *Lincoln's Virtues,* William Lee Miller, p 241

all men, and the fortifying of nullification, i.e., the right of any state to secede. These passports to disaster meant that it would only be a matter of time before one state or another would find itself in enough disagreement to again invoke their right of nullification and react with secession from the Confederacy just as South Carolina did from the Union. In fact Georgia, North Carolina, and east Tennessee had taken formal steps to do just that over disagreements with their Confederate government during the closing months of the war. As president, Lincoln clearly saw this danger, which explains his unbending determination to preserve the Union. Once the Union was divided and weakened, blacks, Mormons, Catholics, the Irish, and who knows who else would no longer have the power of the original Constitution to protect them.

Mr. Lincoln's response to the passage of this bill was much different from his passive nonpolitical response to the Fugitive Slave Act and other current events of the previous five years. The dangers brought upon this nation with the passage of the Kansas-Nebraska Act, together with its accompanying repeal of what Lincoln referred to as a "sacred compact" in the Missouri Compromise, moved him to remarkable action.

He started by studing. He researched speeches, newspapers, the *Congressional Globe,* and history. Some newspapers took notice and reported that Lincoln was "mousing about the libraries in the State House," "nosing for weeks in the State Library, pumping his brain and his imagination for points and arguments" or anything related to events that had led to this cataclysmic debacle at the hands of the highest elected officials of the United States of America.[192] He read Douglas's Senate speeches defending the bill on the one side and those of Charles Sumner, Salmon Chase, and William Seward the most prominent in opposition to it. (The two latter men would be favorites

---

[192] *Lincoln's Virtues* William Lee Miller p 234

for the presidential nomination of 1860 but landed instead on Lincoln's cabinet.) "He [Lincoln] was thinking his way to first principles, clarifying his thoughts about American slavery, and carefully composing the sentences, the paragraphs, the illustrations, to make his points persuasive to an audience of ordinary white Americans on the frontier."[193]

What neither Lincoln nor anyone else could know was that he, a mere retired politician and prairie lawyer with a less than notable national political career, was only six years from the White House and was mounting the most remarkable and unlikely political ascent in United States history. John Wesley Hill declares,

> Abraham Lincoln was a man of God. Recalling his frequent references to Jesus Christ, it would seem altogether fitting to indicate that he set a high standard of Christian manhood...He believed Providence was directing the destiny of the American Union and the march everywhere of human freedom. He accepted the triumph of his cause as the fulfillment of a divine plan.[194]

Senator Stephen A. Douglas became alarmed when Iowa and Maine's Democratic incumbents in the U.S. Senate were defeated, primarily as a backlash to his Kansas-Nebraska Act. So to shore up support in his home state, he launched a whistle-stop campaign to cities and towns throughout Illinois. Fresh from his latest victory in Washington, Senator Stephen A. Douglas returned to Illinois in his luxurious personal train car with a small cannon mounted on the top and a brass band to announce his arrival into the various Illinois communities. His

---

[193] *Lincoln's Virtues* William Lee Miller p 234
[194] *Abraham Lincoln, Man of God*, John Wesley Hill, p xviii

purpose was to foment support for the new law by explaining that the concept of popular sovereignty carried by the Kansas-Nebraska Act was nothing more than granting the citizenry the right to choose their own social institutions, including slavery, and this he presented with his usual passion and eloquence.

A number of faithful and long-time Douglas backers were also displeased with the passage of the Kansas-Nebraska Act and more particularly his leadership role in its success. He was uncharacteristically shouted down in a speech in Chicago. As he moved southward his campaign took him to Bloomington. It was here that Lincoln, the Springfield lawyer, revealed what he was planning to do with his research. Lincoln began his astounding national emergence when Douglas arrived in Bloomington, Illinois to speak to a Democratic gathering on September 29, 1854. The "aroused, thunderstruck, and well-prepared Abraham Lincoln"[195] was about to launch a dramatic single-handed and solitary assault on the corruption that had been passed by the United States Congress and president. Just what he believed would come of his one-man offensive is left for us all to wonder; but what is known is that he pressed forward as if on a divinely inspired mission. He traveled to Bloomington to hear Senator Douglas's speech, and to propose to Douglas that they hold a debate on the dreadful law just passed. His plan took an immediate step backward when Douglas simply refused to debate him. And why would he? Douglas had just won the contest at the highest level in Congress, and the president had signed it into law. Douglas had already won this prize; he had no interest in bringing to the debate podium the same opposing views that he had vanquished in Washington. Plus he knew Lincoln, and he knew Lincoln to be a formidable debater from their numerous encounters in earlier years on opposite sides of the Illinois legislature. Douglas clearly saw that there would be nothing to gain in debating his victory

---

[195] *Lincoln's Virtues*, William Lee Miller, p 238

with a lightweight prairie lawyer. His aim was to recapture the support of his now-troubled local constituency by presenting just his side of the argument and nothing else.

It is important to consider the astounding moral courage of Lincoln in this debate challenge and Lincoln's offensive tactics aimed at the world's most powerful government. Lincoln was nowhere in terms of prominence on the national political scene. Furthermore, what made Lincoln think that his challenge to the most powerful politician in America would be taken seriously? With a long string of successes under his belt as a U.S. senator, including his recent victory with the most hotly debated bill in the history of the U.S. Congress, Douglas was at the top of his game. William Lee Miller wrote, "Even an historian of a later time who was not an admirer of Douglas, Allan Nevins, would write that Douglas 'was doubtless the most formidable legislative pugilist in all our history.'"[196] Miller goes on to say, "Moreover, Douglas was no mild and polite opponent. He was a practiced, powerful debater, full of energy, articulate, sarcastic, scathing, and formidable. From his years at the center of national policy he was full of information that no novice in the provinces could begin to match, and he could call it up in memory at will.[197] "All who watched politics had just seen him in February and March scorch, smash, and skewer the distinguished national figures Chase, Sumner, and Seward, leaving them—in the view of at least his partisans—gasping, vanquished, and silenced."[198] "If that is what this man could do to his opponents of the highest rank in the nation's Capital, what might he do to some mere local adversary out in Springfield?"[199]

And what could Lincoln have possibly imagined would be the outcome of his challenge to Douglas? Lincoln was no doubt

---

[196] *Lincoln's Virtues,* William Lee Miller, p 249

33 *Lincoln's Virtues,* William Lee Miller, p 249

[198] *Lincoln's Virtues,* William Lee Miller, p 249

[199] *Lincoln's Virtues,* William Lee Miller, p 249

aware of Douglas's unmatched prowess as a debater. What could a common citizen, essentially unknown outside of his home state, do to change a bill that had been passed in Congress and signed into law by the president? Yet that is exactly what Lincoln eventually accomplished. History has seen many a man, driven with personal ambition, attempt to seize upon opportunities like this with the intent to establish his own self-promoting and politically ambitious agendas. But one would search in vain for evidence of such intent in Lincoln. Nor would his future debates with Douglas include evidence of intended personal aggrandizement. They would, however, be replete with proclamations to the nation of the basic principles of right and wrong, particularly the moral wrongs of slavery, all forms of injustice, and the dangerous road toward destruction upon which this nation had just been set by its elected leaders with the passage of the Kansas-Nebraska Act. He would soon be heard to say, "Stand with anybody that stands RIGHT, stand with him while he is right and with anybody that stands RIGHT, stand with him while he is right and PART with him when he goes wrong."[200]

Was this man, like the Biblical prophets of old, being moved by the spirit of God in his seemingly fruitless challenge? There is reason to believe, through Lincoln's own expressions, that he in fact believed that God was moving him to this end. Scholars have speculated on his motive for this dramatic reentry into the political arena. William Lee Miller draws on statements made by Lincoln in early adulthood to suggest,

> One reason, surely, was his "thirst for distinction," his desire that his name be known, and that he be "truly esteemed of his fellow men," by rendering himself "worthy of their

---

[200] *Lincoln's Virtues,* William Lee Miller, p 236

esteem." Here was his chance. A related reason, surely, was that this time his longtime rival Stephen A. Douglas might be vulnerable. But the depth and range and daring of his intervention went beyond anything that could be explained by these motives. [201]

Six years later he would confide in a friend by saying, with tears in his eyes, just days before his election as president,

> I know there is a God and that He hates injustice and slavery. I see the storm coming and I know that His hand is in it. *If he has a place and a work for me, and I think he has, I believe I am ready.* I am nothing, but truth is everything. I know I am right because I know that liberty is right, for Christ teaches it and Christ is God.[202]

At the conclusion of the war, to the freed slaves in Richmond who were bowing and addressing him as their savior and redeemer, he said, "You must kneel to God only and thank Him for the liberty you now enjoy. I am but God's humble instrument..."[203] Could Lincoln, on his own, have even imagined that this obscure challenge would be the first step in his road to the White House? Yet somehow Abraham Lincoln, the former and unremarkable two-year congressman, believed that a challenge to Douglas, "who had just mopped the Senate floor with some of the most distinguished of national leaders,"[204] would result in some impact of significance. Lincoln appeared to have had no fear of the defiant Douglas's power in debate.

---

[201] *Lincoln's Virtues,* William Lee Miller, p 250

[202] *Church at War and Peace,* Stephen L. Richards

[203] *The Wit and Wisdom of Abraham Lincoln,* James C. Humes, p 73

[204] *Lincoln's Virtues,* William Lee Miller, p 250

What is rarely suggested as a possible motive for his courageous and dramatic appearance on the national stage is the possibility that much of his motivation came from on high, as Lincoln suggested to his friend—that the spirit of Lincoln's Almighty God could also have been the force behind his remarkable rise. From this point in 1854 onward, Lincoln would assert himself with his characteristic eloquence and humility coupled with a superior intelligence and spirituality for which he had become known all of his life. The "peculiarsome" boy, so kind, obedient, and thirsty for knowledge, this "lawyer who was never known to lie"[205] was about to become the unsponsored conscience for the nation. And to what aim? Some have noted that beginning with his speech in Bloomington, Lincoln's messages took on an uncommon tone, a prophet-like tenor. Referring to this first speech and the many that would follow, Miller observes,

> I suggest it is significant that he completely dropped all of the old Whig topics (the bank, internal improvements, the nativism, Mormon polygamy, temperance) some of which might have helped to promote the Whigs' prospects or his own or to damage Douglas and the Democrats. He would take up no other matters—not in the fall of 1854, and not for the next six years. He concentrated only on slavery. That suggests that he had, melding with his personal ambition, an overriding purpose of great intensity.[206]

After Douglas's refusal to debate, Lincoln listened quietly to his defiant and snarling message in Bloomington. At the con-

---

[205] *Lincoln*, David Herbert Donald, p 149
[206] *Lincoln's Virtues*, William Lee Miller, p 250

clusion, some in the crowd unexpectedly called for Lincoln to give a response, but respecting Douglas's earlier refusal to debate, he declined. However, he announced that he would speak later that evening in a separate meeting, and by candlelight, he gave the first of what would become a long series of messages challenging the immorality of slavery. Because of Douglas' political prowess and the continued national stir caused by the passage of the Kansas-Nebraska Act, Lincoln's challenge was viewed as newsworthy by most major newspapers and was covered by them, as would be nearly all of his upcoming speeches challenging Douglas. Over the next six years, this press coverage would be a catalyst that would help catapult Lincoln into the highest political office in the land by making his name and position known throughout the nation.

Historians have marked this rebuttal speech as the beginning of a new Lincoln. From this point Lincoln's speeches would take on a higher tone. It is important to keep in perspective that in that time there was no shortage of antislavery voices throughout the North. It was a major theme for dozens of the most prominent down to the lesser politicians, not to mention the continuous stream of newspaper and magazine articles on the subject that blanketed the nation. But there would be uniqueness about Lincoln's speeches in comparison to the other political messages of the day. He would focus on the principles of immorality found in slavery, as well as expound on the sanctity of the Union, and would do so without invective or the personal attacks that were so common from the political podiums. Absent also would be impassioned accusations, statements of judgment, aspersions on opponents' characters, and self-promoting themes. His messages would be loftier than those of the other defenders of freedom. His would be focused on principles and on doing one's duty to God and country. In Buffalo he expressed this sentiment: "I must trust in that Supreme Being who has never forsaken this favored land, through the instrumentality of this great and intelligent people."[207]

He would often say that the people had an obligation not just to this nation but also to the rest of the world to protect and defend the liberties afforded them in their Constitution. And he would repeatedly remind his listeners of their responsibility to remember and honor the "Almighty God," the Founding Fathers, the Declaration of Independence, and the Constitution. Lincoln's voice was a new voice, a prophet-like voice in America, with an ability to speak from a spiritual plane devoid of hypocrisy, duplicity, and condescension. His messages were directed to the "better angels"[208] of the souls in Americans. John Wesley Hill said,

> In the light of subsequent events it seems that Lincoln was endowed with more than mortal wisdom and that he was God's chosen instrument to clarify the issues of the inevitable conflict for which the time was now fully ripe.[209]

In his speech that evening to the large Bloomington crowd, Lincoln erupted with deep emotion to once again join the fight against slavery and the Southern states' increasing threats to leave the Union. Lincoln exclaimed,

> It's wrong; it's wrong in its effect, letting slavery into Kansas and Nebraska—and wrong in principle, allowing it to spread to every other part of the wide world, where men can be found inclined to take it. When we were politi-

---

[207] *The Almost Chosen People*, William J. Wolf, p 150

[208] Abraham Lincoln's First Inaugural Address

[209] *Abraham Lincoln, Man of God*, John Wesley Hill, p 115

cal slaves of King George, and wanted to be
free, we called the maxim that "all men are
created equal" a self-evident truth; but now
when we have grown fat, and have lost the
dread of being slaves ourselves, we have become so greedy to be *masters* that we call the
same a "self-evident lie."[210]

He went on to say that the Kansas-Nebraska Act pitched the
nation back into the position of defending the moral essence of
slavery, removing the "principled rejection of slavery—making
the nation morally neutral as between slavery and freedom."[211]
"It assumes there can be moral right in the enslaving of one
man by another."[212]

Senator Douglas was not so much proslavery as he was devoted to other political issues on his agenda. He actually
viewed slavery as a political nuisance, an obstacle to his other
political goals. However, he frequently spoke of black people
with sneering disdain. In Lincoln's counter to Douglas's earlier
speech, he said,

> Judge Douglas frequently and with bitter
> irony and sarcasm, paraphrases our argument
> by saying, "The white people of Nebraska are
> good enough to govern them selves, but they
> are not good enough to govern a few miserable
> Negroes!!!"[213]

> Well I doubt not that the people of Ne-
> braska are, and will continue to be as good as

---

[210] Lincoln Speech, September 26, 1854 in Bloomington, Ill.(LV p.248)
[211] Lincoln Speech, September 26, 1854 in Bloomington, Ill.(LV p.248
[212] *Lincoln's Virtues,* William Lee Miller, p 238
[213] *Lincoln's Virtues,* William Lee Miller, p 239

the average of people elsewhere. I do not say the contrary. What I do say is that no man is good enough to govern another man, without that other's consent. I say this is the leading principle—the sheet anchor of American republicanism.[214]

For some years prior to all of this, starting with the powerful U.S. Senator John C. Calhoun from South Carolina and various other, mostly Southern politicians, including governors from South Carolina and Virginia, the Declaration of Independence was openly derided for its ridiculous clause, as they described it, that "all men are created equal."[215] The debates in the highly divisive Kansas-Nebraska bill centered upon this criticism. Senator Benjamin Franklin Wade argued against this new generation of elected enemies of the Declaration of Independence:

> Mr. President, the advocates of this bill in order to sustain it in principle have rightly judged that the Declaration of Independence must also be superseded and rendered inoperative. I had supposed that the great principles touching upon the rights of human nature set forth in that immortal instrument were universally acknowledged in this country. Judge my surprise when I heard them assailed, denounced, and repudiated, in the Senate of the United States as self-evident falsehoods...The great declaration cost our forefathers too dearly...to be thrown away by their children.[216]

---

[214] *Lincoln's Virtues*, William Lee Miller, p 239
[215] *The Declaration of Independence*
[216] *Lincoln's Virtues*, William Lee Miller, p 246

Interestingly, it was another Northern senator, John Pettit of Indiana, who in the Kansas-Nebraska debates spoke most vehemently against the Declaration of Independence. Lincoln said he "was chief among those who would throw it away, and the one who claimed, and kept on claiming, that the Declaration's statement that all men are created equal was false."[217] To Pettit's denunciations Lincoln continued:

> Nearly eighty years ago we began by declaring that all men are created equal, but now…some have run down to the other declaration, that for SOME men to enslave others is a "sacred right of self-government."[218] These principles cannot stand together. They are as opposite as God and Mammon, and whosoever holds to the one, must despise the other. When Pettit, in connection with his support of the Nebraska bill, called the Declaration of Independence a "self-evident lie" he only did what consistency and candor require all other Nebraska men to do. Of forty odd Nebraska [bill] Senators who sat present and heard him, no one rebuked him. Nor am I apprised that any Nebraska [supporting] newspaper, in the whole nation, or any Nebraska orator, has ever rebuked him. If you support the Kansas-Nebraska Act, then you must agree that the egalitarianism of the Declaration is a "self-evident lie."[219]

---

[217] *Lincoln's Virtues,* William Lee Miller, p 247
[218] *Lincoln's Virtues,* William Lee Miller, p 247
[219] *Lincoln's Virtues,* William Lee Miller, p 247

A decade later, in April 1864 President Lincoln would tell the nation, "I am naturally anti-slavery, if slavery is not wrong, nothing is wrong. I cannot remember when I did not so think and feel."[220] The original Constitution was created with a gaping hole in its side with its forced acceptance of slavery. Lincoln would frequently point out that slavery was a wrong tolerated by the Founding Fathers "only by necessity."[221] In truth, some of the Founding Fathers wanted to end slavery and some did not, and those for slavery made it abundantly clear that they were prepared to abandon the nation-preserving process of Constitution-building should the antislavery Founders press too hard. Had they left in disgust, they would have rendered the entire process of creating the Constitution null and void. Therefore, under these pressures, the Constitution emerged with the unfortunate and infamous three-fifths clause, which stated that in the process of counting state residents for the purpose of establishing the number of House of Representatives seats in the new government, the non-voting Negro counted as three-fifths of a person, which created a significant enhancement of power for the slave states. Over the next six years Lincoln would point out this unfortunate inequity, stating, "In the control of the government…they [the slave States] greatly have the advantage of us."[222] "The slaves do not vote; they are only counted and so used to swell the influence of the white people's vote."[223] He would illustrate the injustice by comparing the states of Maine and South Carolina, both of which had the same number of senators (of course), the same number of House members, and the same number of electoral votes for choosing a president. But Maine had, at that time, twice as many white citizens as South Carolina (which for some time actually had

---

[220] *Lincoln's Virtues,* William Lee Miller, p 247
[221] *Lincoln's Virtues,* William Lee Miller, p 238
[222] *Lincoln's Virtues,* William Lee Miller, p 259
[223] *Lincoln's Virtues,* William Lee Miller, p 259

more slaves than white people). He would then draw the conclusion that equal power for the state with fewer than half the voters meant that "each white man in South Carolina is more than double of any man in Maine."[224] "This principle, in the aggregate, gives the slave States, in the present congress, twenty additional representatives—being more than the whole majority by which they passed the Nebraska bill."[225]

Back in 1846, the Negro slave Dred Scott filed a landmark lawsuit for his freedom. The case slowly traveled up the court system to the U.S. Supreme Court eleven years later, where in 1857 Supreme Court justice Roger B. Taney, a slave owner from Maryland, and the majority of the high judges disgraced this nation with their decision that Negroes were "beings of an inferior order…and altogether unfit to associate with the white race. Furthermore, they possessed no right which the white man was bound to respect."[226] Therefore, wrote the high court, "Blacks were not, and never had been, citizens of this country and thus had no right to sue."[227] With the same opinion, the Supreme Court nullified the Missouri Compromise that had outlawed slavery from certain parts of the West and North, deeming it unconstitutional, null and void, thus giving slavery an open road to the West.

Lincoln reacted with passionate disgust. He argued that Taney had deliberately skewed the record with the claim that blacks had never possessed any rights in America. In fact, the two dissenting judges wrote that in five of the original states, free blacks had been full voting citizens at the time of the writing of the Constitution. Lincoln stated his further reproach with the following statement:

---

[224] *Lincoln's Virtues,* William Lee Miller, p 259
[225] *Lincoln's Virtues,* William Lee Miller, p 259
[226] US Supreme Court Dred Scott Decision, 1857
[227] US Supreme Court Dred Scott Decision, 1857

In those days, our Declaration of Independence was
held sacred by all, but now, to aid in making the bondage of the negro [sic] universal and eternal, it is assailed,
and sneered at, and construed, and hawked at, and torn,
til, if its framers could rise from their graves, they could
not at all recognize it.[228]

Lincoln declared bluntly, that Taney was doing "obvious violence to the plain unmistakable language of
the Declaration [of Independence]," which had once
been held sacred by all Americans and thought to include all Americans. So blatant was the Chief Justice's
misreading of the law, so gross was his distortion of the
documents fundamental to American liberty, that Lincoln's faith in an impartial, rational judiciary was shak-
en; never again did he give deference to the rulings, of
the Supreme Court.[229]

In 1854, Lincoln reluctantly bowed to pressure to run again
for the Illinois state legislature and, without even campaigning
for the position, was elected with the largest number of votes
given to any candidate. Nevertheless, his political zeal had been
rekindled and his eye became focused on a run for United
States senator. When the opportunity opened for him to pursue
it, he resigned from the legislature to become a candidate for
the congressional office, which he saw as a vehicle to continue
his fight against the wrongs in this country and which he now
desperately wanted. But in the process of voting, he suddenly,
and unexpectedly, withdrew from the race so as to shift the
votes for him to his friend and fellow Republican, Lyman
Trumbull, when it appeared that the third candidate, a Demo-

[228] *Lincoln, An Illustrated Biography*, Philip B. Kunhardt Jr.,Philip Kunhardt
III,Peter W. Kunhardt p 106
[229] *Lincoln*, David Herbert Donald, p 201

crat, would win the three-way race through some alleged bribery. By doing so, Trumbull won the election for the good of the antislavery movement and Lincoln was left with another defeat. Friends described him as "disappointed and mortified by the outcome."[230] Lincoln said, "A less good humored man than I, perhaps would not have consented to it."[231] Lincoln was somewhat comforted by knowing that his defeat was a victory for his party and a blistering rebuke to Douglas and his popular sovereignty, and that Trumbull with "endless persistence and a sharp tongue" would make life miserable for the senior senator from Illinois.[232] More importantly, it did open the way for Lincoln to make another run for the U.S. Senate, against Douglas himself, four years later.

By 1855, the Whig Party was dying and a new movement developed, in which Lincoln became heavily involved to organize the Republican Party in Illinois that was also emerging in the rest of country. The new party combined under one umbrella, pooling various conservative factions into a united front in opposition to the scourge of slavery. At the state organizing convention in Bloomington, Illinois, a series of political speeches were being rendered when, again, calls unexpectedly rose up from the crowd for Lincoln to address the convention. He took the stage and with no notes or preparation he spoke for about ninety minutes. Those who were present and who later heard or read his other famous presidential speeches acclaimed that this Bloomington discourse was the best speech of his life. Known as Lincoln's Lost Speech, in it he flatly identified, and categorically proved with crystal clarity, that slavery was the source of this nation's problems. Oddly, there were roughly forty reporters in the crowd of one thousand who were so captivated by the

---

[230] *Lincoln*, David Herbert Donald, p 185
[231] *Lincoln*, David Herbert Donald, p 185
[232] *Lincoln*, David Herbert Donald, p 185

message and delivery that they all failed to take notes of the speech, leaving no reliable record of its contents. One delegate exclaimed, "Never was an audience more completely electrified by human eloquence. Again and again, during the delivery, the audience sprang to their feet, and by long-continued cheers, expressed how deeply the speaker had roused them."[233] Lincoln's young law partner, William Herndon, who was also taking notes as he commonly did, gave up after about fifteen minutes and "threw pen and paper away and lived only in the inspiration of the hour."[234] Herndon summarized the speech as being "full of fire and energy and force; it was logic; it was pathos; it was enthusiasm; it was justice, equity, truth, and right set ablaze by divine fires of a soul maddened by the wrong..."[235] "The audience sat enthralled. Men listened as though transfixed. Reporters forgot to use the pencils in their hands, so that no complete and authentic record of what may have been his greatest speech has ever been found. At the end, the hall rocked with applause. The Republican Party was born in Illinois."[236] A compendium of reports revealed that, in this speech Lincoln elaborated on the following:

1. That there were pressing reasons for the formation of the Republican Party
2. That the Republican movement was very important to the future of the nation.
3. That all free-soil people needed to rally against slavery and the existing political evils.
4. That the nation must be preserved in the purity of its principles as well in the integrity of its ter-

---

[233] http://members.aol.com/RVSNorton/Lincoln2.html
[234] *Lincoln*, David Herbert Donald, p 191
[235] *Lincoln*, David Herbert Donald, p 192
[236] *Lincoln's Lost Speech.htm*, p 1

ritorial parts, and the Republicans were the ones to do it.[237]

John Wentworth, of the *Chicago Democrat,* wrote of the speech, "Abraham Lincoln for an hour and a half held the assemblage spellbound by the power of his argument, the intense irony of his invectives, the brilliancy of his eloquence. I shall not mar any of its fine proportions by attempting even a synopsis of it.[238]

By now Lincoln was fervent in his determination to continue his challenge, but Douglas persisted in not allowing him to share the podium, wanting more than ever to prevent Lincoln's inspiring words from being heard with his. On October 3, Douglas was the keynote speaker for the Illinois State Fair in Lincoln's hometown of Springfield. Rain was expected for that day so the speech was moved to the state house. Again Lincoln was present but instead of sitting in the audience, he paced back and forth in the lobby as he listened intently to Douglas's fiery speech. At the conclusion, as people began to leave the assembly hall, Lincoln suddenly appeared on the stairway and shouted to the dispersing crowd that he would answer Douglas on the morrow. He then, out of fairness, invited Douglas to be present and offered him time following his remarks for rebuttal. Douglas was forced by these circumstances to accept. This gallant stairway challenge would mark the rise of Abraham Lincoln in America. The next day the hall was full to capacity as Lincoln took the podium. Lincoln dismissed as nothing more than a lullaby Douglas's assertion that even with the ability to choose, slavery was unlikely to be admitted by the residents of the new territories. Next, Lincoln addressed Douglas's argument that the sacred right of self-government required that restrictions on

---

[237] *Lincoln's Lost Speech.htm,* p 1
[238] *Lincoln's Lost Speech.htm,* p 1

slavery be removed. Lincoln reached the crux of his disagreement by asserting that the core issue for permitting or excluding slavery depended upon "whether a Negro is *not* or *is* a man."[239] He said, "[Douglas] has no very vivid impression that the Negro is a human; and consequently has no idea that there can be any moral question in legislating about him."[240] But Lincoln argued that the African-American was very much a man and that the Declaration of Independence teaches us that all men are created equal. Because the Negro is a man, there could be no moral right to enslave him. The institution of slavery was founded in the selfishness of man's nature.

The audience was moved by Lincoln's moral outrage as he described "the monstrous injustice of slavery."[241] "There can be no moral right in connection with one man's making a slave of another,"[242] he thundered. "Our revolutionary fathers"[243] knew that slavery was wrong, but for practical reasons they could not eradicate it at the time they organized the new government. "They did not allow the word 'slavery' in the Constitution but permitted only indirect references to it."[244] Lincoln could not hide his indignation at Douglas's claim that he and the proslavery movement were merely acting in the spirit of the Founding Fathers by permitting self-government in the new territories. As Lincoln spoke of the framers of our Constitution, Herndon observed that "he quivered with feeling and emotion" and "his feelings once or twice swelled within [him] and came near stifling" his ability to speak.[245] He also opened their vision to the magnitude of damage that American slavery would mean not just for this nation but for the rest of the entire world: The

---

[239] Lincoln's State Fair Speech, October 5, 1854
[240] Lincoln's State Fair Speech, October 5, 1854
[241] *Lincoln*, David Herbert Donald, p 176
[242] *Lincoln*, David Herbert Donald, p 176
[243] *Lincoln*, David Herbert Donald , p 176
[244] *Lincoln*, David Herbert Donald, p 176
[245] *Lincoln*, David Herbert Donald, p 176

world's best hope depended on the continuation of a strong and free union of all states, united in purpose and resolve. "We are proclaiming ourselves political hypocrites before the world by thus fostering Human Slavery and proclaiming ourselves, at the same time, the sole friends of Human Freedom."[246]

It was another remarkable and moving speech. Women in the audience waved their white handkerchiefs and the men gave loud and continuous hurrahs. With these three speeches in the fall of 1854, Lincoln launched himself from a has-been politician to a formidable contender for the "Little Giant," Stephen A. Douglas—the most feared and powerful politician in America—as word of the obscure challenger to the great Senator Douglas circulated in the nation's newspapers.

By now Lincoln's plan was apparent. Douglas would not debate him. But he could not stop Lincoln from following him and offering to his audience a rebuttal, as he had just done. Privately, Douglas confided to friends that he did not want to share the platform with "the most difficult and dangerous opponent that I have ever met."[247] However, it was too great a political risk to reveal any hesitation; therefore, publicly he changed his stance and welcomed the challenger. After Chicago's debate, a journalist said of Lincoln that he created the impression "on all men of all parties…first, that he was an honest man, and second, that he was a powerful speaker."[248]

By the mid 1850s, Lincoln and other antislavery advocates nervously observed the growing solidarity of Southern states on the promulgation of slavery. "Where earlier Southern statesmen like Thomas Jefferson had hoped for the gradual extinction of the peculiar institution of slavery, a new breed of Fire-Eaters favored its perpetuation, and indeed its extension."[249] Lincoln's

---

[246] Lincoln's State Fair Speech, October 5, 1854
[247] *Lincoln,* David Herbert Donald, p 178
[248] *Lincoln,* David Herbert Donald, p 178
[249] *Lincoln,* David Herbert Donald, p 187

law office subscribed to the rabidly proslavery newspapers, the *Charleston Mercury* and the *Richmond Enquirer*, through which he observed the transformation of slavery from a once-lamented and necessary evil into a celebrated good for slave and master alike. Arguments appeared that described slave labor as preferable to free labor because slaves worked under the security of continuous employment, were given a home, food, and clothing, and thus greater real freedom. Of this Lincoln reminded his listeners, "We never hear of the man who wishes to take the good of it, *by being a slave himself.*"[250]

Events in Kansas became an intense political battleground on slavery. Antislavery organizations in New England began offering financial assistance to free-state immigrants to settle in Kansas. Missouri's proslavery people would have none of that so they did the same by encouraging proslavery settlers, equipped with guns and ammunition, to migrate to the new territory. Violence erupted and at the election of the first territorial legislature, Missourians swamped the polls to successfully fill the legislature with proslavery delegates. Some of their first acts were to make it a felony to question the right to hold slaves in Kansas and a capital offense to give aid to a fugitive slave. The reports of the proslavery success in Kansas moved Herndon and other antislavery men of Springfield to urge "the employment of any means, however desperate, to promote and defend the cause of freedom in the territory."[251] Lincoln intervened with his usual calm to remind his excitable partner and his friends that "physical rebellions and bloody resistances" were wrong and unconstitutional.[252]

Though the more extreme abolitionists of the North offered implausible solutions for the "Negro problem" once the slaves were freed, all were grossly impractical, such as shipping

---

[250] *Lincoln,* David Herbert Donald, p 187
[251] *Lincoln,* David Herbert Donald, p 188
[252] *Lincoln,* David Herbert Donald, p 188

all four million of them back to Africa or the West Indies. On seeing this, Lincoln grew despondent in his accurate realization "that there is no *peaceful* (italics added) extinction of slavery in prospect for us."[253] "The condition of the Negro slave in America…is now as fixed, and hopeless of change for the better, as that of the lost souls of the finally impenitent," he lamented, predicting, "The Autocrat of all the Russias will resign his crown, and proclaim his subjects free republicans sooner than will our American masters voluntarily give up their slaves."[254] He could see no *peaceful* resolution. "The problem is too mighty for me." He lamented, "May God in his mercy, superintend the solution."[255]

---

[253] *Lincoln,* David Herbert Donald, p 187
[254] *Lincoln,* David Herbert Donald, p 187
[255] *Lincoln,* David Herbert Donald, p 188

Chapter Five

The Unlikely President

After two years of skillful maneuverings, the Illinois Republican Convention unanimously voted Abraham Lincoln as the newly formed Republican Party's "first and only choice for the United States Senate...,"[256] to oppose the powerful incumbent, Stephen A. Douglas on the Democratic ticket.

By 1858 during this run for the U.S. Senate against Douglas, Lincoln was convinced, probably more clearly than anyone else in America, that slavery was on the verge of dividing this nation, and that this impending division would run this democracy to oblivion. He told his law partner William Herndon and other friends that he was looking for a universally known figure of speech that would rouse people to the peril of the times. That universally known phrase would come from Jesus, a phrase that Lincoln and nearly all in America knew from their reading in the New Testament, "A house divided against itself cannot stand."[257]

He believed that Jesus's words, better that any others, expressed his clear and ominously accurate vision of the future, and required that the next harrowing question be posed: "Can

---

[256] *Lincoln*, David Herbert Donald, p 205
[257] *Holy Bible*, Matthew 12:25

we, as a nation, continue together *permanently—forever* half slave, and half free?"[258] His friends warned him that such a position was much too controversial and could cost him the race. He said it anyway and he did lose the race. On this he wrote his friend Jesse K. Dubois,

> I refused to read the passage about the house divided against itself to you, because I knew you would ask me to change or modify it, and that I was determined not to do. I had willed it so, and was willing, if necessary to perish with it. That expression is a truth of all human experience: a house divided against itself cannot stand. I want to use some universally known figure expressed in simple language, that it may strike home to the minds of men, in order to arouse them to the peril of the times. I would rather be defeated with this expression in the speech, and to uphold it and discuss it before the people, than to be victorious without it.[259]

Another lawyer and devoted friend, Leonard Swett, said the speech defeated Lincoln in the Senate campaign. In 1866 he wrote to Herndon, musing, "Nothing could have been more unfortunate or inappropriate; it was saying first the wrong thing, yet he saw it was an abstract truth, but standing by the speech would ultimately find him in the right place."[260]

In the Springfield, Illinois statehouse on June 16, 1858 (two and one-half years before his election as president and the emergence of the horrific Civil War), to more than one thousand Republican delegates who had just given him the

---

[258] *Lincoln,* David Herbert Donald, p 187
[259] *Abraham Lincoln, Man of God,* John Wesley Hill, p 116
[260] Abraham Lincoln Online, House Divided Speech

Republican nomination for the U.S. Senate race, Lincoln accurately predicted the calamity and resulting resolution that was at the doorstep of America. The unpopularity of his candor cost him the election but launched him into the White House two years later.

His acceptance speech, later that night, was both memorable and prophetic as he mournfully expressed with startling accuracy the events that he perceived would come to pass for this nation. Referring to the Kansas-Nebraska Act he said,

> Mr. President and Gentlemen of the Convention. We are now in our *fifth* year, since a policy was initiated, with the *avowed* object, and *confident* promise, of putting an end to slavery agitation.
>
> Under the operation of that policy, that agitation, has not only, *not ceased,* but has *constantly augmented.*
>
> In *my* opinion, it *will* not cease, until a *crisis* shall have been reached, and passed.
>
> A house divided against itself cannot stand.
>
> I believe this government cannot endure, permanently half *slave* and half *free.*
>
> I do not expect the Union to be *dissolved*—I do not expect the house to *fall*—but I *do* expect it will cease to be divided.
>
> It will either become *all* one thing, or *all* the other.
>
> Either the *opponents* of slavery, will...place it where the public mind shall rest in the belief that it is in the course of ultimate extinction; or its *advocates* will put it forward, till it shall become alike

lawful in *all* the States, *old* as well as *new*—*North* as well as *South.*[261]

What followed was a series of Lincoln-Douglas debates that captured the nation's interest as two of country's most gifted orators went head to head. There would be seven debates in each of seven congressional districts of Illinois. The notoriety of Stephen A. Douglas's popularity and influence in Washington, coupled with the oddity of the eloquent backwoodsman, made the 1858 Illinois senatorial race "the most interesting political battle-ground in the Union," according to the *New York Times.* The debates opened in Ottawa, a town of nine thousand residents, drawing nearly ten thousand anxious listeners. Reporters reveled in the sharply contrasting candidates' appearance and style. Douglas was a short and stout man reaching only to Lincoln's shoulder when standing side by side—a pose that the five feet, two inch Douglas avoided. Lincoln, tall and painfully thin, spoke in a piercing tenor voice that at times became shrill but carried well for large audiences to hear. Douglas's voice was booming and authoritative; he used graceful gestures and bowed charmingly when applauded; in contrast, Lincoln's movements were awkward, and when he bowed he looked like a jackknife trying to close and open. Douglas traveled in a splendid private train, apportioned for comfort and entertaining. Lincoln traveled contentedly in a regular passenger car that allowed him unending opportunities to meet with the citizenry of the state.

Throughout the debates, Douglas spoke on the morality of choice, that each state and territory had the constitutional right to decide for or against slavery, clearly with the unspoken design that on this entire continent white men would be free to pursue mountainous wealth off the lifelong toil of the Supreme

---

[261] *Lincoln*, David Herbert Donald, p 206

Court-defined "beings of a lesser order." In fact, Douglas said of the Dred Scott ruling that blacks belong to "an inferior race, who in all ages, and in every part of the globe…had shown themselves incapable of self-government."[262] On another occasion he said, "this government of ours is founded on the white basis. It was made by the white man, for the benefit of the white man, to be administered by white men."[263]

Lincoln, on the other hand, carried his theme on principles that were free of the duplicity of those of Douglas, stating, "the issue that will continue in this country when these poor tongues of Judge Douglas and myself shall be silent…is the eternal struggle between these two principles—right and wrong—throughout the world."[264] He centered his messages on the absolute humanity of the black race, and therefore the immorality of enslavement of them or any human being. And he would speak on the consequential dangers of a divided nation on this immense issue. In the one-hundred-day campaign, Douglas would travel 5,227 miles and give 130 speeches; Lincoln traveled 4,350 miles by boat, train, and carriage, to give 63 speeches. As highly popular as they were, in the end the debates seemed to have done little to change political stances of the tens of thousands of listeners and millions of readers throughout the country; most of those for slavery remained for slavery still, and those against it continued their momentous task to eradicate it. It was generally concluded that Douglas carried the earlier debates, with Lincoln gaining strength to edge out Douglas in the final debates.

When the electoral votes were counted in January 1859, Lincoln garnered forty-six votes and Douglas received fifty-four. Douglas would remain on Capitol Hill for another term and Lincoln would remain in Springfield, in deep disappointment,

---

[262] *Lincoln*, David Herbert Donald, p 201
[263] *Lincoln*, David Herbert Donald, p 210
[264] *Lincoln*, David Herbert Donald, p 224

fearing that his political career might now be over. Lincoln said of Douglas, "With me the race of ambition has been a failure— a flat failure; with him it has been one of splendid success."[265] Once again, Lincoln saw that he had allowed to slip away another opportunity to bring to fruition the inner promptings he had carried for much of his life: that he was to be part of something unknown yet significant in the eyes of God and of mankind. What he did not foresee was the impact that the debates would have on the minds of the people of America, because now, nearly everyone in America knew of Abraham Lincoln and the strength of his message.

As 1860 approached, newspapers throughout the country began surfacing a number of names as potential candidates for the upcoming presidential election, and a handful mentioned Abraham Lincoln as an outside contender. Neither he nor most everyone else seemed to take the suggestions very seriously. Of all the names suggested, Lincoln was clearly the least qualified of the group. When asked about it, Lincoln would respond, "I must in candor, say I do not think myself fit for the Presidency."[266] David Herbert Donald in *Lincoln* sums up Lincoln's viability for a run at the presidency:

> Without family tradition or wealth, he had received only the briefest of formal schooling. Now fifty years old, he had no administrative experience of any sort; he had never been governor of his state or even mayor of Springfield. A profound student of the Constitution and of the writings of the Founding Fathers, he had limited acquaintance with the government they established. He had served only one term in the House of Representatives, and for the past ten years

---

[265] *Speech of Hon. Reed Smoot in Congress. and Lincoln*, David Herbert Donald, p 208

[266] *Lincoln*, David Herbert Donald, p 235

he had held no public office. Though he was one of the founders of the Republican Party, he had no close friends and only a few acquaintances in the populous Eastern states, whose votes would be crucial in the election. To be sure, his debates with Douglas had brought him national attention, but he had lost the senatorial election both in 1855 and in 1859.[267]

Dismissing his chances for the presidency, one Boston correspondent remarked scornfully, "As for Lincoln I am afraid he will kick the beam again as he is in the habit of doing."[268]

Coupled with these political disadvantages, we find in Abraham Lincoln a lifetime of unmatched devotion to God, and a profound conviction that God would not have this nation divided. As president, after the second bloody battle of Bull Run, he said, "I have talked with God. It is His cause, and the Union is His. As He willeth, so it will be."[269] He believed deeply that the abomination of slavery somehow had to be eradicated if this nation's freedoms were to survive, and that the sacred yet threatened Constitution needed a strong and principled nation to protect it so that the constitutionally guaranteed freedoms might preserve "freedom for the free."[270]

Lincoln's humble statements about feeling unfit for the presidency, though meekly honest, did not reflect his deep interest in the office. Competing on the Republican ticket against other notable and successful politicians, such as William H. Seward, former governor of New York; Salmon P. Chase, former governor of Ohio; and the celebrated explorer John C. Fremont, was a formidable undertaking. Recognizing his weak position against these better-qualified rivals, Lincoln

---

[267] *Lincoln*, David Herbert Donald, p 236
[268] *Lincoln*, David Herbert Donald p. 236
[269] *Abraham Lincoln Man of God*, John Wesley Hill, p 280
[270] Lincoln's 1862 Speech to Congress

wisely undertook a series of subtle steps to consolidate his strength and influence rather than formally announcing his candidacy. To create a wider circulation of his ideas, he quietly compiled and published his debates with Douglas. The 268-page book entitled *Political Debates Between Hon. Abraham Lincoln and Hon. Stephen A. Douglas, in the Celebrated Campaign of 1858, in Illinois* became an immediate best seller. In December 1859 he published his autobiography.

Indicative of the growing Eastern fascination with this unlikely candidate from Illinois was the welcomed invitation by New York voters to lecture in Manhattan with two other notable presidential candidates: Cassius Clay and Edward Bates. The day of the scheduled evening speech, Lincoln caught his first glimpse of Broadway, had his picture taken by the soon-to-be world-renowned Civil War photographer Mathew Brady, and to historian George Bancroft he quipped, "I am on my way to Massachusetts where I have a son at school, who, if reports be true, already knows much more than his father."[271] That evening he was warmly introduced by Henry Ward Beecher to the filled Cooper Union, and New Yorkers got their first look at the awkward candidate. Many expected "something weird, rough and uncultivated."[272] And at first glance they were not disappointed. George Haven Putnam wrote this of his impressions:

> The long ungainly figure, upon which hung clothes that, while new for the trip, were evidently the work of an unskilled tailor; the large feet; the clumsy hands, of which…the orator seemed to be unduly conscious; the long gaunt head capped by a shock of hair that seemed not to have been thoroughly brushed out made a pic-

---

ture which did not fit in with New York's conception of a finished statesman.[273]

Nevertheless, the speech that he delivered erased any evidence of a backward frontiersman. Lincoln passionately attacked as a sacrilege, Douglas's assertion that popular sovereignty was merely an extension of the desires of the Founding Fathers. Lincoln disclosed his extensive research of these great politicians, revealing that of the thirty-nine signers of the Constitution, at least twenty-one demonstrated by their voting records that they perceived the federal government to have the power to control slavery in the national territories, deflating Douglas's claim that they intended the states and territories to decide. Lincoln wisely made no denunciation of his fellow Republican rivals, portraying the Republicans as a party of moderates with a mission to preserve the legacy of the Founding Fathers against the radical assault of the proslavery element. "Let us have faith, he admonished, "that right makes might, and in that faith, let us, to the end, dare to do our duty as we understand it."[274] His delivery was frequently interrupted by enthusiastic applause, and when he closed, the capacity crowd jumped as one to its feet, amidst more applause punctuated with hat- and handkerchief-waving. Noah Brooks of the *New York Tribune* exclaimed, "He's the greatest man since St. Paul." A Harvard student told his father, "It was the best speech I ever heard."[275] The following day, four New York papers printed the speech in its entirety. It was immediately published in pamphlet form and issued as a Republican tract in newspapers from New York, Chicago, Albany, and Detroit. In all, it was a superb political development for the unannounced candidate. During his two weeks in New England, he would speak nearly every day.

---

[273] *Lincoln,* David Herbert Donald, p 238
[274] *Lincoln,* David Herbert Donald, p 239
[275] *Lincoln,* David Herbert Donald, p 239

In spite of his success in New England, he still expressed doubt that he could be given the nomination, but from that time he made no attempt to conceal his interest in it. A friend inquired about his intentions and he replied, "I will be entirely frank. The taste is in my mouth a little."[276] Tradition dictated that candidates should not openly campaign for office, believing that the office should seek the man, thus requiring the efforts of others to make it happen. After a night of reflection, Lincoln consented to allow a number of friends, including John Wentworth in Chicago and Judge David Davis, to quietly work toward it. These friends knew that Lincoln's integrity was a potential liability in the aggressive campaign arena. Judge Davis said, "Lincoln has few of the qualities of a politician and cannot do much personally to advance his interests, because he was such, 'a guileless man.'"[277] While his managers were set to the task, Lincoln remained on the sidelines. He deflected requests for political statements by saying, "When not a very great man begins to be mentioned for a very great position, his head is likely to be a little turned."[278]

One week prior to the Republican National Convention in Chicago, the Illinois State Republican Convention was held in Decatur. As Lincoln lacked a campaign slogan like President Harrison's "Log Cabin and Hard Cider" and Andrew Jackson's "Old Hickory," one of Lincoln's supporters, Richard Oglesby, a young and ambitious politician from Decatur, sought one out for Lincoln's bid as the Illinois Republican nominee for president. Consulting with the aged John Hanks, a cousin to Lincoln's mother Lucy, Oglesby located a split rail fence near Decatur that Hanks and Lincoln had built thirty years prior. On the first day of the convention, during a recess in the voting for governor, Oglesby introduced the elderly Hanks and, with an assistant, marched

---

[276] *Lincoln*, David Herbert Donald, p 241
[277] *Lincoln*, David Herbert Donald, p 242
[278] *Lincoln*, David Herbert Donald, p 242

down the aisle carrying two of the old fence rails decorated with flags and streamers, upon which were written:

ABRAHAM LINCOLN
The Rail Candidate
FOR PRESIDENT IN 1860
Two rails from a lot of 3,000 made in 1830 by Thos. Hanks and Abe Lincoln—whose father was the first pioneer of Macon County

The crowd erupted into a deafening cheer and applause for Lincoln, who was called to the stand and blushingly confirmed that he had indeed built a cabin and split the rails thirty years ago. The cheers that followed his remarks suggested that even his friends had underestimated Lincoln's popularity. He would now be labeled "The Rail Splitter," which would package him as a self-made man. The next day Lincoln was unanimously selected as the Illinois Republican choice for president of the United States for Chicago's national convention the following week.

In Chicago, as was the tradition in political conventions, it was unseemly for the candidates to attend and appear to pursue the offices. Lincoln, who desperately wanted to be there, told a friend that "he was almost too much of a candidate to go, and not quite enough to stay home."[279] He stayed home. This pressure to not openly seek the office did not prevent, however, the nonstop political wrangling, positioning, agreements, promises, and bribes, from occurring as each candidate's managers labored feverishly for the nomination. There were whisperings of unethical collusions throughout, but Lincoln's men knew that he would have no part of them. In fact, one friend telegrammed Lincoln encouraging him to consider a deal with certain other

---

[279] *Lincoln*, David Herbert Donald, p 242

aspirants, saying, "I know that you have no relish for such a Game, but it is an old maxim that you must fight the *devil with fire.*"[280] Lincoln responded tersely, "Make no contracts that will bind me."[281]

On Friday, May 18, the day for the delegates to cast their votes, Lincoln passed part of the nervous day playing "fives," a form of handball, with some men in the vacant lot next to the *Illinois State Journal,* which housed the telegraph machine and operator. As was the usual procedure, the delegates in Chicago would cast their votes in rounds and the first candidate to garner 233 votes would win the nomination. In the first round William Seward received 173 votes, Lincoln 102, Bates 48, Cameron 50, and Chase 49. In the second round, Seward's votes increased to 184; Lincoln's also increased to 181, with all the other candidates losing in number. In the third round, Seward received nearly the same number, whereas the majority of the remaining delegates flocked to Lincoln's corner, and the final tally gave Lincoln 364 votes out of a possible 466. Seward's delegates then followed suit and backed Lincoln as well, making Abraham Lincoln the unanimous choice for the Republican nomination for president of the United States. The nomination was won with no hidden promises or contracts. Leonard Swett, another member of Lincoln's campaign committee, wrote a friend a few days later saying, "No pledges have been made, no mortgages executed."[282] That was also Lincoln's understanding as he assured Joshua Giddings that "The responsible position assigned me, comes without conditions, save only such honorable ones as are fairly implied." Upon receiving the news of his victory by telegraph, he approached his ballplayer friends and joked, "Gentlemen, you had better come up and shake

---

[280] *Lincoln*, David Herbert Donald, p 249

[281] *Lincoln*, David Herbert Donald, p 249

[282] *Lincoln*, David Herbert Donald, p 250

my hand while you can—honors elevate some men."[283] Then he headed for home, telling them, "There is a little woman at our house who is probably more interested in this dispatch than I am."[284] A key to Lincoln's victory was the fact that—although there were those who did not agree with his political views—because of his regard for everyone, including opponents, he had said nothing offensive of his opponents, making it difficult for them to speak negatively of him. This attribute served him well once again.

The next day a delegation from Chicago arrived at Lincoln's home to officially notify him of the nomination. Lincoln was tense because he and Mary had argued just before their arrival. Mary thought it proper to offer liquor to the guests; Lincoln did not want to serve alcohol. A little later he explained to the distinguished entourage, "Having kept house for sixteen years, and having never held the 'cup' to the lips of my friends then, my judgment was that I should not, in my new position, change my habit in this respect."[285] They were each served a glass of water.

The Springfield residents were beside themselves to think that one of their own was a candidate for president and they flocked to the Lincoln home on Eighth and Jackson streets to express their support. Outside of Springfield, the northern half of the nation wanted to know about this little-known candidate and Lincoln was flooded with telegrams, letters, photographers, and reporters. Few in the South had interest in him. Nearly two hundred thousand additional autobiographical sketches were printed and distributed. The convention selected Hannibal Hamlin of Maine to be the vice presidential running mate with Lincoln. Lincoln would run against three other presidential candidates, including fellow Illinoisan Ste-

[283] *Lincoln,* David Herbert Donald, p 251
[284] *Lincoln,* David Herbert Donald, p 25
285 Lincoln Among the Reformers: Tempering the Temperance Movement, LUCAS E. MOREL, *Journal of the Abraham Lincoln Association,* Winter 1999, Vol 20, No 1

phen A. Douglas and former vice president John C. Breckenridge from Kentucky; both were from the split-apart Democratic Party—the result of the proslavery radicals' calculated move earlier that year, at the Democratic Convention in South Carolina, to split the party and force a Republican win. The fourth candidate was John Bell. Lincoln would remain on the sidelines pledging to make no political speeches during the campaign, saying only that if elected he would procure "Justice and fairness to all."[286] His primary opponent, Stephen A. Douglas, ignored tradition and unabashedly campaigned to promote himself in the race. Lincoln, remaining in Springfield, confessed to bouts of boredom during the long campaign process, while huge rallies were taking place throughout the North in his absence, conducted by his campaign committee and fellow Republicans. Oddly, his silence became his best offense because it gave his opponents little to criticize.

State elections took place one month prior to the November 6 presidential election, and all eyes were on these important results. The Republicans had conducted a brilliant campaign resulting in several historically Democratic states voting Republican, boding well for Lincoln in November. Following the state returns Lincoln wrote to his former opponent Seward and said, "It now really looks as if the Government is about to fall into our hands. Pennsylvania, Ohio, and Indiana have surpassed all expectations."[287]

On Election Day Lincoln was reluctant to vote, not wanting to appear to vote for himself. Nonetheless, sensing the importance of the voting process and at the urging of friends, he walked to the voting station amidst cheers from the local citizens, cut off the top portion of the ballot containing his name and the others for president, and cast his votes for his choice in

---

[286] *Lincoln*, David Herbert Donald, p 254
[287] *Lincoln*, David Herbert Donald, p 255

the other races. That evening he joined the Republicans in the capitol to hear the returns as they arrived by telegraph. After years of success and influence in Illinois, Stephen A. Douglas also watched with his Democratic supporters, as his home state of Illinois went Republican and backed Lincoln, as did Indiana and a number of other Western states. But the critical returns would be those from the Eastern states. By ten o'clock word arrived that Pennsylvania had surprisingly voted Republican. It wasn't until two o'clock that word finally arrived that the important state of New York also went Republican, sealing the election for Lincoln. Abraham Lincoln, the Rail Splitter and Self-Made Man, would be the next president of the United States, and he won it ominously, without a single vote from ten of the Southern states. Lincoln recalled, "I went home, but not to get much sleep for I then felt as I never had before, the responsibility that was upon me."[288] Days later the final tally registered 180 electoral votes for Lincoln, 72 for Breckenridge, 39 for Bell, and 12 for Stephen A. Douglas.

Predictably, the South did not take the election of the "nigger-loving"[289] Lincoln well. The day after his victory, the people of Pensacola, Florida hung his effigy by the neck. The *Dallas Herald* wrote, "Evil days are upon us";[290] the *Augusta Constitutional* declared, "The South should arm at once."[291]

It took the unprecedented division of the northern and southern Democratic Party to transform Lincoln's 39.8 percent majority of the popular vote into an electoral vote majority. Es-

---

[288] *Lincoln*, David Herbert Donald, p 256

[289] *Abraham Lincoln, An Illustrated Biography*, Philip B. Kunhardt Jr.,Philip Kunhardt III,Peter W. Kunhardt p 133

[290] *Abraham Lincoln, An Illustrated Biography*, Philip B. Kunhardt Jr.,Philip Kunhardt III,Peter W. Kunhardt p 133

[291] *Abraham Lincoln, An Illustrated Biography*, Philip B. Kunhardt Jr.,Philip Kunhardt III,Peter W. Kunhardt p 133

tablished leaders of his Republican Party were more than willing to remind him that he was the least credentialed president in history. His strongest qualification was his undistinguished two-year term in the House of Representatives. His largest executive responsibility was that of senior partner in the two-lawyer firm of Lincoln and Herndon in Springfield.

It was a bitter defeat for Douglas but one he saw coming. The Fire-Eaters of the South could likely have had proslavery Douglas as their president had they not divided the Democratic Party, but ignoring their promise of support for Douglas's presidential run in exchange for his muscle in passing the Kansas-Nebraska Act six years earlier, they wanted more. They wanted a perceived national crisis to which the Southern states could rise up in a self-righteous defense of their immoral source of wealth and thus appear to be reacting with reason and justice as they, with impunity, would separate themselves from this nation. An antislavery president would be just that perceived crisis.

In early February 1861, just days prior to the Lincoln family's second move to Washington, President-elect Lincoln made one last visit to his beloved stepmother, now seventy-three and widowed in Coles County. He went to the small two-room cabin in Goosenest Prairie that he had helped his father build, that Sarah Bush Lincoln now shared with her daughter. There he presented her with a black woolen dress and paid his respects to his deceased father by carving T.L. into two stakes and placing them at the head and foot of his grave. He then bade her farewell, feeling fearful that this would be his final farewell to the loving woman who restored motherly warmth to his young and grieving boyhood by loving him as her own son. Of this final farewell, Sarah recalled later, "I did not want him elected—was afraid somehow or other...that something would happen to him…and that I should see him no more."[292] Her loving stepson tried to comfort her by saying, "No no mama, trust in the Lord and all will be well. We will see each other again."[293] Sadly, his mother's premonition would prove to be accurate.

On a cold and rainy February 11, 1861, the Presidential Special, a train consisting of only two cars painted a bright yellow, hissed and steamed as it awaited the president-elect's arrival at the Springfield train station to carry him to Washington and the most severe crisis to ever face any United States president. Lincoln had requested that his departure be done quietly and without fanfare, but an estimated one thousand friends and well-wishers surrounded the train station and waited anxiously for Springfield's favorite son to arrive.

That morning Lincoln made one last visit to his law office with his law partner William Herndon, who recorded the following exchange: "'Billy,' he said, 'over sixteen years together, and we have not had a cross word during all that time, have we?' 'No, indeed we have not,'[294] was Billy's reply. 'Don't take the sign down, Billy; let it swing, that our clients may understand that the election of a president makes no change in the firm of Lincoln & Herndon. If I live, I'm coming back, and we will go right on practicing law as if nothing had ever happened.'"[295] Then the two went down the stairs and across the town to the railroad station, Lincoln never to return alive. Herndon recorded, "The sorrow of parting from his old associations was deeper than most persons would imagine."[296] He said that Lincoln was experiencing of late a "feeling which had become irrepressible that he would never return alive."[297]

[292] *Abraham Lincoln, the Boy the Man*, p 104
[293] *Lincoln*, David Herbert Donald, p 271
[294] *Lincoln*, David Herbert Donald, p 272
[295] *Lincoln*, David Herbert Donald, p 272
[296] *The Eloquent President*, Ronald C. White, Jr., p 10
[297] *The Eloquent President*, Ronald C. White, Jr., p 10

Lincoln had resolved to make no speech that day or at any of the dozens of stops that were planned along the way except for a select few pre-designated locations. For security purposes, Mary and their two youngest sons left the night before and would meet up with Lincoln in Indianapolis. Their oldest son Robert would accompany his father. Lincoln stepped out on the platform amidst a chorus of cheers and calls for a speech. A reporter near the new president observed, "Lincoln's face was pale, and quivered with emotion so deep as to render him almost unable to utter a single word."[298] Moved with emotion at the fond support of so many friends, he removed his beaver hat and motioned for silence. The nation had heard nothing from their new leader for the four months since his election and in the face of the recent alarming events of secession, they were desperate to hear from this relative stranger into whose hands they had placed the survival of the God-given inalienable rights enjoyed by the nation. The reporters eagerly set their pencils at the ready at this unexpected opportunity to record his extemporaneous remarks.

Struggling to gather himself, and with the warmest sincerity, he said:

> My friends, no one, not in my situation, can appreciate my feelings of sadness at this parting. To this place, and the kindness of these people, I owe everything. Here I have been a quarter of a century, and have passed from a young to an old man. Here my children have been born, and one is buried. I now leave, not knowing when, or whether ever, I may return, with a task before me greater than that which rested upon Washington. Without the assistance of that Divine Being, who ever attended him, I cannot suc-

---

[298] *The Eloquent President*, Ronald C. White, Jr., p 4

ceed. With that assistance I cannot fail. Trusting in Him, who can go with me, and remain with you and be everywhere for good, let us confidently hope that all will yet be well. To His care commending you, as I hope in your prayers you will commend me, I bid you an affectionate farewell.[299]

James C. Conkling, a close friend to Lincoln, recorded that "Many eyes were filled to overflowing." And of Lincoln he said, "His breast heaved with emotion and he could scarcely command his feelings sufficiently to commence."[300] Lincoln's plea for the prayers of his friends elicited choked exclamations from the crowd of "We will do it, we will do it."[301] This farewell speech contained nothing specific regarding the national crisis and no words to draw political support for himself as one would expect from a politician. But rather, Lincoln chose to speak of his love for his friends and of his faith in his Maker. Of the 152 words in the short address, 63 were devoted to the omnipotence and omnipresence of the Almighty.

In the four months from Lincoln's November 1860 election to his inauguration in the following March, he made no public statements or formal addresses. Instead, he quietly observed the unraveling of this nation while President James Buchanan finished out his term. Politicians in Washington could not agree on how to respond to the startling secession of the Southern states. Some called for a constitutional amendment to offer even more appeasements for the Southern slave-owners' grievances. The House of Representatives recommended a constitutional amendment that would prohibit any further interference with slavery in hopes of placating the southern Fire-Eaters. The Senate offered up additional concessions to pacify their rebellious

---

[299] *The Eloquent President*, Ronald C. White, Jr., p 3
[300] *The Eloquent President*, Ronald C. White, Jr., p 22
[301] *The Eloquent President*, Ronald C. White, Jr., p 19

neighbors to the south. But Lincoln, observing all of this solemnly in Springfield, would have none of anything suggesting compromise with the rebellion. He considered compromise to be nothing more than bribes to the secessionists. He resolutely told a visitor, "I will suffer death before I will consent…to any concession or compromise which looks like buying the privilege to take possession of this government to which we have a constitutional right."[302] He privately told a friend his conviction on the matter that he would take with him to the White House:

> The right of a State to secede is not an open or debatable question; it had been settled in Andrew Jackson's time, during the nullification crisis. It is the duty of a President to execute the laws and maintain the existing Government. He cannot entertain any proposition for dissolution or dismemberment. No state can, in any way lawfully, get out of the Union, without the consent of the others; and…it is the duty of the president, and other government functionaries to run the machine as it is.[303]

Lincoln was resolute in his commitment to preserve the Union but his faith in the Supreme Court had been shattered three years earlier by the disgracing Dred Scott decision, so he entered the Presidency looking first to God and then to his Congress and cabinet, to establish his presidential foundation.

In the twelve days and nights that his train rumbled across the states from Springfield to Washington, Lincoln would be seen by more Americans than any other president before him.

---

[302] *Lincoln*, David Herbert Donald, p 268
[303] *Lincoln*, David Herbert Donald, p 269

He would in fact, give nearly one hundred speeches during the twelve-day journey. It became just too difficult to be unresponsive to the cheering and admiring crowds and the occasional lavish receptions. Lincoln, in his meekness so uncharacteristic of a politician, enunciated again and again that the celebrations en route were not about a person but about an office and a nation. He insisted that the guest lists at these locally planned receptions should not be made up primarily of partisans, but should include representatives of all parties.

He was wary of impromptu speeches, knowing how easily a misspoken or misinterpreted word or phrase could ignite even more instability in the nation that he now saw teetering at the edge of a cliff, and he was keenly aware that President Buchanan continued as president until the March 4 inauguration. But the national and local newspapers were gobbling up every word he spoke for their anxious readers back home. Millions in America read details of the journey and of his speeches. His enemies in the South were as anxious to read them as anyone, as they looked for clues signaling his course of action as president.

Lincoln used these speeches to reveal to the citizens of America the principles upon which he had based his life and that would now form the foundation upon which he would lead this country. The point he made over and over again was that he viewed himself as an instrument in God's hands, that God's will would be sought and then followed. And he assured them that God would see them through this national crisis that had so recently appeared. In one speech he referred to himself as "The humblest of all individuals that have ever been elected to the Presidency."[304] In New Jersey, he declared, "I shall be most happy indeed if I shall be an humble instrument in the hands of the Almighty, and of this his almost cho-

---

[304] *Lincoln*, David Herbert Donald, p 275

sen people…"[305] With this theme he elaborated on his belief that Americans were "God's chosen people"[306] who had yet to fully conform to His ways. In Indianapolis he referred to himself as a mere instrument, "an accidental instrument, perhaps I should say"[307] to work God's will as president. In Trenton he revealed his belief that his role as president came "not only from the people but from *the Almighty*,"[308] and that the present crisis was about nothing less than the *salvation* of the nation. He punctuated this point by referring to Jesus' New Testament injunction to Peter in Matthew 16:18 that Peter's mission was to build His Church with the assurance that "the gates of hell will not prevail against it."[309] Sensing the uncertainty fostered by the gravity of the current crisis, Lincoln also calmed America with his wit and wisdom. There were frequent reports of cheering laughter from the crowds.

He often ended his speeches with this sobering question that he put to his listeners for them to consider: "Shall the Union and shall the liberties of this country be preserved to the latest generation?"[310] To be sure, few in America saw the gravity of this division as clearly as Lincoln. It would be critical for him to open their vision as to its gravity. This question illustrated the great chasm that divided the mission of President Lincoln from the ambition of the Southern political leaders. Lincoln, deeply aware that the actions of today are the consequences of tomorrow, saw his role as that of preserving this nation as God had designed it. He feared that the recent events of secession had the potential to weaken and eventually disintegrate this nation and its sacred constitutional liberties as they were established by

---

[305] *The Eloquent President*, Ronald C. White, Jr., p 23
[306] *The Eloquent President*, Ronald C. White, Jr., p 54
[307] *Lincoln*, David Herbert Donald, p 275
[308] *The Eloquent President*, Ronald C. White, Jr., p 54
[309] *The Eloquent President*, Ronald C. White, Jr., p 31
[310] Speech in Indianapolis, February 11, 1861

the Founding Fathers, for the future benefit of unborn generations of Americans and the world. The aim of those in the South had no apparent regard for the future impact of their intentions. Their purpose was clear: to secure the ability to continue the amassing of their own personal wealth through slavery, enabling them to continue unmolested in their hedonistic aristocracy, with no apparent regard for the damage they were designing for the future generations of this nation or the world.

As the train rolled into Philadelphia, Lincoln approached his visit and planned speech at Independence Hall, which had been scheduled to fall on George Washington's birthday, with a deep reverence for the momentous Declaration of Independence, which was born therein.

> I am filled with deep emotion finding myself standing here in the place where were collected together the wisdom, the patriotism, the devotion to principle, from which sprang the institutions under which we live...I have never had a feeling politically that did not spring from the sentiments embodied in the Declaration of Independence.[311]

Lincoln was consumed with the conviction that the liberties of this remarkable and free nation, that were won and organized by the Founding Fathers and loyal patriots, had been severely eroded and weakened. He saw his role and that of all other political leaders as standing in defense of those hard-won liberties. He had been deeply troubled by the mob violence and disregard for Constitutional freedoms that had been pervasive for decades from New England to the Gulf Coast. He believed that the threat to this government would not come from a transatlantic military force but rather from foes and forces that "must spring

---

[311] *Abraham Lincoln, an Illustrated Biography,* Philip B. Kunhardt Jr.,Philip Kunhardt III,Peter W. Kunhardt p15

up amongst us. If destruction be our lot, we must ourselves be its author and finisher. As a nation of freemen, we must live through all time, or die by suicide."[312]

Horace Greeley, editor of the *New York Tribune*, joined Lincoln's entourage in Buffalo. Greeley would be the most outspoken and most listened-to newspaper editor during the upcoming war. Greeley and many other editors would feel it their duty to advise President Lincoln in print and in private on how he should execute his office. Greeley observed that "The power of Mr. Lincoln is not his presence or his speech, but in the honesty and gloriously refreshing sincerity of the MAN."[313] He went on to say, "His passage through the country has been like the return of grateful sunshine after a stormy winter day. The people breathe more freely and hope revives in all hearts."[314] In the coming years, Greeley, along with nearly everyone else, would turn more critical as the war intensified.

At a whistle-stop outside Albany, New York, Lincoln received word that Jefferson Davis had taken the oath of office as president of the Confederacy, while thousands of cheering Southern citizens exulted at the momentous event. Davis's inauguration included many religious references, which included an invocation and a kiss to the Bible by Davis at his swearing in. This was followed by a dance on the American flag by the popular actress Maggie Smith.

Lincoln's Presidential Special wasn't the only train being closely watched by the nation. On February 11, the newly elected president of the Confederacy, Jefferson Davis, was also zigzagging the South by train from his plantation in Mississippi to the new Confederate capital in Montgomery, Alabama. The headline of the *New York Times* captured the irony with two column headlines placed side by side:

---

[312] *The Eloquent President*, Ronald C. White, Jr., p 16
[313] *The Eloquent President*, Ronald C. White, Jr., p 48
[314] *The Eloquent President*, Ronald C. White, Jr., p 48

"The New Administration"   "The New Confederacy"

Earlier, on February 4, delegates from six Southern states gathered in Montgomery with the purpose of creating the new government for a separate nation. To the bitter disappointment of Robert Barnwell Rhett, who had earned for himself the dubious distinction as being the Father of the Secession and leader of the radical South Carolina delegation, Jefferson Davis was unanimously elected as provisional president of the Confederacy, with Lincoln's old friend Alexander Stephens as provisional vice president. Rhett had long envisioned and labored hard for a separate Southern nation, and he had always envisioned it with himself at the helm. But at the Montgomery Convention, his politics were too extreme for the other delegates and they went with Davis. The embittered Rhett returned to Charleston, and through his newspaper the *Charleston Mercury* became a harsh critic of Davis and his administration. He firmly believed that he was responsible for this great Southern political victory and that he deserved to lead the new nation. Two years later, he ran for a seat in the Confederate Congress and was again defeated, which only added to his indignant bitterness.

Chapter Six

"I, Abraham Lincoln, Do Solemnly Swear"

It was no secret that Lincoln's life was in danger. On March 1, Horace Greeley's newspaper article titled "Mr. Lincoln on His Way" reported that "large rewards have been openly proffered in the Cotton States to whosoever would take his life before the 4th of March."[315] In the final days of the journey to Washington, DC, Allan Pinkerton, head of the Pinkerton National Detective Agency, uncovered a detailed plot to assassinate Lincoln in Baltimore, where anti-Lincoln sentiment was rampant; this was not the first threat to be detected on the trip to Washington but it was certainly the most credible. Nearby Baltimore was a strongly pro-Southern city with a history of street and mob violence. After considerable private discussions, Lincoln reluctantly agreed to secretly change his travel plans that would take him through Baltimore at a different time, late at night, and thus avert the threat in Baltimore. This secret train ride into the capital became a source of ridicule for Lincoln by Democratic-leaning newspapers. He arrived in Washington at 6:30 a.m., several hours ahead of schedule. There was no presi-

---

[315] *Lincoln, an Illustrated Biography*, Phillip B. Kunhardt, Jr., Phillip B. Kunhardt III., And Peter W. Kunhardt, p 20

dential reception; he and Ward Hill Lamon, his trusted bodyguard, arrived alone, unannounced and unrecognized, which was a portent of the aloneness he would feel over the next four years of a long, painful war and presidency.

With all the cheering along his train ride to Washington, there was also derision expressed through the anti-Lincoln newspapers. The *Baltimore Sun* reported, "He approaches the capital of the country more in the character of a harlequin. There is that about his speechification which, if not for the gravity of the occasion, would be ludicrous."[316] In Massachusetts, the *Springfield Republican* flatly said, "Lincoln is a 'simple Susan.'"[317] The nation's most highly regarded orator, Edward Everett, whose two-and-a-half-hour speech some two years later at Gettysburg would be completely overshadowed by Lincoln's brief masterpiece, evaluated Lincoln's whistle-stop speeches as reflecting a new president who "is evidently a person of very inferior cast of character, wholly unequal to the crisis."[318]

After his arrival to Washington, the ten days leading up to his inauguration were filled with Lincoln's receiving countless visitors while he sandwiched in the selection of his cabinet—consisting of three of his opponents in the race for president and three former Democrats—and preparations for his inaugural speech and for taking over the presidential office. Lincoln was an admirer of Thomas Jefferson and particularly Jefferson's policy on republicanism, which was described by the term "Jefferson simplicity."[319] Unlike previous presidents, President Jefferson welcomed to the White House "the humble mechanic and the haughty aristocrat with the same unaffected cordiali-

---

[316] *The Eloquent President,* Ronald C. White, Jr. p 59
[317] *The Eloquent President,* Ronald C. White, Jr. p 59
[318] *The Eloquent President,* Ronald C. White, Jr. p 60
[319] *Recollections Of Abraham Lincoln,* Ward Hill Lamon, p 80

ty."[320] Jefferson espoused the ideal that he, as president, was the servant of the people, not their master. Lincoln embraced this view, interpreting it as the right way to conduct his life and his presidency. He was likely influenced again also by Jesus' New Testament teachings on leadership: that the greatest in the kingdom is to live his life as if the least and the servant of all, reinforced by the many examples of this virtue in His mortal life.

Ward Hill Lamon, a trusted friend and former law partner in Illinois, was Lincoln's appointment as marshal of the District of Columbia; his primary responsibly was to keep Lincoln alive during his presidency and he would be with the president probably more than any other. Lamon recalled:

> Lincolnian simplicity was, in fact, an improvement on the code of his illustrious predecessor. The doors of the White House were always open. Mr. Lincoln was always ready to greet visitors, no matter what their rank or calling—to hear complaints, their petitions, or their suggestions touching the conduct of public affairs. The ease with which he could be approached vastly increased his labor. It also led to many scenes at the White House that were strangely amusing and sometimes dramatic.[321]

Lamon heard Lincoln say numerous times during his four-year term, "There is no smell of royalty about this establishment."[322]

---

[320] *Recollections Of Abraham Lincoln*, Ward Hill Lamon, p 80
[321] *Recollections Of Abraham Lincoln*, Ward Hill Lamon, p 80
[322] *Recollections Of Abraham Lincoln*, Ward Hill Lamon, p 6

Lincoln was pleased with the visit from his friends of the Illinois delegation in Washington, which included his long-time rival, the vanquished presidential candidate Stephen A. Douglas, with whom Lincoln had a particularly cordial visit. At a later reception, the proslavery Douglas, who was opposed to the secession movement of the Southern states, urged the president-elect to persuade the Republicans to compromise with the South for the sake of preserving the Union, and pledged that he and his Democratic followers would not try to gain political advantage from the crisis. "Our Union must be preserved," Douglas said solemnly. "Partisan feelings must yield to patriotism. I am with you, Mr. President, and God bless you."[323] Lincoln was touched by Douglas's expression and responded, "With all my heart I thank you. The people with us and God helping us, all will yet be well."[324] When Douglas left the reception, Lincoln exclaimed to another visitor, "What a noble man Douglas is!"[325]

The wealthy and influential New York merchant William E. Dodge paid the new president a visit to warn him that only concessions to the South could prevent a national bankruptcy, telling Lincoln that he and his fellow merchants looked to him to determine "whether the grass shall grow in the streets of our commercial cities." Lincoln, looking quizzical, surprised his haughty visitor by saying that he preferred to see the grass grow in the fields and the meadows but that as president he would defend the Constitution and "let the grass grow where it may."[326] Nearly every evening prior to the March 4 inauguration, he and Mary would receive visitors at the lobby of the Willard Hotel consisting of politicians, office-

---

[323] *Lincoln*, David Herbert Donald, p 280
[324] *Lincoln*, David Herbert Donald, p 280
[325] *Lincoln*, David Herbert Donald, p 280
[326] *Lincoln*, David Herbert Donald, p 280

seekers, well-wishing citizens, and many others like Dodge, offering their advice on how the new president should address the problems facing the nation. The Lincolns received all cordially, with Mary being an enthusiastic, informed, and gracious hostess.

Never before had an inauguration taken place in such a tense and dangerous atmosphere. Riflemen lined the rooftops and cannon were set near the capital to nervously guard the life of the new United States president as he made his way from the Willard Hotel toward the Capitol in a cavalry-flanked horse-drawn carriage accompanied by the outgoing and worn-out president, James Buchanan. Many of the Washington residents were overwhelmingly sympathetic to the South and unabashed in their opposition to Lincoln. Wild rumors swirled, fed by many of the discontented Southerners who now felt trapped in Washington and fearful of their planned return to their home Southern states. They speculated about imminent attacks on Washington, or assassination attempts on the president-elect, and about plans for reinforcing Fort Sumter to keep the Federals from taking back control of *their* fort.

These Southern sympathies were firmly entrenched in many of Washington's social and political circles. For the first seventy-two years of the federal government, Southern leaders had been dominant in Congress. Washington was a slaveholding city and even though both Abraham and Mary were technically Southerners, having both been born in Kentucky, their new domicile was dangerously hostile territory for them. The citizens of Washington had tolerated the Democrat Buchanan, but this Lincoln, a Republican, was viewed by many locals to be a most unwelcome intrusion. Even though he won the election, it was done with an overwhelming majority of electoral votes from the North and not one from south of the Mason-Dixon Line. Inauguration day, 1861, was far different from the fifteen previous;

this one was tense and subdued, with the capital city sparsely decorated compared to years past.

At noon on March 4, the carriage and entourage of President James Buchanan and President-elect Lincoln proceeded down Pennsylvania Avenue, which was lined with what appeared to be as many soldiers and sharpshooters as citizens. Few of the anti-Lincoln locals attended the event, but some twenty-five thousand, mostly from the nearby Northern states, were present on that cold and gray day. Lincoln and Buchanan entered the Capitol building's north side through a boarded passageway built expressly to block a clear shot from an assassin's rifle. Shortly, Lincoln emerged from the Capitol to the platform built on the east side with the still unfinished Capitol dome above him. Introduced by his old friend, Edward Baker, Lincoln rose to address the audience. He was momentarily distracted with no place to put his tall stovepipe hat when Stephen A. Douglas, sitting behind him, stepped forward saying, "Permit me sir,"[327] and held his hat during the ceremony.

With his inaugural address Lincoln intended to, as clearly and unequivocally as possible, communicate his executive position with the same clarity and honesty he had utilized throughout his personal and political life. He wanted the nation to know that he believed there to be no constitutional right for any state to secede from the Union; that he, as the president of the United States, had a solemn obligation to defend the Union, to which he would publicly swear an oath in but a few moments. He wanted to express that he had no intention of shrinking from that solemn presidential responsibility. He wanted to make clear that, even though he despised slavery, he had no intention of interfering with it in the states where it was lawfully practiced; and finally, he wanted them to know that he considered

---

[327] *Lincoln*, David Herbert Donald, p 283

the people of the South to be his friends and fellow citizens, not enemies.

He opened his address, saying:

> In compliance with a custom as old as the government itself, I appear before you to address you briefly, and to take, in your presence, the oath prescribed by the Constitution of the United States, to be taken by the President before he enters on the execution of his office.[328]

In this his first official presidential utterance he demonstrated a pattern of referring to himself in the third person, something he would do repeatedly. He told some during the next four years who called him Mister President to simply "Call me Lincoln."[329] Driven by a lifelong avoidance of self-aggrandizement, now becoming the most influential and powerful politician in the nation brought him a humble uneasiness that would be present throughout his presidency. Lincoln's high-pitched voice had a remarkable carrying power that could be heard distinctly over a considerable distance. The reporter from Washington's *National Intelligencer* wrote that his voice was heard "quite intelligible by at least ten thousand"[330] of the estimated twenty-five thousand that were present.

Lincoln continued:

> I hold, that in contemplation of universal law, and of the Constitution, the Union of these states is perpetual. Perpetuity is implied, if not expressed, in the fundamental law of all national governments. It is

---

[328] *The Eloquent President,* Ronald C. White, Jr., p 77

[329] *Anecdotes of Abraham Lincoln and Lincoln's Stories: Including Early Life...,* By Abraham Lincoln, James Baird McClure, Rhoades & McClure, 1879

[330] *The Eloquent President,* Ronald C. White, Jr., p 80

safe to assert that no government proper, ever had a provision in its organic law for its own termination…One of the declared objects for ordaining and establishing the Constitution was "*to form a more perfect union.*"[331]

I have no purpose, directly or indirectly, to interfere with the institution of slavery in the States where it exists. I believe I have no lawful right to do so, and I have no inclination to do so.[332]

Lincoln, as always, was being completely forthright here. Always apart from the ever-mounting abolition movement, he had never been a part of any plan to eradicate slavery from any state, because the Constitution and dozens of laws did in fact allow and support slavery. Lincoln always abided by the law. He was, however, well known to be an ardent opponent to the expansion of slavery in the territories and in future states to the west.

Lincoln believed that there remained many in the South who opposed secession from the Union and who were being coerced to support it. He also believed that it was the design and actions of a minority of Southern radical yet influential men, almost all slave owners and particularly in South Carolina, who were the authors of this national crisis. Of them he said, "[they] seek to destroy the Union at all events, and are glad of any pretext to do it."[333] These radical Fire-Eaters, as they were pleased to be called, promptly placed the blame for war on Lincoln. According to them, he should have done as Buchanan and the United States Congress had done: simply allow them to leave the Union, and with them take the government's military installations and arse-

---

[331] *The Eloquent President*, Ronald C. White, Jr., p 83
[332] *The Eloquent President*, Ronald C. White, Jr., p 81
[333] *The Eloquent President*, Ronald C. White, Jr., p 85

nals within their boundaries. Lincoln went on in his inaugural speech to clearly state the gravity of their actions and to plainly express his determination to do his sworn duty as president of the United States: to these Southern radicals he firmly declared:

> In *your* hands, my dissatisfied fellow countrymen, and not *mine* is the momentous issue of civil war. The government will not assail you. You can have no conflict, without being you yourselves the aggressors. *You* have no oath registered in Heaven to destroy the government, while I shall have the most solemn one to "preserve, protect and defend it."[334]

If there was to be armed conflict, Lincoln was determined that it would not be the North that would initiate bloodshed. The Southern radicals of South Carolina, in their shortsightedness, were quick to oblige. Starting with the first group of rebelling Southern states, followed by the expropriation of the government's military installations and arsenals that resided in their respective states, the South was clearly the instigator of the war. They fired upon a government supply ship in Charleston Harbor en route to its military base at Fort Sumter, and then fired again on, and took by force, Fort Sumter, culminating in the formation of a confederate government on U.S. government soil. "Plainly," Lincoln warned them, "the central idea of secession, is the essence of anarchy. No state, upon its own mere motion, can lawfully get out of the Union...and acts of violence, within any State or States, against the authority of the United States, are insurrectionary or revolutionary..."[335] With this clarity he extinguished any hopes of compromise. He would act on his duty to defend and uphold the Union.

---

[334] *The Eloquent President*, Ronald C. White, Jr., p 87
[335] *The Eloquent President*, Ronald C. White, Jr., p 62

In plaintive warmth and sincerity he brought his speech to its conclusion:

> I am loath to close. We are not enemies, but friends. We must not be enemies. Though passion may have strained, it must not break our bonds of affection. The mystic chords of memory, stretching from every battlefield, and patriot grave, to every living heart and hearthstone, all over this broad land, will yet swell the chorus of the Union, when again touched, as surely they will be, by the better angels of our nature.[336]

At the conclusion of the speech, the eighty-four-year-old Chief Justice Roger Taney stepped forward to swear in the new president. With his left hand on an open Bible, and right hand raised to the square, Lincoln repeated the oath of office:

> I, Abraham Lincoln, do solemnly swear that I will faithfully execute the office of President of the United States, and will, to the best of my ability, preserve, protect, and defend the Constitution of the United States.[337]

To the astonishment of the Fire-Eaters, he would keep this solemn promise.

Never before had the nation been so thirsty to hear an inaugural address, for never before had one been given in such a state of national crisis. Newspapers across the country anxiously waited for the telegraph-transmitted message to put to print. In New York, special editions were printed at noon and one thirty

---

[336] *The Eloquent President*, Ronald C. White, Jr., p 62
[337] *The Eloquent President*, Ronald C. White, Jr., p 92

with part of the speech in the first edition and the rest of the speech in the following one for its readers to devour and for a slick doubling of newspaper sales for the day. Reaction to the speech was predictably mixed. The *Charleston Mercury* wrote that the speech from "The Ourang-Outang [sic] at the White House [was] the tocsin of war...[338] The paper excoriated Lincoln's "lamentable display of feeble inability to grasp the circumstances of the momentous emergency."[339] The *Richmond Enquirer* censured the speech as "the cool, unimpassioned, deliberate language of a fanatic."[340] The *New York Times* observed that "Before the Inaugural has been read in a single Southern State, it is denounced, through the telegraph, from every Southern point, as a declaration of war."[341] In this instance, the South was right: there would be war. They were wrong, however, in their blaming of Lincoln for causing the war. Abraham Lincoln was almost alone in his determination to preserve the Union and to save the fragile Constitution as they were originally formed, and quite certainly the only man strong enough in principle, resolve, and meekness before God to carry it through. This unbending defense of the sacred Union and Constitution would trigger the sad and unfortunate four years of bloodletting in America.

His great speech was received with mild applause. The audience heard no magic solution to the crisis, only his expressed determination to defend the Constitution. Lincoln could have taken advantage of the speech and the listening ear of all Americans, as most politicians would, to muster even more support for himself as the champion of the North by vilifying the South, but Lincoln was not interested in doing so. He never had been one to seek unmerited support. This speech was spoken plainly

---

[338] *Lincoln,* David Herbert Donald, p 284
[339] *The Eloquent President,* Ronald C. White, Jr., p 95
[340] *The Eloquent President,* Ronald C. White, Jr., p 95
[341] *The Eloquent President,* Ronald C. White, Jr., p 95

and from his heart, as he always had done and as he would continue to do throughout his presidency, seeking only to do what was right and not concerning himself with whatever political ill might come his way by defending the right. To Lincoln the secession movement was not legal so he viewed himself as still president of all of the United States, including the citizens in the Southern states.

After the inaugural ball that evening, as Lincoln entered his new living quarters in the White House, he was handed a note: Fort Sumter, South Carolina was in grave danger. This nation's darkest days had now arrived.

The next morning, Lincoln's first day as president, he received the detailed message from Major Robert Anderson at Fort Sumter, stating that he had only enough provisions for his small detachment at the fort to last about six weeks and that, based on the massive firepower that the Charleston militias now had aimed directly on Fort Sumter, Anderson would need an additional twenty thousand men to secure the fort for the government. The future of the nation rested on Fort Sumter and all eyes, North and South, were on it. Lincoln could simply order Anderson to abandon the fort and concede that the Southern states' unlawful taking of federal forts and arsenals would be allowed and by so doing they would have their Confederate nation, as was their desire. Or, if he and the government were to defend its right to exist, Fort Sumter gradually became the looming target of its defense.

The government was hardly prepared for such a monumental crisis. The House of Representatives had just adjourned and the congressmen were heading home, his cabinet had not yet been approved or assembled, and Lincoln had never worked at an executive level. He had always worked on his own. The delegation and coordination among massive government departments was completely foreign to him. It had been ten years since he was even a government-elected official when he completed his only term in the House of Representatives, and now he found himself as the inexperienced chief executive with the nation on the brink of civil war. This lack of managerial experience became quickly evident and did not inspire confidence in those around him. The new president was well aware of his own inexperience. At first he attempted to do everything himself, as he had always conducted his own business for years. Later he admitted to an Illinois friend that "when he first commenced doing the duties, he was entirely ignorant not only of the duties, but of the manner of doing the business of the presidency."[342]

It is stunning that the gargantuan events of secession, which took place in the 118 days between Lincoln's November 6 election and his inauguration on March 4, were done with Congress in session and with that body doing nothing to stop the disintegration of the nation. President Buchanan also turned spectator, saying, "Congress alone has power" to decide the legality of secession.[343] "But," observed Ward Hill Lamon, "Congress behaved like a body of men who thought the calamities of the nation were no special business of theirs."[344] Those congressmen from the Deep South were merely looking for the proper time to resign their elected offices and return to their home states; those from the middle slave states could but watch to see how these movements would affect them, and, as the French minister observed, the leaders from the Northern states were a "mere aggregation of individual ambitions."[345] Lamon continued:

> In the philosophy of their politics it [secession] had not been dreamed of as a possible thing. Even when they saw it assume the shape of a fixed and terrible fact,

[342] *The Eloquent President*, Ronald C. White, Jr., p 100
[343] *Recollections of Abraham Lincoln*, Ward Hill Lamon, p 57
[344] *Recollections of Abraham Lincoln*, Ward Hill Lamon, p 57
[345] *Recollections of Abraham Lincoln*, Ward Hill Lamon, p 57

they could not comprehend its meaning. The nation was going to pieces, and Congress left it to its fate. The vessel, freighted with all the hopes and all the wealth of thirty millions of free people was drifting to her doom, and they who alone had power to control her course refused to lay a finger on the helm.[346]

People continued to pour into to the White House to advise the new president, or ask for presidential appointments, or just to satisfy their curiosity and meet their new leader. To the chagrin of his staff, Lincoln would not turn them away, so the business of running a country in crisis was constantly being interrupted. John Hay, Lincoln's secretary, observed:

> There was little order or system about it. Those around him strove from beginning to end to erect barriers to defend him against constant interruption, but the President himself was always the first to break them down.[347]

To Senator Henry Wilson's admonition that "You will wear yourself out," Lincoln replied, "They don't want much; they get but little, and I must see them."[348] Again, Hay remarks upon the dilemma, "It would be hard to imagine a state of things less conducive to serious and effective work, yet in one way or another, the work was done."[349]

Lincoln's inexperience quickly produced widespread criticism of his administrative ability, and with it came others pointing to their chief executive's lack of education. Lincoln was sur-

---

[346] *Recollections of Abraham Lincoln*, Ward Hill Lamon, p 58
[347] *The Eloquent President*, Ronald C. White, Jr., p 100
[348] *The Eloquent President*, Ronald C. White, Jr., p 100
[349] *The Eloquent President*, Ronald C. White, Jr., p 100

rounded by college, military academy, and law school graduates, but the United States, at its most critical time, was now being led by a man with less than one year of formal education. However, the humble attributes of greatness possessed by Lincoln were not available in these learning institutions; they, instead, were divine in nature and would prove to be more than adequate. Ronald C. White, Jr., concluded that what Lincoln lacked in formal education, he made up in his gift of expression; he was an artist with words. "He had risen above political peers with more education and more political experience because he could articulate his political vision in spoken words that could both inform and inspire."[350]

There was a somewhat noble yet critically damaging condition shared by many early Americans up to the time of the Civil War, and yet this condition is virtually extinct today. It is the strongly embraced notion of states' rights. The states' rights stand was a major stumbling block for the Founding Fathers, many of whom were suspicious of a national government. They felt that the states were best suited to governing themselves; and this decision was in spite of the near disaster that followed the winning of their independence from England, when disagreements and strife between states nearly brought this country to utter ruin. This deep allegiance to one's home state was widely celebrated in early America as demonstrated by many patriots, including Thomas Jefferson. Jefferson's love of his home state of Virginia ran much deeper than his devotion to the United States. He referred to his fellow Virginians as his countrymen and to Virginia as his country. For a time, he spoke of the United States Congress as a "foreign legislature," and even referred to the Union as a Confederacy. These sentiments were widely held by early Americans for more than four score and seven years since the Declaration of Independence. It was this

[350] *The Eloquent President*, Ronald C. White, Jr., p 10

same devotion to state that influenced Robert E. Lee's decision to reject Lincoln's request that he lead the Union army when his home state of Virginia joined the rebellion, even though Lee was opposed to secession.

"Until his dying days, Thomas Jefferson regularly propounded local self-government above all else, supporting states' rights against the Union."[351] He was a strong proponent of the Tenth Amendment to the Constitution that limited federal power in relation to the states. "In 1800, he soberly warned that a 'single consolidated government would become the most corrupt government on earth.'"[352]

While Jefferson was president, some states in New England were dissatisfied over his economic policies and took dangerous steps toward secession. To this Jefferson responded, "Whether we remain in our confederacy, or break into Atlantic and Mississippi confederacies, I do not believe very important to the happiness of either part," adding, "separate them if it be better."[353]

Such states' rights sentiments were again expressed when in 1832 South Carolina made a near break from the Union, over disagreements with President Andrew Jackson's policies. Jackson's administration responded by making "nullication" or secession from the Union illegal, a point to which Lincoln often referred. But these sentiments persisted on up to December 1860, when South Carolina became the first of eleven states to secede based on the perceived right of a state to leave the Union when dissatisfied with it.

Charleston, South Carolina was a beautiful coastal city of forty thousand residents, the second-largest city in the South, and due to the enormous wealth brought by the plantation owners and merchants, it was also a very progressive and prosperous city.

---

[351] *April 1865*, Jay Winik, p 11
[352] *April 1865*, Jay Winik, p 11
[353] *April 1865*, Jay Winik, p 11

While the secession fever was present in varying degrees throughout the South, the citizens of Charleston provided most of the leadership to the movement. The opening scene of secession took place when the radical Fire-Eaters from Charleston forced a major division within the Democratic Party in earlier 1860, dashing the favored Stephen A. Douglas's chances to be elected president and catapulting the Republican candidate, Abraham Lincoln, into the forefront of the race. This was a calculated move by the Fire-Eaters, who actually wanted an antislavery Republican president to be elected, believing that this would create enough alarm in Southern slave owners and politicians to finally push them to support secession. Their calculations were accurate. Just days after Lincoln's election, South Carolina became the first of eleven states to withdraw from the Union, with the focal point of the two adversaries becoming South Carolina's bombardment of, capture of, and refusal to return the federal government's Fort Sumter in Charleston Harbor.

The Civil War at Charleston records the feelings of Charleston's citizens on hearing the news of their state's secession:

> While sobriety and restraint prevailed within Institute Hall as the Ordinance of Secession was being signed on December 20, 1860, wild excitement swept the streets outside. When, at last the president of the convention arose to proclaim the State of South Carolina an independent commonwealth, jubilation followed. Business was suspended. The pealing of church bells mingled with the roar of saluting guns. Old men ran shouting through the city. Everyone entitled to wear a uniform went home and put it on.[354]

---

[354] *The Civil War at Charslton*, Arthur Wilcox and Warren Ripley, p 2

Representatives were promptly dispatched to all parts of the South to carry the message that South Carolina had declared its independence and now urged her sister states to join her. By Christmas 1860, even though few expected there to be war, enthusiasm for soldiering had become a craze in Charleston. The militiamen were the darlings of the community. Citizens of all classes joined to defend their new nation from the Yankees and to enjoy the admiration of their neighbors. The best families of Charleston led this jubilant parading, ceremoniously taking their places in the militia ranks as well as accepting commissions. "One company had an aggregate wealth of more than a million dollars."[355] Shortly, six more states joined the rebellion, with the remaining southern states following suit some weeks later.

An island in Charleston Harbor housed Fort Sumter, a fortification built during the War of 1812 for protection against enemy ships. A small detachment of federal troops, commanded by Major Robert Anderson, was stationed across the harbor from Fort Sumter, at the run-down Fort Moultrie. The citizens were not overly concerned with this detachment because Major Anderson was a fellow Southerner from Kentucky who had just replaced Massachusetts-born Colonel John L. Gardner, and they mistook him as sympathetic to their cause. Upon his arrival, however, Major Anderson, observing the secession zeal that was taking place in Charleston, grew concerned with the vulnerable position of his small contingent of troops at Fort Moultrie in the event of an uprising. He immediately requested from his superiors permission to transfer across the harbor into the vacant Fort Sumter that would provide them better protection. The beleaguered lame-duck President Buchanan's administration clearly recognized the volatility of events in Charleston— the hotbed of the secession movement—and was looking intently for Lincoln's inauguration day in March, to pass its trou-

---

[355] *The Civil War at Charslton*, Arthur Wilcox and Warren Ripley, p 2

bled nation on to the unfortunate successor. Not wanting to incite further problems, Buchanan's War Department responded to Major Anderson's request by granting him full discretion to decide for himself whether or not to move his small garrison of sixty-five men to Fort Sumter. Two weeks later, on the night of December 26, one day after South Carolina's legislature voted to officially secede from the Union, Major Anderson's detachment secretly disabled the cannons of Fort Moultrie to prevent their use against them, and quietly floated across the bay to Fort Sumter. That morning the guardship *Nina* raced to the city with news that Union troops were observed on the ramparts of Fort Sumter. To add to their alarm, the citizens awoke to the view of smoke curling up from Fort Moultrie, as Major Anderson had ordered the wooden gun carriages burned as a defensive measure. It was all perceived as a Union offensive against Charleston; the residents were enraged at this apparent challenge to their newly obtained sovereignty.

December 28, 1860
The Charleston Mercury
The Events of Yesterday

The report that the defenses of Fort Moultrie had been so shamefully mutilated, naturally aroused great indignation in the city. People immediately sought the steeples and cupolas of the public buildings, and telescopes were brought into active requisition, to gratify the general curiosity. Little, however, could be descried beyond a dense smoke issuing from within the ramparts, and large gangs of men at work unloading the cargos of schooners into Fort Sumter.

Emboldened by their newborn independence that had been officially declared the day before, South Carolina governor F. W. Pickens ordered that the nearby federal fort named Castle Pinckney be captured in retaliation to Anderson's occupation of Fort Sumter. Only one officer, a Lieutenant Meade, one sergeant with his family, and a crew of four mechanics and thirty civilian laborers occupied Castle Pinckney. The day after Anderson's move to Fort Sumter, Colonel J. J. Pettigrew received orders from the governor to organize on the Citadel Green in Charleston one hundred and fifty young men, eager for the glory of military victory. Dressed smartly in their winter uniforms, complete with knapsacks, blankets, and revolvers, they boarded the *Nina*, which crossed the harbor and tied up at the Castle Pinckney wharf at about four p.m. Lieutenant Meade observed their approach and locked the gates. With scaling ladders, Colonel Pettigrew led the ascent of the castle walls. Climbing over the parapet he was met by Lieutenant Meade, whereupon Colonel Pettigrew announced that he was taking over the work on the fort by order of the governor. Meade refused to acknowledge the authority of the governor to take over the fort, and then added the obvious that he had no means to defend it; by that time Colonel Pettigrew's men had scaled the walls and opened the gate. Refusing to accept capture as a prisoner of war, as there was no war, Lieutenant Meade negotiated considerate treatment for his men and himself and they left the Castle in the hands of the sovereign commonwealth of South Carolina. A palmetto flag taken from the *Nina* was triumphantly raised over the fort. Although bloodless, this confiscation of federal property is considered by many to be the first overt act of the Civil War. That same evening, a detachment of two hundred and twenty-five Charleston militiamen conducted a similar bloodless capture of the vacated Fort Moultrie. Charleston citizens were jubilant as their road to secession continued with such perfection.

Viewing South Carolina as no longer part of the United States, its leaders began demanding that the federal government turn over Fort Sumter. The sight of the Stars and Stripes flying over Fort Sumter was now seen as a foreign presence and an affront to their "national" sovereignty. They appealed to President Buchanan, who surprised them by refusing to surrender Fort Sumter or any other federal arsenal or installation residing in the South. In fact, he sent a merchant steamer, *Star of the West*, with tons of supplies and two hundred additional men to reinforce Major Anderson's small contingent. Upon its entry into the harbor, shore batteries on both sides awaited anxiously for orders to fire on the unarmed vessel. The order finally came from Major P. F. Stevens, to thirty-nine eager Citadel cadets manning the artillery on the Morris Island battery. Young G. W. Haynes had the dubious honor of firing the first shot of the Civil War, as he sent a cannonball roaring over the top of the *Star of the West*. Others opened fire and forced the ship back to sea.

On March 1, the newly installed president of the Confederacy, Jefferson Davis, ordered General Pierre Beauregard, ironically a friend and former West Point pupil of Major Anderson's, to take command of the Charleston defenses with orders to diffuse tensions incited by Robert Barnwell Rhett, William L. Yancey, Louis T. Wigfall, and their fellow Fire-Eaters of Charleston. To the new Confederate leaders, a peaceful separation was in sight and they saw no need—nor did their plans call—for war.

Some in Lincoln's new cabinet pressed him to abandon the fort as a signal of the North's peaceful intentions, but Lincoln was not interested in yet another in a long string of concessions to the rebels. On April 6, Lincoln ordered another relief expedition to Charleston Harbor. It was preceded by a letter to Governor Pickens, informing him of Lincoln's intention to resupply the fort with nonlethal provisions, as well as informing the governor that no ammunition, weapons, or reinforcements were aboard the ship; only food, water, and essential stores for Anderson's men. Pickens responded with derision and consulted with Jefferson Davis, who ordered Beauregard to demand that Anderson surrender the fort. The Charleston militiamen in their snappy uniforms manned the guns surrounding the island fort and waited eagerly for orders to fire on Fort Sumter.

Mary Chesnut was in Charleston during these anxious days. She had been in Washington just weeks earlier where her husband, James Chesnut, a Princeton graduate, served as a moderate U.S. senator. But when Lincoln was elected, he followed his fellow Southern politicians in abandoning their oaths of offices and left Washington for their Southern homes to support the rebellion. He returned to Charleston where he became a delegate to the Secession Convention. In Charleston he was appointed as aide-de-camp to General Beauregard and Jefferson Davis. Mary Chesnut and Mrs. Varnia Davis, were close friends before, during and after the war. For about a year, during Jefferson Davis's Confederate presidency in Richmond, Mary and James were neighbors to the Davises. The Chesnuts had been wealthy planters and slave owners from South Carolina, although Mary often spoke out on her opposition to the institution.

In their early married years, they lived with Chesnut's father, who was one of the wealthiest slave owners in the South. Here they lived the most opulent life that the era could offer. Mary wrote of the place as "magnificent, elegant, luxurious—with everything that a hundred years or more of unlimited wealth could accumulate."[356] Yet she was unhappy there and was anxious to move on with her own married life. Mary wrote of her father-in-law that he was "the last of the lordly planters who ruled this Southern world. He is a splen-

---

[356] *Mary Chesnut's Civil War*, p xxxiv

did wreck…as absolute a tyrant as the Czar of Russia, the Khan of Tartary, or the Sultan of turkey."[357] She was indignant at what she took to be (although no one spoke of it) "his brood of colored [mulatto] children"[358] that were in abundance among his hundreds of slaves.

Mary was an avid diarist, and her Civil War diaries are prized accounts of the coming horrific four years. She would chronicle events of the entire war from the perspective of women in the South and their own emotional battlefields. For Mary and James, the rebellion would leave their lives in ruin, like the majority of the aristocracy of the once-proud South. In the final months of the war, while her husband General Chesnut fought for the rebellion, Mary would become a hungry and homeless refugee with countless others who were in the destructive path of General Sherman as he ripped a devastating swath through the South. After the war, Mary and General Chesnut would spend the rest of their lives in poverty and saddled with huge prewar debts that exceeded their holdings.

April 4, 1861

A ship was fired into yesterday and went back to sea.

Is that the first shot? How can one settle down to anything? One's heart is in one's mouth all the time. Any minute this cannon may open on us….[359]

April 6, 1861

The plot thickens. The air is red-hot with rumors.

Things seem to draw near a crisis.

---

[357] *Mary Chesnut's Civil War*, p xxxv
[358] *Mary Chesnut's Civil War*, p xxxv
[359] *Mary Chesnut's Civil War*, p 41

The Gregg's told me my husband was in a minority in the convention. So much for cool sense, when the atmosphere is phosphorescent.[360]

April 7, 1861

Governor Manning walked in, bowed gravely, and seated himself by me. Again he bowed low, in mock heroic style and, with a grand wave of his hand, said, "Madame, your country is invaded." [Referring to the new country of South Carolina] "There are six men-of-war outside the bar.

Governor Pickens and Beauregard are holding a council of war. Mr. Chesnut [her husband] then entered and confirmed the story.

Wigfall next entered in boisterous spirits. He said, "There was sound of revelry by night, &c&c. The men went off immediately and I crept silently to my room, where I sat down for a good cry.

No sleep for anybody last night. The streets were alive with soldiers, men shouting, marching, singing.

Wigfall, the stormy Petrel, in his glory. The only thoroughly happy person I see.[361]

The eyes of the nation were fixed on Charleston Harbor. Neither side wanted war. At the height of the tension, Robert Toombs, the new Confederate secretary of state, wrote prophetically in a letter to Jefferson Davis:

---

[360] *Mary Chesnut's Civil War*, p 41
[361] *Mary Chesnut's Civil War*, p 43

The firing on that fort will inaugurate a civil war greater than any the world has yet seen...you will lose us every friend at the North. You will wantonly strike a hornet's nest, which extends from mountain to ocean. Legions now quiet will swarm out and sting us to death. It is unnecessary. It puts us in the wrong. It is fatal.[362]

With President Lincoln's supply ship just over the horizon, on April 12, the first gun fired upon Fort Sumter and was followed by a barrage that lasted thirty-six hours. Major Anderson returned fire from the fort. The extremely thick walls of the fort repelled most of the exploding shock but hot shot from the explosions caused numerous fires inside the fort. More than three thousand rounds of shot and shell were fired at the fort and yet remarkably no one was killed on either side. Finally, as fires raged out of control inside the fort, Major Anderson, being desperately short on supplies for his men, ordered the lowering of the American flag and surrendered the fort to Colonel Louis T. Wigfall. Anderson's men were allowed to vacate the fort, peacefully board their vessels, and proceed northward. With the "foreigners" expelled, the Confederate Stars and Bars were raised in a hail of cheers and jubilation. Surely there could not have been a happier people than the proud citizens of Charleston, South Carolina. The celebrations in Charleston were repeated throughout the South. What a remarkable victory they had gained over their hapless and stunned foreign neighbors to the north.

Lincoln and his cabinet and Congress faced a quandary as to how to respond to the Southern rebellion, and the people of the North were growing impatient. The Charlestonians' open aggression and attack of Fort Sumter brought everything into fo-

---

[362] *The Civil War at Charleston*, p 5

cus. Lincoln believed that if the South Carolinians made the fatal mistake of attacking Fort Sumter that it would electrify the Northern populace to action; he was right. To the horror of the Southern citizens, and the surprise of the instigators of rebellion, the day after the hostile taking of Fort Sumter, Lincoln issued a proclamation declaring that the obstruction of the laws in the Southern states was the work of "combinations too powerful to be suppressed by ordinary course of judicial proceedings," and called for seventy-five thousand volunteers to "suppress said combinations, and to cause the laws to be duly executed."[363]

At the same time, he summoned a special session of Congress, to meet on July 4. The appeal was received with euphoric enthusiasm in the Northern states. Democrats united with Republicans in their indignation over South Carolina's affront to their government by attacking Fort Sumter and they rallied behind their new president. The day before issuing the proclamation, Lincoln had a two-hour private conversation with an ailing Stephen A. Douglas to elicit his input and support. The nation's leading Democrat emerged from the meeting with a press release stating that while he was "unalterably opposed to the administration on all its political issues," he was prepared to sustain the president in the exercise of all his constitutional functions to preserve the Union, maintain the government, and defend the federal Capital."[364] A few days later, Douglas returned to Illinois and worked heroically to persuade western Democrats to join him in supporting President Lincoln. By April his health deteriorated as he suffered from acute rheumatism and from the effects of excessive drinking and smoking. In June, at the age of forty-seven, he passed away at his home in Chicago.

Lincoln's Northern supporters were confident that they were significantly stronger than the South. There were some twenty

---

[363] *Lincoln*, David Herbert Donald, p 296
[364] *Lincoln*, David Herbert Donald, p 296

million people in the North compared to the South's nine million. The North was enormously superior to the South in manufacturing and railroad miles. Many were confident that this uprising would be over in short order. This bluster was sounded in many newspapers. The *Chicago Tribune* predicted success "within two to three months at the furthest," because "Illinois can whip the South by herself."[365] The *New York Tribune* boasted "that Jeff. Davis & Co. will be swinging from the battlements at Washington…by the 4th of July,"[366] and the *New York Times* also predicted victory in thirty days. President Lincoln was not so optimistic.

> At hearing the "boastful contrasts of Northern enterprise and endurance, with Southern laziness and high mindedness, he warned them against overconfidence. He reminded them that the Northerners and Southerners all came from the same stock and had 'essentially the same characteristics and powers. Man for man the soldier from the South will be a match for the soldier from the North and *visa versa.*'"[367]

The Northern states' leaders promptly appealed for volunteers, and young men eagerly stepped forward, anxious for the excitement of soldiering and reclaiming their broken Union. In a letter to President Lincoln, Renewick Dickerson of New Hampshire wrote, "I have but one son of seventeen Summers, he is our only child, a man of stature—We are ready to volunteer, to fight for the integrity of the Union."[368] Another young

---

[365] *Lincoln,* David Herbert Donald, p 295
[366] *Lincoln,* David Herbert Donald, p 295
[367] *Lincoln,* David Herbert Donald, p 295
[368] *Lincoln,* David Herbert Donald, p 297

volunteer wrote, "Woe to the rebel hordes that meets them in battle array. We are wound up to the very pinnacle of patriotic ardor."[369] It was a different story in the upper Southern states, as they showed little support, even though they were still part of the Union. The governor of North Carolina wrote the president: "I can be no party to this wicked violation of the laws of the country, and to this war upon the liberties of a free people. You can get no troops from North Carolina!"[370] The governors of Virginia, Tennessee, and Arkansas shared the same sentiment and all four promptly withdrew from the Union. Within a couple of weeks they joined the Confederacy, which then moved its capital to Richmond, Virginia. From the West, Governor O. P. Morgan of Indiana pledged ten thousand men "for the defense of the Nation and to uphold the authority of the Government."[371]

But the most immediately problematic state was Maryland, which nearly surrounded the capital city and controlled the only railroad access and several roads to Washington. Maryland's governor, Thomas Hicks, telegraphed the president: "The excitement is frightful. Send no troops here."[372] The following day, the Sixth Massachusetts Regiment, marching on its way to Washington, was attacked by Maryland secessionists as they neared Baltimore on their way to defend Washington. Four soldiers and some civilians were killed. Realizing the critical nature of Maryland's support, Lincoln responded that he would not have his troops march through Baltimore. Doubting that this arrangement would last, he also said, "If I grant you this concession, that no troops shall pass through the city, you will be back here to-morrow demanding that none shall be marched

---

[369] *Lincoln*, David Herbert Donald, p 297
[370] *Lincoln*, David Herbert Donald, p 297
[371] *Lincoln*, David Herbert Donald, p 297
[372] *Lincoln*, David Herbert Donald, p 297

around it."[373] Again, he was right. Shortly thereafter, Governor Hicks asked him to stop sending troops through Maryland. A committee from Baltimore called on Lincoln at the White House a few days later, to reinforce their demand and to insist that Lincoln, on any terms, make peace with the Confederacy. Lincoln responded in one of his rarely seen moments of wrath:

> "You would have me break my oath and surrender the Government without a blow," he exploded. "There is no Washington in that—no Jackson in that—no manhood nor honor in that. Our men are not moles, and can't dig under the earth; they're not birds, and can't fly through the air," he reminded the committee.[374] "Go home and tell your people that if they will not attack us, we will not attack them; but if they do attack us, we will return it, and that severely."[375]

For the next few days Washington was essentially under siege and Lincoln and his government were virtually defenseless. Along with the exit of Southern politicians went dozens of high-ranking Southern military leaders as well. Marylanders continued their resistance by destroying the railroad bridges linking Baltimore with the North and cutting telegraph lines. The militia volunteers, though on their way, had not yet arrived, a Confederate assault from Virginia was feared any day, and it was rumored that the pro-South remaining residents would join in the invasion. Day by day, Lincoln languished in waiting for his militias. Finally, on April 25, the first militia arrived followed by several others, making the capital safe for the time being.

---

[373] *Lincoln*, David Herbert Donald, p 298
[374] *Lincoln*, David Herbert Donald, p 298
[375] *Lincoln*, David Herbert Donald, p 298

Chapter Seven

The Unraveling of a Favored Nation

The war was all but begun. The "combination" of South Carolina radicals, as Lincoln would sometimes refer to them, driven by greed, had led out in the secession parade and then punctuated their rebellion with their open aggression at Fort Sumter. Much attention is give to the firing on Fort Sumter, but the real breaking apart of this nation occurred quietly in the weeks prior to Lincoln's inauguration when the Southern states planned and carried out their rebellion while President Buchanan and Northern lawmakers passively looked on. Southern U.S. senators, congressmen, cabinet members, judges, and military generals left their posts, forsook their oaths of office, and abandoned the greatest nation ever to be formed in history. Most of President Buchanan's cabinet was sympathetic and even complicit with the rebellion. In the four months between Lincoln's election and inauguration they committed a number of treasonous acts. Howell Cobb, the Secretary of the Treasury from Georgia, "managed to destroy the credit of the Government, and when, on December 10th, he resigned...he left the treasury

empty."[376] Just before the Secretary of War John B. Floyd resigned to become a Confederate general, he "partly disarmed
the free States and sent soldiers belonging to the regular Army
so far away as to not be available until the conspirators should
have time to consummate the revolution."[377] "Isaac Toucy, of
Connecticut, Secretary of the Navy under Buchanan, scattered
the Federal ships to distant seas, and left the Government without a navy."[378]

John Wesley Hill writes,

> So bold were the secessionists that they actually
> planned to prevent Lincoln's inauguration...Buchanan
> was clay in the hands of Jefferson Davis, Cobb,
> Toombs, and their disloyal associates. The govern-
> ment was in the power of conspirators who were plot-
> ting its overthrow. Treasonable messages were actually
> sent back and forth between the desks of high offi-
> cials. No attempt was made to interfere, much less to
> arrest open and avowed traitors.[379]

The approaching war would be the worst kind and the worst
ever for this almost chosen people. It would take place on
American soil and the combatants would be fellow citizens, in
some cases brother against brother. Lincoln said toward the end
of the war: "War is most terrible and this of ours in its magnitude and duration is one of the most terrible the world has ever
known."[380] Lincoln believed that through it, the people of this
nation would feel in an awful way, the chastening hand of the
Almighty God as some six hundred twenty-three thousand men

---

[376] *Abraham Lincoln, Man of God*, John Wesley Hill, p 157
[377] *Abraham Lincoln, Man of God*, John Wesley Hill, p 157
[378] *Abraham Lincoln, Man of God*, John Wesley Hill, p 157
[379] *Abraham Lincoln, Man of God*, John Wesley Hill, p 157
[380] *The Wit and Wisdom of Abraham Lincoln*, p 46

and boys would die in the space of four years while millions of others—their loved ones—would mourn their loss and endure the economic devastation that accompanied the war. The survivors would bear these pains for the rest of their lives—a sobering reminder that, if Lincoln was correct, the judgments of an offended God can be quick and terrible.

The months between Lincoln's inauguration in March 1861 and the first major battle of the war in July were strained. Would there really be war? Did this new president have a plan, and if so what was it? Recognizing that although he was elected in November, he would not become president until March, Lincoln remained largely silent in terms of public remarks during those first months of the crisis, and the resentment of the insurgents in the South would fester for this new awkward president, for having the audacity to hint of resisting their rebellion. Although keenly aware of the risk of war, the Southern Fire Eaters had bet against it. They had accurately anticipated that the North would numbly look on as sympathetic Southern officials walked away from their elected offices. They knew that there were those in the North who would welcome the separation. But they had not planned on the chastening hand of the Almighty God coming in to play through a president whose primary objective in office was to do the Great Creator's will. How dare Lincoln call for seventy-five thousand militia volunteers and suggest responding with force?

In the North, citizens were growing impatient for a quick victory and many launched their own share of criticism toward their silent new president as well. What the citizenry of this nation could not realize so early in his term of office was that their new "uneducated" president would execute his office from a higher ground than any other politician since George Washington, and that he had, in fact, risen above his more educated and experienced political peers through his self-imposed personal governance on principles of righteousness, morality, and truth as delineated in the Bible. When he would communicate, it would be done with his transcendent and inspiring ability to articulate his vision. He would employ this attribute on July 5, to Congress in a special session, which he called for the purpose of fulfilling the Constitution's requirement for congressional approval to authorize and fund the defense of the South's open aggression toward the United States.

Hoping against hope for any possible way to prevent bloodshed, in April Lincoln launched a plan to cut off the primary source of wealth and military supplies by use of a naval blockade along the Southern shores. The focus of the blockade would be the best-defended harbor in the new Confederacy, Charleston, South Carolina. The rich Southern states' economy was heavily dependent on its exports of cotton, tobacco, and other agricultural products to its buyers in Europe, and the Southern aristocracy had become deeply attached to the luxuries they had grown accustomed to purchasing from across the Atlantic. On May 11, the federal ship *Niagara* took station just outside Charleston Harbor, the first of many others that would follow. Together they would conduct the painfully slow strangulation of the Southern economy with the repelling and interception of much of the flow of guns, ammunition, and goods that would now be willingly sold to the South by England. At first many ships easily slipped by the blockading naval vessels, and the jubilant Charleston elite would mockingly hold "blockade dinners" featuring wines and other fineries from England that had slipped through the comically porous blockade. But in the coming months such celebrations would cease and the jubilation would turn to numbing despair as many of the blockade-running ships would be captured or turned away by the Northern navy, and as reports of loved ones' deaths on the battlefields would flood the South, as well as the North, for the next four years. While the Confederacy did little but scoff at the ineffectiveness of the initial blockade, Lincoln's new naval secretary,

Gideon Wells, was aggressively recruiting any vessel he could find, outfitting merchant ships and ferry boats with guns to expand the blockade. In eight months there were seventy-nine vessels blocking trade on the Southern coastline, with more on the way, and many of those at Charleston Harbor.

The blockade did bring legitimate fears by Lincoln and his government that England would become involved on the side of the Confederacy. After losing in the Revolutionary War and the War of 1812 the English were giddy at the thought of the United States imploding under the strain of their own internal strife. But they were also very concerned at the threat to their flow of cotton, rice and other U.S. imports being disrupted by a war and now the blockade. Knowing this, Jefferson Davis made appeals for their assistance and the English responded by becoming the Confederacy's primary source of weaponry and other military necessities, and by challenging the blockade through the courts, but to no avail; the Lincoln administration insisted that the blockade was legal, and it would not be lifted until the war was over.

The months of April, May, and June of 1861 saw a flurry of activity around Washington. With most of the pro-rebellion residents vacating back to their home Southern states, military units from the west and the north streamed into the capital. Eager for a brief and glorious fight for their nation, they were a common sight drilling and camping around the Capitol and the White House. Forts sprang up around Washington and tents dotted the hillsides. To prepare for the inevitable, and foreseeing the worst, Lincoln called up additional volunteers, this time for three-year terms of duty. Without waiting for congressional authorization, he also expanded the regular U.S. Army by adding eight regiments of infantry, one of cavalry, and one of artillery, then ordered the enlistment of eighteen thousand seamen in the Navy.

In the first months of his presidency Lincoln turned down numerous requests for appearances and speeches. It wasn't until July 5 that the American people would receive a message, given to Congress, from their president. It would be the first of nearly one hundred speeches and communications that he would give during his presidency. The Thirty-seventh Congress assembled in marked contrast to some seventy-five years of Democratic Party dominance. Now Republicans held strong majorities in both houses; secession had reduced the Democratic majority by nearly one-half. The text of President Lincoln's first address to Congress and to the nation was hand-delivered by his secretary John Nicolay and was read to the assembled congressmen by a clerk. Thomas Jefferson, as the nation's third president, felt that a president addressing Congress appeared too monarchal and kingly so he initiated the custom of having all of his addresses read by someone else. This practice would be continued by all U.S. presidents until Woodrow Wilson broke the tradition in 1913, when he addressed Congress in person for his State of the Union speech.

In Lincoln's message, he pointed to the Confederacy's new declaration of independence that had removed the phrase "all men are created equal." It included his vision that this crisis at hand was much more than the dividing of a nation, but that the weakening of this government also weakened the defense of the U.S. Constitution, and this condition would affect not just the nation, but also the entire world, then and in the future. One can only wonder if this nation and the dozens of other democratic nations of today, with their own constitutions, their own freedoms of religion and other blessed liberties that are patterned after the original version by our Founding Fathers, would be in existence had Lincoln not had the resolve to defend it against this nearly successful assault.

Referring to the rebellion, he said:

And this issue embraces more than the fate of these United States. It presents to the family of man the question, whether a Constitutional republic, or a democracy—a government of the people, by the people—can, or cannot, maintain its territorial integrity against domestic foes.

This is essentially a People's conflict. On the side of the Union, it is a struggle for maintaining in the world, that form and substance of government, whose leading object is, to elevate the condition of men—to lift artificial weights from all shoulders; to clear the paths of laudable pursuits for all; to afford all, an unfettered start, and a fair chance in the race of life.[381]

While Lincoln's fight was to save the Union, he here expressed in his first address to Congress and the nation that its preservation was much more than the end; it was a means to a greater end, one through which the whole world would be richly benefited. William J. Wolf said that Lincoln saw America "as an impregnable fortress, vulnerable only to violence from within."[382] He could see that this rebellion would severely weaken the democracy and the weakened democracy would become a vulnerable one. Lincoln's fight was to preserve the liberties of the Constitution for generations yet unborn throughout the world by keeping the United States united as states, and therefore strong against any internal or external enemy of the Constitution, which grants and protects the right to worship, to assemble, to speak freely, etc.

Lincoln understood the importance of identifying the crisis for what it was, not for how the Confederacy wanted it to be

---

[381] *The Eloquent President*, p 98
[382] *The Almost Chosen People*, William J. Wolf, p 58

identified. He used this speech to differentiate between the terms secession and rebellion. Referring to the leaders of the rebellion, he said:

> It might seem, at first thought, to be of little difference whether the present movement at the South be called "secession" or "rebellion." The movers, however, well understand the difference. At the beginning they knew they could never raise their treason to any respectable magnitude by any name which implies <u>violation</u> of law. Accordingly they commenced by an insidious debauching of the public mind. They invented an ingenious sophism…With rebellion thus sugarcoated, they have been drugging the public mind of their section for more than thirty years.[383]

Although as president, he would occasionally use the term "civil war," he would not use "secession" or "Confederacy" because he did not recognize the right of independent government to exist within the boundaries of the United States. He used instead the term "rebellion" more than four hundred times during his presidency to refer to the national emergency. To Lincoln, the conflict was not a war between two governments but rather an insurrection of influential individuals from the South who joined "in combinations too powerful to be suppressed by the ordinary course of judicial proceedings."[384]

In the next twenty-eight days, the special session of Congress would pass more than seventy provisions, most of which were in the defense of preserving the Union. This uncommon unity of purpose was a mostly under-recognized product of Lincoln's leadership. From the beginning of his presidency, he

---

[383] *The Eloquent President*, p 120
[384] *Lincoln*, David Herbert Donald, p 302

influenced the hearts and minds of the North's leaders and citizens to form a unified sense of purpose in their cause, using his clear communication of the basic principles of right versus wrong. Just weeks earlier, the North was filled with citizens and politicians who wanted to offer concessions to the South and many others who felt the Southern states should be allowed to separate from the Union and form their own government.

The weeks leading up to Lincoln's address to the special session of Congress were punctuated by a number of small skirmishes between the assembling military forces, most of which were won by the Confederates. This was not as it was supposed to be. Demand from Northerners for a Union military advance against the Southern "marauders" became intense. On May 23, the all-important state of Virginia ratified its ordinance of secession placing the Confederate border on the border of Washington; and with the assembled Confederate forces in Virginia, virtually at Washington's doorstep, numbering an estimated one hundred thousand, Lincoln felt compelled to move federal troops across the Potomac and to occupy Alexandria to ensure the safety of the nation's capital. As a result, the Virginia troops stationed there were greatly outnumbered, and they withdrew. Elmer Ellsworth, a young Union officer in that occupation who was beloved by Lincoln almost as a son, saw, after the retreat, a Confederate flag flying above a hotel there, a flag that could be seen by Lincoln with his spyglass from the White House. Young Ellsworth dashed up the stairs and tore it down. On his way down the stairs, he was shot and killed by the hotelkeeper. Lincoln grieved and wept openly at Elmer's funeral that was held in the White House. The president wrote his heartbroken parents: "So much of promised usefulness to one's country and of bright hopes for one's self and friends, have rarely been so suddenly dashed, as in his fall."[385] Young Ellsworth's tragic

---

[385] *Lincoln*, David Herbert Donald, p 306

death, something that would have gone virtually unnoticed had it happened a few months later merely because this tragedy would be repeated thousands of times before the end of 1861, reinforced the clamor of politicians, citizens, and newspapers for a call to action.

Up to this point Lincoln had been intentional in his delay of battle and bloodshed, but soon after this event he ordered an advance against the large Confederate forces stationed dangerously close to Washington, in Manassas, Virginia. On June 29, Lincoln and his cabinet met with their military advisors to discuss the plan. Believing Confederate general P. G. T. Beauregard to have thirty-five thousand men at Manassas, they proposed an attack before their numbers could be reinforced. General Beauregard had been recently called up from the South Carolina front to lead the Virginia troops, while General Robert E. Lee, fresh from his declining of Lincoln's appeal to lead the Northern forces, was sent to direct the military affairs at Charleston. Lee was a reluctant secessionist who two months earlier stated,

> If Virginia stands by the old Union so will I. But if she secedes (though I do not believe in secession as a constitutional right, nor that there is sufficient cause for revolution) then I will still follow my native State with my sword, and if need be, with my life.[386]

It took a week for the Union army to marshal its advance, an extremely costly week because during that delay, the number of Confederate soldiers swelled with reinforcements from the Shenandoah Valley. This planned assault was well known in Washington and the army's advance was followed by a corps of

---

[386] *Civil War Website West Virginia*

curious spectators including six U.S. senators, at least ten representatives, scores of newspaper reporters, and many of what
one reporter referred to as "the fairer, if not gentler sex,"[387]
who brought picnic baskets with them in their buggies as they
watched the unexpected carnage from the hillside above the
battleground. Assured by his armed forces leader, General Win-
field Scott, that victory would be theirs, Lincoln nervously went
to church on that Sunday morning, July 21, as the Battle of Manassas (also referred to by the Confederacy as Bull Run) began.
In midafternoon, Lincoln went to the general-in-chief's office
and found General Scott taking his afternoon nap. Scott awoke
long enough to tell Lincoln that preliminary reports of the battle
indicated no major concerns and he again assured Lincoln of
victory before dropping off again to sleep. At six o'clock, news
arrived at the White House that the Union army was in full re
treat. The Confederate army had prevailed again. By nightfall on
that summer Sunday, more than forty-eight hundred men from
both sides lay dead on the battlefield, with another twenty-
seven hundred wounded. The ever-empathetic Lincoln knew all
too well the depth of anguish that the loss of a loved one can
bring, after experiencing the death of his infant brother, his
dearly loved mother, his only sister and sibling, his sweetheart
Ann Rutledge, and his son Eddie (and he and Mary were just
months away from the death of their cherished son Willie). He
grieved knowing the key part he now played in the death of the
se thousands of men and boys. For a man such as Lincoln, who
could not pass a small pig mired in the mud without stopping to
release it and ease its suffering, the next four years of unrelenting casualty reports would bring him untold sorrow, and he
would anguish with the rest of the nation through the long crisis.

---

[387] *Lincoln*, David Herbert Donald, p 307

Letter of Union army Major Sullivan Ballou to his wife, prior to the first major battle of the Civil War at Manassas, in which he was killed:

My very dear Sarah:

The indications are very strong that we shall move in a few days—perhaps tomorrow. Lest I should not be able to write again, I feel impelled to write a few lines that may fall under your eyes when I shall be no more...

Sarah my love for you is deathless, it seems to bind me with mighty cables that nothing but Omnipotence could break; and yet my love of country comes over me like a strong wind and bears me unresistably on with all these chains to the battlefield.

I have, I know, but few and small claims upon Divine Providence, but something whispers to me—perhaps it is the wafted prayer of my little Edgar, that I shall return to my loved ones unharmed. If I do not my dear Sarah, never forget how much I love you, and when my last breath escapes me on the battle field, it will whisper your name. Forgive my many faults, and the many pains I have caused you. How thoughtless and foolish I have often times been! How gladly would I wash out with my tears every little spot upon your happiness...

But, O Sarah! If the dead can come back to the earth and flit unseen around those they loved, I shall always be near you; in the gladdest days and in the darkest nights...always, always, and if there be a soft breeze upon your cheek, it shall be my breath...Sarah do not mourn me dead; think I am gone and wait for thee, for we shall meet again.[388]

The sentiments of the South following their great victory at Manassas are reflected in Mary Chesnut's diary entries.
Mary Chesnut's Diary, July 22, 1861:

> Mrs. [Jefferson] Davis came in so softly that I did not know she was here until she leaned over me and said—"A great battle has been fought—Jeff Davis led the center, Joe Johnson the right wing, Beauregard the left wing of the army. Your husband is all right. Wade Hampton is wounded. Colonel Johnson of the Legion killed—so are Colonel Bee and Colonel Bartow."

> I had no heart to speak. She went on in that same desperate calm way to which people betake themselves when under greatest excitement. "Bartow was rallying his men, leading them into the hottest of the fight—died gallantly, at the head of his regiment.
> The president telegraphs me only that "it was a great victory." Still I was stunned. Then I was so grateful. Those nearest and dearest to me were safe still.

> Then she began in the same concentrated voice to read from a paper she held in her hand. "Dead and dying cover the field. Sherman's battery taken. Lynchburg regiment cut to pieces. Three hundred of the legion wounded."

---

[388] *The Civil war: An Illustrated History,* p 82-83

Today I met my friend Mr. Hunter. I was on my way to Mrs. Bartow's room—begged him to call at some other time. I was too tearful just then for a morning visit from even the most sympathetic person.

A woman from Mrs. Bartow's country was in a fury because they stopped her as she rushed to be the first to tell Mrs. Bartow that her husband was killed. It had been decided that Mrs. Davis was to tell her. Poor thing! She [Mrs. Bartow] was lying on her bed. Mrs. Davis knocked. "Come in." When she saw it was Mrs. Davis, she sat up, ready to spring to her feet—but then there was something in Mrs. Davis's pale face that took the life out of her. She stared at Mrs. Davis—and then sunk back. She covered her face.

"Is it bad news for me?" Mrs. Davis did not speak. "Is he killed?"

Today [Mrs. Bartow] said [that] as soon as she saw Mrs. Davis's face—and then she could not say one word—she knew it all in an instant—she knew before she wrapped the shawl around her head.[389]

This painful drama was for but one of the thousands fallen the day before.

Mary Chesnut's Diary, July 24, 1861:

---

[389] *Mary Chesnut's Civil War*, p 105

Mrs. Davis's drawing room last night was brilliant, and she was in great force. Outside a mob collected and called for the president [Jefferson Davis]. He did speak. He is an old war-horse...His enthusiasm was contagious. (The president took all the credit to himself for the victory—said the wounded roused and shouted for Jeff Davis and the men rallied at the sight of him and rushed on and routed the enemy. The truth is, Jeff Davis was not two miles from the battlefield, but he is greedy for military fame).[390]

Up North, concern now turned to the safety of Washington. Would the Southern forces move on to attack the now-vulnerable capital? Hurriedly, the retreating armies were reassembled and at the ready for any assault on the city, which did not occur. Lincoln and the entire North were stunned, both at the thousands of men whose lives were snuffed out in the one-day battle and at their defeat. Lincoln responded by visiting the torn and bloodied wounded in the surrounding makeshift hospitals and encouraging the troops in the nearby forts. He assured them that as their commander-in-chief he would make sure that they had all necessary supplies to be successful in this conflict. At one of these visits, a disgruntled officer complained to Lincoln that Colonel William Tecumseh Sherman had threatened to shoot him like a dog for planning to go to New York without leave. Lincoln would, more than ever, have to set aside his compassionate tendencies in order to shore up his new responsibility as commander-in-chief so as to win this war. He knew victory would only come with the dedication and commitment of all in the North. He responded to the officer in a stage whisper so that the surrounding soldiers would hear his

---

[390] *Mary Chesnut's Civil War*, p 109

reply, "Well, if I were you, and he threatened to shoot, I would not trust him, for I believe he would do it."[391]

The immediate political reaction in the North to this unexpected defeat was to rally behind Lincoln. Both houses of Congress assembled and voted unanimously, declaring "that this war is not waged...for any purpose of conquest or subjugation, nor purpose of overthrowing...established institutions [meaning slavery]...but to defend...the Constitution and to preserve the Union."[392] This of course was the same personal position that Lincoln had expressed and would continue to reinforce. Many believed that a crushing defeat of the Confederates at Manassas would likely have ended the war and opened the door to reunification; instead an appalling horror lay ahead for both sides.

In the South they were jubilant as expressed in this letter to Mary Chesnut by Mary Sophia Stark, sister-in-law to the former South Carolina governor, John Hugh Means:

July 28, 1861

Many thanks to you, my dear Mrs. C for your kind letter...Such tidings we have had! Exultingly singing and praising God with one voice and the next moment finding us low at His footstool in weeping and prayer and deep humility. His mercies abound and we will not sully the bright glories of the 21st by more than natural tears, in grieving over our brave soldiers. I think every man on that battlefield on our side was a hero. And we must admit that a portion of the "bad cause" fought as bravely as ours, but the heart and principle were wanting, and so God gave us the victory. Our brave and no-

---

[391] *Lincoln*, David Herbert Donald, p 308
[392] *Lincoln*, David Herbert Donald, p 307

ble men! May the merciful God of battles shield them every moment.

Tell Mrs. Preston her dear old mother turned out today for a national thanksgiving. But our ministers were all absent, and she had to go back home without joining in the public praise, but God has heard her hosannas and prayers.

I was delighted at the appropriation from [Confederate] Congress, consecrated as it was by prayer, fasting, and tears. God bless you all.
Mary Stark[393]

The North had its own national day of fasting as well. The proclamation was passed by both houses of Congress and very willingly approved and signed by Lincoln. Of this day-of-fasting proclamation, William J. Wolf said, "The themes of this remarkable document are a further development of his prophetic understanding of the nation's history."[394] In the proclamation Lincoln declared that governments must recognize the lordship of God over their existence. "They must contritely confess their faults as a nation and as individuals."[395] He went on to declare to the American people in this fast-day proclamation that the present conflict was the chastisement of God, saying that men would do well "to recognize the hand of God in this terrible visitation."[396]

For the next few months Lincoln had a modicum of relief from the intense political pressures that beset him before the defeat of Bull Run or Manassas. The nation now realized that it

---

[393] *Mary Chesnut's Civil War*, p 117
[394] *The Almost Chosen People*, William J. Wolf, p 119
[395] *The Almost Chosen People*, William J. Wolf, p 119
[396] *The Almost Chosen People*, William J. Wolf, p 119

would take time to build the kind of army that could defeat the growing and confident Southern forces. It was during these months that Lincoln was able to turn some attention to his family in their new spacious home. At first, they were overwhelmed by the thirty-one rooms of the Executive Mansion. But except for the dining room, the first floor was open to all visitors; anybody who wanted could stroll in and out of the Lincolns' home at any hour of the day and on into the evening. And stroll in they did; the White House was nearly always full of visitors, office-seekers, and church groups on missions to pray with the new president and correct his misguided vision and handling of the crisis at hand. On the second floor almost half of the rooms were also public, so that the private quarters of Lincoln's "mansion" turned out to be surprisingly constricted. Sons Willie and Tad frequently mingled with the soldiers of the Bucktail Pennsylvania regiment quartered on the south White House grounds, and found great diversion in conducting their own military maneuvers with the neighborhood boys they had recruited. The boys commandeered the White House rooftop for their fort, complete with painted logs for cannon, which they earnestly fired at imagined Confederates across the river. Once a great commotion was heard from the upstairs oval room and the startled occupants rushed in to find the president of the United States on his back in a playful wrestle with Tad, Willie, and their friends. Often he was seen walking with his boys to the woods to enjoy time together. Lincoln cherished such times because they were rare while in the White House. Lincoln was said to have worked harder than any other president, continually engaged in the mountain of work before him, from sunup to late at night.

The presence of children in the White House was a novelty and the boys were showered with gifts from the public: a pony for Willie was especially beloved as were the two goats that were occasionally seen occupying hallways and rooms in the

White House. On one occasion Tad harnessed one of the goats to a chair, which he used as a sled, and drove the goat into the East Room where a reception was being held; with the women holding their hoop skirts and Tad hollering, he and the goat circled the room and exited out the door again.

As president, Lincoln by and large discontinued his daily practice of reading the newspapers; the caustic editorials had become especially unsettling. He had come to the conclusion that there was nothing now in the papers that he did not already know. Besides, he kept his fingers on the pulse of the American public through his "public opinion baths"[397] as he called them: the unending throng of visitors whom he was loath to turn away. From early morning to dusk, visitors filled the Executive Mansion, sometimes lined up to the outside grounds, waiting for an audience with the president. Day after day Lincoln displayed remarkable patience with these visitors, some of whom brought requests that bordered on the ridiculous and others whose intent was to take an inordinate amount of the president's time. In such cases, he would reach to his seemingly unending store of stories or would change the subject abruptly to a topic so completely unrelated so as to disarm the visitor and create an opening for Lincoln to end the interview.

> Justice Carter, District of Columbia Supreme Court justice, related the following: one particularly verbose man from Pennsylvania, who had already called on Lincoln a number of times before, became unusually persistent with Lincoln, and knowing that the president had a delegation waiting for him, still refused to leave. Suddenly, while the man was in mid-sentence, Lincoln arose from his

---

[397] *The Life and Works of Abraham Lincoln*, Henry Clay Whitney, p 261

chair, walked to the wardrobe in the cabinet chamber, and removed a small bottle. Looking gravely at his visitor, whose head was very bald, he asked, "Did you ever try this stuff for your hair?" "No sir, I never did." "Well," said Lincoln, "I advise you to try it, and I will give you a bottle. If at first you don't succeed, try, try again. Keep it up. They say it will grow hair on a pumpkin. Now take it and come back in eight or ten months and tell me how it works."[398] The astonished man left the room instantly and without a word, with the bottle in hand. Judge Carter walked in just after the Pennsylvania man's exit and found Lincoln unable to restrain his laughter at the success of his strategy. The judge insisted in hearing of the incident before he would proceed with his business."[399]

General Wilson related, "On arriving at the White House, I found a Congressman in earnest conversation with the President. Looking at me as if I were an intruder, the politician stopped, and Mr. Lincoln said, 'It is all right—we are going out together so turn on your oratory.' So the member resumed talking vigorously for five minutes or more, in behalf of his constituent, an applicant for some office. The President, looking critically at the right side of his face and then on the left, remarked, in an earnest manner, 'Why, how close you shave, John!' That was the

---

[398] *The Wit and Wisdom of Abraham Lincoln*, Edited by Anthony Gross, p 90
[399] *The Wit and Wisdom of Abraham Lincoln*, Edited by Anthony Gross, p 90

way in which he baffled the office-seekers; and, although the Congressman was disappointed, of course, he could not avoid laughing. After his departure I said, 'Mr. President, is that the way you manage the politicians?' And he answered, 'Well, you must not suppose you have all the strategy in the army.'"[400]

Certain officials in the government employ were very anxious to get absolute control of certain monies to be distributed by them. These monies were formerly controlled by [another entity] and they came to the President with this plea. He knew what they wanted, and responded to their proposal with the following story: 'You remind me very much like a man in Illinois whose cabin burned down, and, according to the kindly custom of early days in the West, his neighbors all contributed something to start him again. In his case they had been so liberal that he soon found himself better off than before the fire, and got proud. One day a neighbor brought him a bag of oats, but the fellow refused it with scorn, and said, "I am not taking oats now; I take nothing but money."'[401] With this he dismissed the misguided and disappointed delegation.

The second half of 1861 brought a string of more bad news for the North. The loss at Manassas was followed by the battles of Ball's Bluff and the battle for Missouri, both of which were

---

[400] *The Wit and Wisdom of Abraham Lincoln*, Edited by Anthony Gross, p 89
[401] *The Wit and Wisdom of Abraham Lincoln*, Edited by Anthony Gross, p 90

again won by the Confederacy, and the naval blockade of the Southern ports was still too porous to have even a negligible impact. Adding to Lincoln's worries was the troublesome development that England was considering a formal recognition of the Confederate States of America. While the North was mired in setbacks, the South was euphoric with its success.

The tide turned temporarily in late 1861, with a run of Union victories beginning with the capture by the U.S. Navy of Port Royal and with the taking of Fort Henry and Fort Donelson by the little-known General Ulysses S. Grant. These victories were followed by a Union victory at Nashville, the first state capital in the Confederacy to be taken. But with the victories came the additional death counts of tens of thousands of soldiers. In April 1862, General Grant won again at Shiloh, the bloodiest battle of the war thus far, but the victory left the North stunned with its thirteen thousand Union casualties; the Confederacy suffered more than ten thousand.

On November 7, 1861, a ragtag group of U.S. warships smothered the outgunned defenses of Port Royal, some few miles south of Charleston, South Carolina, until General Robert E. Lee ordered the abandonment of the Confederate defenses, allowing the Stars and Stripes to once again fly in South Carolina. This Union victory struck a debilitating blow to the Confederacy. Their blockading ships would no longer have to return far up north to be resupplied. This could now be done from Port Royal, and would allow them to push the blockade even farther south.

Mary Chesnut's Diary , November 8, 1861:

Mullbury Plantation, South Carolina

192

The Reynoldses came, and with them terrible news. The enemy are effecting their landing at Port Royal.[402]

November 9, 1861
Utter defeat at Port Royal. DeSaussure's and Dunovant's regiments cut to pieces.

General Lee sent them, they say. Booted and bridled and gallant rade he. So far his bonnie face has only brought us ill luck.[403]
Such a meeting we had—all the churches joined to pray. They sung:

> Dread Jehovah! God of Nations
> From thy Temple in the skies
> Hear thy people's supplication
> Now for their deliverance rise.

Not one doubt is there in our bosoms that we are not the chosen people God. And that he is fighting for us. Why not? We are no worse than Jews, past or present, nor Yankees.[404]

November 11, 1861
Yesterday Mr. John DeSaussure came, absolutely a lunatic. He was in a state of abject fright because the negroes show such exulta-

---

[402] *Mary Chesnut's Civil War*, p 228
[403] *Mary Chesnut's Civil War*, p 230
[404] *Mary Chesnut's Civil War*, p 233

tion at the enemies making good their entrance at Port Royal.[405]

November 12, 1861

Went to the turnout at Mullberry for Mr. C. Met only Minnie Frierson. She says they are hanging negroes in Louisiana and Mississippi, like birds in the trees, for an attempted insurrection.

A genuine slave-owner born and bred will not be afraid of negroes...Here we are mild as the moonbeams and as serene. Nothing but negroes around us—white men all gone to the army.[406]

Mrs. Reynolds and Mrs. Withers, two of the very kindest and most considerate of slave-owners, aver that the joy of their negroes at the fall of Port Royal is loud and open. There is no change of any kind whatever with ours.[407]

Charleston is being fortified on the land side. When the enemy overran James Island, the negro men went to the fleet, but the women and children came to us. So many more mouths to feed—a good way to subdue us by starvation.

How they laugh at our calamity. And mock when our fear cometh. The enemy grins at us. We jeered so when they ran at Manassas. It is

---

[405] *Mary Chesnut's Civil War,* p 233
[406] *Mary Chesnut's Civil War,* p 233
[407] *Mary Chesnut's Civil War,* p 233

slow work raising regiments now. The best fighting material went off at the first tap of the drum. But the recruiting goes on, for better or for worse.[408]

Letter from John S. Preston
Mill House
Charleston, S. C.
14 Nov. 1861

I will be at Charleston for some days (Yankees permitting) and would be glad to hear from you. Great terror prevailing here, and no preparations. Neither troops nor defenses! I regard the city [Charleston] is in hourly peril. I believe it could be taken in six hours. I believe they will have Charleston within thirty days.

General Lee is here, visiting the defenses. He is never hopeful and does not seem in particular good humor concerning things here.

John S. Preston[409]

November 16, 1861
We fasted and prayed—and we think our prayers are answered, for lo! good news has come. Another ship with ammunition and arms has slipped into Savannah. If our prayers are to be so effective, let us all spend our days and nights on our knees.[410]

---

[408] *Mary Chesnut's Civil War*, p 236
[409] *Mary Chesnut's Civil War*, p 237
[410] *Mary Chesnut's Civil War*, p 237

The war's death and misery that rocked America in 1861, and which turned out to be only the tip of the looming iceberg in magnitude as compared to what lay ahead in the coming three years, again shrouded the Lincoln family in February 1862. Their eleven-year-old son Willie fell ill with what the doctor diagnosed as the "bilious fever"—probably typhoid fever. It is believed that Willie contracted the illness from the polluted White House water system. A few days later their son Tad came down with the same fever. With their hearts still aching over the death of their three-year-old Eddie a few years earlier, they were horrified at Willie's worsening condition. That February, Lincoln and Mary endured their own personal crisis of sitting up nights with their sick sons, adding to the pressures of a wartime presidency. On February 20, Lincoln emerged from Willie's room and announced to his secretary, John Nicolay, in a voice choked with grief: "Well, Nicolay, my boy is gone—he is actually gone!"[411] Then he wept the grieving tears known only to those parents who have lost a child. Looking at his lifeless son he tearfully said, "He was too good for this earth...but we loved him so."[412] Mary was so devastated that she could scarcely look after their other son Tad. The president would often be seen lying on Tad's bed to comfort the sick and now grieving boy at the death of his older brother. One can only imagine their dread at the thought of losing Tad also. Thankfully, Tad did recover but Lincoln could not hide his grief over Willie's death. For weeks after, every Thursday, the day on which Willie left them, Lincoln would shut himself up in his room so as to grieve and weep alone. As time passed the frequency of these grieving sessions diminished but continued still. Months after Willie's death, an aide recalled traveling with Lincoln as he read

---

[411] *The Eloquent President,* p 336
[412] *The Eloquent President,* p 336

passages out loud from Shakespeare. And from *King John* he recited from memory Constance's lament for her lost son:

> And, father cardinal, I have heard
> you say
>   That we shall see and know our
> friends
>   In heaven
> If that true, I shall see my boy
> again.

The aide recorded that as Lincoln recited this, his voice trembled and he wept.

During the war it became fashionable for newspaper editors throughout the North to take it upon themselves the role of adviser to President Lincoln on all aspects of the war and the government. This was due in large part to Lincoln's meek and sincere willingness to listen to outside counsel, but it also served to increase their newspaper sales as they elevated themselves in the eyes of their readers. These letters to Lincoln *from* the editors totaled more than three hundred during the war, many of which were ceremoniously and personally delivered and read by the editors to the president. Naturally, this important exchange with the president of the United States would then be reported as a follow-up in their newspaper. Lincoln was very aware of the impact of the newspapers on public opinion yet did nothing to discourage them in this endeavor, and on selected occasions he used their involvement with the affairs of the government to promote his own agenda. Particularly influential were the New York papers, with Horace Greeley, editor of the *New York Tribune*, emerging as the self-appointed chief-of-staff of the New York newspaper generals. In August 1862, Greeley wrote one of these advising letters but added a twist by publishing it as an open letter in his *New York Tribune* under the caption "The

Prayer of Twenty Millions." In it Greeley charged that Lincoln was "strangely and dangerously remiss"[413] in not proclaiming emancipation now. Abolitionists in the North were ecstatic at the anti-slavery Lincoln's election in 1860. They were equally dismayed when he took no action toward emancipation. Greeley's open letter that gave expression to these anti-slavery yearnings contained a number of inaccuracies upon which Greeley based his dissatisfaction with the new president. This open letter created a firestorm of public opinion for and against his challenge to Lincoln as it was republished in newspapers across the North. But to Greeley's and the nation's surprise, Lincoln "did not blink, but raised the stakes" [414] with an immediate reply using his own open letter that he sent to the *National Intelligencer* in Washington. Newspapers North and South immediately picked up his response. It was written in two parts; the first was an introduction, and the second was a crystal-clear statement that demonstrated Lincoln's practice of thoroughly evaluating all sides of an issue, acting on principle, and then skillfully communicating his view in the most concise of manners. Throughout the nation, North and South, public opinion ran the gamut on every issue, but with the war all opinions were felt and expressed with heightened intensity, and Lincoln would hear this range of opinion daily through his "public opinion baths"[415] provided by the unending stream of White House visitors. With his open letter completely devoid of partisan politicizing, he communicated his position unequivocally clear to be, as always, founded on principles and not politicking, and addressed Greeley's inaccuracies with a remarkable combination of authority and saintly humility:

---

[413] *The Eloquent President,* p 125
[414] *The Eloquent President,* p 126
[415] *The Life and Works of Abraham Lincoln,* Henry Clay Whitney, p 261

As to the policy I "seem to be pursuing" as you say, I have not meant to leave any one in doubt.

I would save the Union. I would save it the shortest way under the Constitution. The sooner the national authority can be restored, the nearer the Union will be "the Union as it was". If there be those who would not save the Union, unless they could at the same time <u>save</u> slavery, I do not agree with them. If there be those who would not save the Union unless they could at the same time <u>destroy</u> slavery, I do not agree with them. My paramount object in this struggle is to save the Union, and is <u>not</u> either to save or destroy slavery. If I could save the Union without freeing any slave I would do it; and if I could save it by freeing <u>all</u> slaves I would do it; and if I could save it by freeing some and leaving others alone I would do that.

ABRAHAM LINCOLN TO
HORACE GREELEY, AUGUST 22, 1862[416]

In one short paragraph Lincoln expressed volumes. And what is of greatest importance is what was not said. This was not a typical statement of a politician, frequently manipulating or shrouding messages to appease his constituency or enhance reelection potential. This element was absent in this message as it would be absent in all of his presidential messages. As president, his personal interests were not observed to rise above his sense of duty to simply do the right thing "as God

---

[416] *The Eloquent President*, p 125

allows us to see the right."[417] There was no finger-pointing or accusations in this letter, nor would there be in any of Lincoln's communications. Neither were there justifications or rationalizations for decisions made or not made for the purpose of rallying support. For those in the South, he emerges again unequivocal in his resolve to oppose the rebellion and restore "the Union as it was."[418] It had to be chilling for the Southern rebels to observe the magnitude of his resolve to restore the Union. What they thought to be an abolitionist president turned out to be "an humble instrument in the hands of the Almighty"[419] whose sense of purpose and spiritual intelligence was unmatched among mortal men of his day. That Lincoln despised slavery was never in question; but when the strength and power of the Constitution became compromised with disunion of the states, he had but one objective, and the only way he would free the slaves would be if he could see clearly that it would contribute to the saving of the Union and the Constitution.

The introduction paragraph in Lincoln's open letter response to Greeley has been largely overlooked in its importance, but a closer look will provide a revelatory view into the singular character of this most magnanimous of men. Greeley's intelligence and respected character paled in comparison to Lincoln's in the exchange. Some of Greeley's facts were inaccurate, and his perception erroneous in his attack on Lincoln's administration. Which begs the question, how does one with exceptional intelligence, spirituality, morality, and resolve correct and confront another without offending? Moreover, how does such a one effectively lead in humility? Lincoln's first paragraph in this open letter is a masterpiece of expression from

---

[417] Lincoln's Second Inagural Address
[418] Lincoln's letter cited above
[419] *The Eloquent President,* p 23

one whose heart was one of "malice toward none and charity of all."[420]

> I have read yours of the 19th addressed to myself through the New York Tribune. If there be in it any statements, or assumptions of fact, which I may know to be erroneous, I do not, now and here, controvert them.[421]

Without saying it, Lincoln presents the magnitude of Greeley's affront by expressing his personal criticism toward Lincoln in his newspaper for all to see. Lincoln always respected our nation's freedom of expression, but he was not one to employ this freedom to degrade or discredit another. To Lincoln, this was a right, but it was a moral wrong in which he would not engage. Here Lincoln, always one to avoid judging another, as Jesus taught all believers to do, subtly points out the fact of what was done, making it clear that although he perceived the affront, he would not lower himself to indulge in the same open criticism. This unwillingness was not a smug public demonstration of piety but rather a sincere compliance with Jesus' Biblical example and teachings, along with his continued high regard for his accuser in spite of his public and inaccurate criticism.

There were most certainly statements and assumptions of fact that Lincoln knew to be erroneous. But Lincoln would not, before the entire nation, point out Greeley's errors and thereby discredit him as Greeley had done to Lincoln. Instead, Lincoln chose simply to turn the other cheek rather than defend his honor and his position by publicly correcting his accuser.

---

[420] Lincoln's Second Inaugural Address
[421] *The Eloquent President*, p 140

> If there be in it any inferences which I may
> believe to be falsely drawn, I do not now and
> here, argue against them.

Again Greeley did make inferences that were falsely drawn,
which Lincoln clearly saw. Yet again, although Lincoln vaguely
acknowledges them, he would not specify them, thereby avoiding the infraction of God's commandment to "Judge not that ye
be not judged" found in Matthew 7:1. Lincoln—with the purest
of Godly humility combined with presidential authority and, as
he believed, authority of one chosen and raised up by the Almighty Himself—merely acknowledges the presence of such
falsely drawn inferences in Greeley's letter.

> If there be perceptible in it an impatient
> and dictatorial tone, I waive it in deference to
> an old friend, whose heart I have always sup-
> posed to be right.

Lincoln's question as to the presence of impatience and a
dictatorial tone expressed that Greeley's affront was not just
toward Lincoln the man, but also unintentionally toward God,
who was moving in His judgment as He bared his arm in righteous indignation at the sins of this people. But again, instead of
addressing Greeley's insolence, Lincoln turned the other cheek.
This final sentence in his introductory paragraph is in essence a
public statement of genuine forgiveness to Greeley, as Lincoln
looked beyond the personal affront and recognized a sincere
desire in Greeley to see the end to slavery. Lincoln ends the
revelatory paragraph by publicly bearing the public reprimand
with a Christ-like patience and then compliments his attacker
with a reference to their friendship and the goodness of Greeley's heart.

Here we catch another glimpse of Lincoln's true greatness. Greeley has not addressed his criticism to a mere man or a mere president of the United States. It was unknowingly addressed to a prophet-like instrument of God with a mission "greater than that of Washington;"[422] a man who had mastered better than probably any other man the art of complete obedience to Jesus of Nazereth's standards of personal conduct, and whose extraordinary faith allowed God to move through him with His omnipotent power. Lincoln was certainly aware, and had frequently and humbly expressed, that God was guiding him in his vital presidential role, and his only purpose would be God's purpose. In a letter to the Reverend Byron Sunderland, who called upon the president toward the end of 1862, Lincoln wrote,

> I hold myself in the present position and with the authority vested in me, as an instrument of Providence. I am conscious every moment that all I am and all I have is subject to the control of a Higher Power and that Power can use me or not use me in any manner and at any time in His wisdom and might as may be pleasing to Him.[423]

All of these divine attributes applied here by Lincoln were demonstrated even more purely, of course, by Jesus Himself as he walked among much lower mankind; yet He, the All Powerful, did so with the purest of humility and Godly love for his less advanced subjects. Lincoln had made it a lifelong endeavor to mirror Christ's example of humility, obedience, and purity; and we, looking back now at Lincoln's life, can see the examples of his abasing of himself, his sense of service to all, and his love

---

[422] *The Eloquent President*, p 3
[423] *Lincoln*, David Herbert Donald, p 257

for God and all mankind, as he became, at the hand of God, one of the most exalted men of all time. Above Lincoln's great accomplishments of saving the Union and the Constitution and ending slavery, it might be considered that Lincoln's crowning achievement was his life lived in such a righteous way, the way Jesus the Redeemer had instructed and demonstrated that all believers should live. It is quite possible that Lincoln honored God more with his personal life of obedience and meekness than with all of the marvelous political accomplishments for which he, to this day, is remembered and revered.

December 1861 stilled for good the shouts of triumph with which the Charleston citizens had received news of the fall of Sumter into their hands and victory at Manassas. Neither of these conquests had achieved what the South Carolinian elite had confidently expected with their rebellion: independence from the most favored nation on earth and the end of fighting. A feeling of elation had persisted—despite some sobering set-backs—but it was finally swept away by the Union's occupation of nearby Port Royal, the general retreat of Confederate troops at the Union's presence, and an unexpected enemy: fire.

On the night of December 11, a fire broke out in Charleston that did not stop until nearly a third of the beautiful city lay in ashes. General Robert E. Lee was roused from a relaxing evening in the parlor of the modern Mills House Hotel, where he was boarding, by the thick smoke, and he and the other tenants were forced to flee the flames without being able to collect their belongings. By morning, the fire had obliterated some five hundred residences, five churches, and numerous commercial buildings. Also falling victim to the inferno was the nearly new Institute Hall, the birthplace of the Southern rebellion where the Secession Convention delegates of South Carolina voted unanimously to secede from the United States, one year earlier. Some would say the razing of Institute Hall was God's retribution for the rebellion. This great fire also devoured the heart of the once proud Charleston citizens. Staggered by uncountable losses, the residents settled down to endure the war that they had initiated. Reconstruction of their homes, churches, and businesses was far beyond their wartime resources, and the swath of ruin remained like a dreadful scar across the once-shining city through the end of the war.

Chapter Eight

"Thenceforward, and Forever Free"

Within ten years of Columbus's arrival to the Americas, Spain was transporting and selling African slaves for huge profits, with all maritime nations of Europe following suit. Over the next two hundred and fifty years England would transport more slaves than all the other nations combined. Between 1680 and 1688, England had 249 slaving ships. By 1783, that number dilated to 878 vessels dedicated to the kidnapping and selling of human beings for slave labor. The primary destination ports in American were not in the South but in the North: mostly in Massachusetts and Rhode Island. The major export from the northern states was dedicated to the lucrative slave trade; it was rum, which was used to purchase the captured Africans. Rum was the foundation of New England's economy, with the most respectable citizens engaged in its production and sale. Even preachers and philanthropists were advocates. One such clergyman who had grown wealthy in the rum trade "always returned thanks on the Sunday following the arrival of a slaver that the Africans could enjoy the blessings of a Gospel dispensation."[424] During this era the Southern colonies had neither

---

[424] *Invasion of the Southern States,* p 10

rum production nor slaving ports, until South Carolina opened its port for slave trading in 1803.

> It is calculated that between the years 1527 and 1866, slaving ships docked on American soil 27,233 times to dispense their human cargo of more than twelve million African men, women, and children for sale into slavery. And due to the horrible conditions on the slaving ships, it is also estimated that one and one half million perished on the open sea in route to the Promised Land.[425]

The horror of filth, disease, and death of the slaving ship's voyage was only momentarily relieved upon arrival to the American shores, as the Africans would then be herded in chains from the ship to the slave market where it was customary to break up the families. The father might be sold to a planter in Maryland, the mother to the Carolinas, and the children scattered from Virginia to Louisiana, joining other second- and third-generation slaves, but unable to speak with or understand them. All hope of ever seeing or hearing from their loved ones again was all but extinguished.

The profitability of slavery was a heady narcotic. In 1793, South Carolina produced ninety-four thousand pounds of cotton. By 1811, with a large infusion of slaves into the labor force, the state exported thirty million pounds of cotton. In the three coastal parishes of Georgetown, Charleston, and Beaufort in South Carolina, African slaves comprised 85 percent of the total population. The enormously rich white planters personified the new promise of opulent prosperity that the compromised Constitution now afforded them. With the use of slave labor, men

---

[425] *The Negro*, W.E. Dubois, *An Eyewitness History of Slavery in America From Colonial Times to the Civil War*, Dorothy and Carl Schnieder, p 38,

whose fathers were poor pioneers or subsistence farmers were suddenly amassing unimaginable fortunes, and they were not about to let this source of excess slip through their fingers. At that time, the earnings of the common white man laboring with his own hands would generate an average of $125 a year. One slave woman could generate about $250 in profit from her labor in a year. The children born to a slave woman whether by her husband or through rape by the slave master or his friends could sell for as much as $1,200. The buying and selling of human souls, much like the buying and selling of livestock, was nearly as profitable as the labor they produced. It is estimated that white men fathered five hundred eighty-eight thousand mulatto children during the two and a half centuries of slavery in America. None of these victimized slave women had even the slightest hope of justice and retribution for these crimes of the white men who dominated them. In 1857, the Supreme Court's Dred Scott decision insured the injustice by declaring that the blacks "are beings of an inferior order" and had no right to pursue justice in the courts of America.

Since the turn of the nineteenth century the Southern states' lawmakers also dominated the halls of Congress and the courts as a result of the unfortunate three-fifths clause in the Constitution. They succeeded in passing an array of laws that defended an uncompromising suppression of the freedoms of speech and of the press so far as slavery was concerned. Southern newspapers were forced to be nearly unanimous in their support of slavery. Southern censorship banned talk or printing of materials that expressed opposition to slavery. *The Impending Crisis* (1857), written by Hinton Rowan Helper, was a widely read economic argument blaming slavery for the backwardness and poverty of the poor whites and small farmers in the South. Threats from proslavery residents forced Helper from his North Carolina home for writing the book.

In reply to a letter from his former master, former slave Henry Bibb wrote:

> You may perhaps think hard of us for run-
> ning away from slavery, but I have but one
> apology to make, which is this: I have only to
> regret that I did not start at an earlier peri-
> od…To be compelled to stand by and see you
> whip and slash my wife without mercy when I
> could afford her no protection, not even offer-
> ing myself to suffer the lash in her place, was
> more than I felt it to be the duty of a slave hus-
> band to endure…My infant child was also fre-
> quently flogged by Mrs. Greenwood for crying,
> until its skin was bruised literally purple. This
> kind of treatment was what drove me from
> home and family to seek a better home for
> them.[426]

For slaves who were insolent or disobedient, whipping was the most common form of discipline administered by slave masters. Nearly all plantations had whipping posts prominently displayed as a reminder of impending punishment for any varie-ty of misdeeds. An errant slave would be stripped, tied to the whipping post, and then brutally whipped. Often the other slaves would be forced to watch, including the victim's family. The whip became the emblem of the slave owner's authority. The threat of selling off children or a spouse or of nailing an errant slave to a barn by his or her ear was also an effective means for maintaining submission. Any amount of hitting, slapping, and kicking was regarded as a prudent measure for training slaves. President Millard Fillmore's passage of the New

---

[426] *Life and Adventures of Henry Bibb, 1849*

Fugitive Slave law in 1850, in which a federal marshal who did not immediately arrest an alleged runaway would be fined up to $1,000 together with penalties for aiding any runaway, made any attempted escape extremely dangerous.

Austin Steward, a slave for twenty-two years, chronicles his ordeal:

> When eight years of age, I was taken to the "great house," or the mansion of my master to serve as an errand boy, where I had to stand in the presence of my master's family all the day and a part of the night, ready to do anything which they commanded me to perform. I slept in the same room with my master and mistress. This room was elegantly furnished with damask curtains, mahogany bedstead of the most expensive kind, and everything else about it was of the most costly kind. And while Mr. And Mrs. Helm reposed on their bed of down, with a cloud of lace floating over them, I always slept upon the floor, without a pillow, or even a blanket, but, like a dog, lay down anywhere I could find a place. Capt. Helm was not a very hard master; but generally was kind and pleasant, terrible when in a passion. Mrs. Helm was a very industrious woman—sewing, knitting, and looking after the servants; but she was a great scold,—continually finding fault with some of the servants, and frequently punishing the young slaves herself, by striking them over the head with a heavy iron key, until the blood ran; or else whipping them with a cowhide, which she always kept by her side. The older servants she would cause to be punished by having them severely whipped by a man, which she never failed to do for every trifling fault. Mrs. Helm appeared to be uneasy unless some of the serv-

ants were under the lash. She came into the kitchen one morning and my mother, who was the cook, had just put down dinner. Some food spilled and that invoked the wrath of my master, who came forth immediately with his horse whip, with which he whipped my poor mother most unmercifully—far more severely than I ever knew him to whip a horse.

I once had the misfortune to break the lock of master's shotgun. I confessed the truth. But oh, there was no escaping the lash. I was commanded to take off my clothes, which I did, and then master put me on the back of another slave, my arms hanging down before him and my hands clasped in his. Then master gave me the most severe flogging that I ever received, and I pray to God that I never again experience such torture. And yet Capt. Helm was not the worst of masters.[427]

The growing opposition to slavery in the Northern states created a unifying solidarity among the powerful slave owners of the Southern states in their resolve to protect their continued use of slaves. In the North, in 1843, the Liberty Party was organized in open opposition to slavery and in 1848 the Free-Soil Party appeared with a similar objective. Harriet Beecher Stowe's *Uncle Tom's Cabin*, published in 1852, had a profound impact on the sentiments of the nation as she brought to life the horrible suffering of the American slave. The expansion of slavery became the South's tactic for protecting it. They saw the impracticability of promoting slavery in the Northern states, but there was fertile ground for the expansion of slavery into the western territories culminating in the eventual creation of a second na-

---

[427] Austin Steward, Twenty-Two Years a Slave, 1857

tion: a Confederacy of slave states—a cause championed by, among others, Stephen A. Douglas, who was, ironically, a Northerner from Illinois. The combination of radicals in the South looked with wary anticipation at the 1860 presidential election for any signs of a strong antislavery candidate who could challenge their own proslavery choice for the executive office. Sensing that the mounting antislavery pressure would eventually be too much to withstand, they plotted to make the monumental move to secede should an antislavery candidate be elected. Much to the relief of many in the South, the hands-down favorite in this election was the leading Democrat Stephen A. Douglas.

With the victory of George Washington over Cornwallis in Yorktown and the subsequent peace treaty with Great Britain, signed in Paris in 1783, the independence of each state was recognized and this newest nation was jolted again by the harsh realities that lay before it. The Continental Congress was bankrupt from the enormous cost of the war, and Congress's efforts to raise revenue for the fledgling nation were ignored by the states that were struggling with their own problems. Damaging disputes between the states intensified over river rights and border tariffs. The money printed by the Continental Congress was nearly worthless, so states printed their own, which within months suffered the same fate. The penniless war veterans returned home to their failing farms and businesses only to find that the ardently promised military pay would never arrive or would be paid in worthless Continental currency. With no money anywhere, the debts that had accumulated in the freedom fighters' absences came due, resulting in an alarming number of foreclosures and property confiscations by the banks. Many families became homeless and destitute. George Washington and other leaders realized that without the taxing powers being granted to Congress, the less-than-united states were facing an internal implosion of chaotic proportions.

For four years the new Americans languished under these dire conditions until 1787, when James Madison wrote letters to leading representatives from all states urging them to attend a Constitutional Convention in Philadelphia; something had to be done. Seventy-four delegates were commissioned to participate, nineteen of whom declined, and Rhode Island sent no representative, ignoring the convention altogether. By the second day of the convention, the Articles of Confederation, by which the un-united states had attempted to govern themselves, were abolished, leaving them with no system of government; there could be no turning back, as a new government now had to be organized. There were many challenges, but two obstacles posed the most significant threat to this harrowing process. The first challenge was to create a system whereby smaller and less populated states could be equally represented with the larger states. Ron Carter, in his book *Prelude to Glory,* summarized the chaos:

> Their differences exploded. Debate became hot, angry, then accusatory. The small states had openly declared that they would not become the pawns and the doormats for the larger states. Before they would allow it, they would break from the union and go their own way. The large states had indignantly made it known that they would not allow their citizenry to be crippled by the interests of the small states. After days of debate the brilliant proposal emerged of a bicameral congress where the Senate would be equally represented and the House of Representatives would be represented according to population. A vote was taken, and for one day the existence of the United States hung by the tiniest thread, and was saved only by the absence that day of two delegates who would have opposed the Constitutional proposal, and the

vote of one big state delegate in favor of the small states.[428]

They then moved on to address the second great stumbling block: slavery. Once again, any perceived threat to the institution of slavery and the slave-state representatives were prepared to walk away from the unfinished business of the convention. As Lincoln would often say, the problem of slavery was just too expansive, too well entrenched in the colonial economy to be fully addressed at that time. So for the sake of creating a nation-saving Constitution, an unfortunate compromise was forced into the fabric of the Constitution in which non-voting slaves would be counted as three-fifths of a person when determining the number of representatives each state would send to the House of Representatives. That compromise in the Constitution, without mentioning the term slave or slavery, legitimized slavery in America. Debate went on with little progress until a delegate proposed a thirteen-year delay on the matter. The three-fifths compromise was reluctantly accepted and a much more destructive stalemate was averted. Today we venerate all of these Founding Fathers for their accomplishment—maybe some receiving more honors than they merited.

When the Constitution was adopted, some states insisted that they had a right to nullify all laws not specifically delegated to the government by the several states. The following year Kentucky stepped further by adding that if a state should decide that the national government had acted contrary to the agreement, the state could declare those laws null and void. These exceptions became the basis for the South's claim that the Constitution granted them the right to secede and to enjoy the fruits of slavery.

---

[428] *Prelude to Glory*, Ron Carter

By the mid 1850s, slavery had become a prominent and highly volatile political issue. A divisive chasm was rending the nation. Senator Charles Sumner, a close friend and confidant to President Lincoln, gave an antislavery speech on the Senate floor, where he was brutally attacked by Preston S. Brooks, a congressman from South Carolina. Sumner was beaten so fiercely there in the Senate chamber that he remained out of public life for three years. Congressman Brooks was forced to resign, but returned to South Carolina a hero, and was, a short time later, triumphantly reelected to Congress. By that time the bitterness and hatred broiled to the point that congressmen, senators, and gallery observers were carrying pistols and bowie knives into the halls of Congress.

In April 1860, the Democratic National Convention convened in Charleston, South Carolina. The most radical faction of the proslavery movement demanded that the Democratic platform require that every state, North and South, guarantee the right to own slaves. This radical position was far too harsh and too impractical to take forward, and carried the potential to divide the party. Ironically, the division and weakening of their own Democratic Party was exactly what these radicals wanted. This discord in their convention over slavery split the party in two when delegates from South Carolina and seven other Southern states walked out of the convention with their candidate nominee, Southern-rights champion and former vice president John C. Breckenridge. The remaining fragment of the party nominated their own candidate, Stephen A. Douglas. This division resulted in both Democratic candidates having but little chance of winning the election. Two weeks later at the convention in Chicago, the Republican Party nominated Abraham Lincoln as its candidate for the presidency. Lincoln, if elected, would be the first real threat to the Southern states' prized institution of slavery, because all of the previous U.S. presidents were either proslavery or soft on issue. South Carolina promptly pledged secession should Lincoln be elected. The extremists of slavery had set the stage for the debilitating division of this nation.

The split in the Democratic Party was seen by many to be disastrous for the party in that it severely weakened their position and placed the Republican dark horse, Abraham Lincoln, into contention in the race for the presidency. The Fire-Eating slave-owner politicians for years had lobbied for a separate Southern confederation of states, free from the growing annoyance of the Northern onslaught against slavery. The most prominent Fire-Eater was Robert Barnwell Rhett, known as the Father of Secession. He was a slave owner, a lawyer, and prominent politician from Charleston, South Carolina. He was also an owner-editor of the rabidly anti-Union and proslavery newspaper *Charleston Mercury*, to which Lincoln subscribed in Springfield so as to follow the anti-Union sentiments in the South. As early as the 1830s Rhett and his group of Fire-Eaters were outspoken proponents of nullification, the right of a state to refuse to obey laws passed by the federal government. With the mounting pressure from the North against slavery, the proslavery Fire-Eaters calculated that the election of an antislavery president would provide the opportunity to execute their separation from the North. Fully aware that the federal government could consider responding with force, they believed that if secession was done as a united effort by a large block of Southern states, the North would lose its will to reunite the country by use of military confrontation and would acquiesce to the division.

Fellow Fire-Eater William L. Yancy was an Alabama state legislator and U.S. congressman, and one of the most extreme advocates for states' rights and slavery. He insisted that Southerners had the right to take their slaves into western territories. In 1858, he proposed the creation of a Southern Confederacy. He, too, believed that a Republican president would pose a significant enough threat to slavery to convince Southern politicians, who were nearly all wealthy aristocrats, that they must withdraw from the Union in order to preserve their source of wealth generated by slave labor. The third major player in the Fire-Eater movement was Louis T. Wigfall, born and educated in South Carolina. He moved to Texas where he served in the Texas legislature and later in the U.S. Senate. As a senator, he became a leading and belligerent voice for slave-owner rights. He also played a significant role in dividing the Democratic Party in the South Carolina Convention along with his fellow Fire-Eaters. These "fire-eating Yancys and Rhetts, Hammonds and Wigfall," writes William Lee Miller, "with their prickly uncompromising sense of Southern 'honor,' their haughty contempt for the mere clerks and mechanics and merchants of the North, their fantastic self-aggrandizing dream of a slave empire stretching southward"[429] did as much to incite the rebellion as nearly all others combined.

One can look long and deep for an honorable motive in the rebellion by the radical secessionists. Nowhere to be found in their efforts was a projected outcome leading to a stronger or safer nation, or one that improved the lives of all Americans. One can only find this immense effort motivated by a single aim: the amassing of mountainous wealth by a small minority. This wealth and status would be generated by the oppression, degrading, beating, and selling of millions of human beings, all at a cost of dividing an entire nation. A more dramatic example of unrequited greed cannot be matched in American history. It must not be forgotten that the remaining spacious and opulent Southern plantation mansions so admired today are remnants of the greatest disgrace in this nation's history. By 1858, exports from the North totaled $45,308,541. Those from the Southern states, with half the population, were $193,405,961; the South-

---

[429] *Lincoln's Virtues*, William Lee Miller, p 228

ern Fire-Eaters were not about to allow anything to interfere with their gargantuan flow of wealth, no matter the cost.

Slave owners in the South liked to avoid the words "slave" and "slavery," preferring instead to use softer terms such as "property," "domestic institution," and "peculiar institution" to describe the practice of enslaving people of African descent. This was especially true after their defeat in the Civil War. They also had a preference for describing the reason for their secession as their constitutional right to leave the Union when such Union would pass laws that were contrary to any state's desires and interests. By so doing they were able to cloak the inhumanity of the distasteful subject of human enslavement, to the point that many even denied that slavery was the core issue of the Civil War. Such denial exists today in some circles. Charles W. Dew, in his book *Apostles of Disunion,* lays out the facts on this important matter. Of his book, Dwight T. Pitcaithley, Chief Historian for the National Park Service, says, "The South knew why it had to secede from the Union and said so through letters and speeches of its secession commissioners. With stunning clarity [we are reminded] that race and slavery were at the center of the march toward secession."[430] The "states' rights" principle was their argument of choice for gaining relief from the mounting antislavery sentiment and the legislation that they feared was coming their way with the 1860 presidential of election in which the "Black Republicans" elected their "Black President," as Southerners frequently referred to the new Republican Party and to President Lincoln.[431] This vehicle also became their medium to cover up their true designs in protecting their source of wealth through the forced labor of slaves.

In fact, not once in Jefferson Davis's inaugural address to the new union of Confederate states on February 18, 1861 did he mention the institution of slavery. His justification for seces-

---

[430] *Apostles of Disunion*, Charles W. Dew, (back cover)
[431] *Apostles of Disunion*, Charles W. Dew, p 22

sion was articulated as resistance to Northern tyranny and a defense of states' rights. According to Davis, the abandoning of the Union by the Southern slave states was merely the assertion of their "right which the Declaration of Independence of 1776 had defined as inalienable."[432] He went on to claim that this secession was not revolutionary; the time had merely arrived when it was necessary for Southerners "to preserve our own rights and promote our own welfare."[433] What were those rights that were being denied those in the South? Davis did not specify. But it was articulated by Alexander H. Stephens, the new vice president to Jefferson Davis and an old friend of Lincoln, to a large and enthusiastic crowd in Savannah, Georgia one month later. Fresh from the Confederate constitutional convention held days earlier, Stephens made the following declaration regarding the South's new constitution (with its removal of references to the equality of the races). He told the crowd that their new constitution "has put at rest forever all the agitating questions relating to...the proper status of the Negro in our form of civilization." Thomas Jefferson and the Founding Fathers had believed "that the enslavement of the African was in violation of the laws of nature; that it was wrong in principle, socially, morally, and politically," Stephens said. "Those ideas, however, were fundamentally wrong. They rested upon the assumption of the equality of the races. This was an error," he continued. "Our new Government is founded upon the opposite idea; its foundations are laid, its cornerstone rests, upon the great truth that the Negro is not equal to the white man; that slavery, subordination to the superior race, is his natural and moral condition."[434]

A Jefferson Davis biographer wrote that Davis expressed dismay "at the lack of political tact exhibited by his Vice-

---

[432] *Apostles of Disunion*, Charles W. Dew, p 13
[433] *Apostles of Disunion*, Charles W. Dew, p 13
[434] *Apostles of Disunion*, Charles W. Dew, p 14

President" in this "rabble-rousing address at Savannah."[435] And yet, just a few weeks following this address by Stephens, Davis spoke with equal candor on the slavery issue to the Confederate Congress on April 29, 1861. He declared that Congress in the North had engaged in "a persistent and organized system of hostile measures against the rights of the owners of slaves in the Southern States."[436] He went on to describe, and correctly so, how "fanatical organizations…were assiduously engaged in exciting amongst the slaves a spirit of discontent and revolt; means were furnished for their escape from their owners; and agents secretly employed to entice them to abscond."[437] Davis also remarked that the new majority Republican Party, gripped by "a spirit of ultra fanaticism," was determined to deny slave owners access to the territories and would surround the South with "states in which slavery should be prohibited…thus rendering property in the slaves so insecure as to be comparatively worthless."[438] With the possible exception of the fanaticism charge, Davis was accurate on this point also.

It was true that the slave owners and their families had always been deathly afraid of the slaves turning on them. Some plantations had hundreds of slaves who with ease could have revolted against their masters, and in isolated incidences they did. And with the antislavery sentiment that was reverberating from the North and being heard and observed by the slaves in the South, this fear was mounting. The seceding states, as one, spoke as if they had no choice but to move in this direction in order to protect their families *and* their fortunes. But there had always been another option at their disposal: nothing stopped them from simply setting their slaves free and rehiring them to work in the fields for pay. This option was never acceptable to the slave own-

---

[435] *Apostles of Disunion*, Charles W. Dew, p 14

[436] *Apostles of Disunion*, Charles W. Dew, p 14

[437] *Apostles of Disunion*, Charles W. Dew, p 14

[438] *Apostles of Disunion*, Charles W. Dew, p 14

ers for the reasons so well expressed by the Mississippi delegation: freeing the slaves "would lead to loss of property and degradation."[439] The only property to be lost was the slaves themselves, but there would be no loss of a workforce; the plantation owners could have hired and paid black and white workers to work their fields, and gone from making exorbitant profits to more moderate ones.

The only *degradation* that would have taken place is that they would have gone from filthy rich to a comfortably wealthy economic status. In short, this approach would have cost them money. They were unwilling to accept that. They were ready to sacrifice the freedoms of this land by deserting it rather than have their enormous profits tampered with. As Lincoln recognized and expressed, these firebrands were but a small minority of the Southern population; the vast majority were common farmers and merchants who owned no slaves, people with nothing to gain from secession.

In a short time, other states would secede from the North, each rewriting their own constitutions, and the original inspired document was in danger of becoming a mere relic in a museum. Jefferson Davis also comes very close to expressing the root cause of slavery and their tenacious hold on it: money. In his concern for the devaluation of slave owners' "property in the slaves" there is no mistaking that "property" to be their investment in the buying and selling of people for the purpose of enslavement, and the potential loss of production and revenue that would result should they ever be freed. The love of money, the "root of all evil" according to the Bible, was the root cause of slavery and the Civil War. Davis was not through with his self-implicating utterances and he went on to describe slavery itself as an institution that "a superior race had used to transform brutal savages into docile, intelligent, and civilized agricul-

---

[439] *Apostles of Disunion*, Charles W. Dew, p 14

tural laborers,"[440] which in the South now numbered more than three million.

After the war, and from his prison cell at Fort Warren, Alexander Stephens claimed he was misquoted in his now infamous Cornerstone Speech of 1861 in Savannah in which he stated that Thomas Jefferson and the Founding Fathers were wrong in believing that all men are equal. Stephens insisted that "The reporter's notes, which were very imperfect, were hastily corrected by me and were published without further revision and with several glaring errors."[441] If this Savannah speech had been misquoted, so then was his Atlanta speech, which he gave just eight days earlier. In that speech, he concluded by saying that the framers of the Confederate constitution had "solemnly discarded the pestilent heresy of fancy politicians, that all men, of all races, were equal, and we had made the African *inequality* and subordination, and the *equality* of white men, the chief cornerstone of the Southern Republic."[442] Stephens continued his postwar backslide by saying that "there could be no greater violence...done to the truth of History than to refer to the Southern opponents of Northern Consolidationists as a Pro-Slavery Party."[443]

Jefferson Davis, in his book titled *The Rise and Fall of the Confederate Government*, written some twenty years after the war in 1881, continued the cover-up. He said the "sectional hostility" that developed before 1861

> was not the consequence of any difference on the abstract question of slavery. It would have manifest itself just as certainly if slavery had existed in all the States, or if there

[440] *Apostles of Disunion*, Charles W. Dew, p 15
[441] *Apostles of Disunion*, Charles W. Dew, p 15
[442] *Apostles of Disunion*, Charles W. Dew, p 15
[443] *Apostles of Disunion*, Charles W. Dew, p 16

had not been a negro in America. The truth remains intact and incontrovertible, that the existence of African servitude was in no wise the cause of the conflict, but only an incident. The South had fought for the noblest of principles...[444]

Dozens of historical records are crystal clear to the contrary. During that disastrous four-month period of November 1860 through February 1861, between Lincoln's election and his inauguration, the Southern rebels launched a vast and organized campaign to fan the fire of rebellion by sending "commissioners" to the governments of all the Southern states with the "now or never" message of secession. The well-documented speeches of these traveling commissioners and those of the subsequent state secession conventions that were held are replete with one message, leaving no doubt that the protection and advancement of slavery was the driving force behind the rebellion against the government of the United States.

The flash point of secession came in South Carolina on December 20, 1860, when it became the first state to secede. But the secession fires were already burning hot in Mississippi, Alabama, Florida, Georgia, Louisiana, and Texas as well, all of which followed South Carolina with their own secession conventions that severed all ties to the United States government. A combined secession convention consisting of these seven seceding states was then held in Montgomery, Alabama in early February 1861. In that convention they removed two of the pillars of the original Declaration of Independence. "We the people" was replaced by "We the deputies" making them a government *of* the people but not *by* or *for* the people; the rulers would now rule, not the people. And second, they removed "all

---

[444] *Apostles of Disunion*, Charles W. Dew, p 17

men are created equal," closing and locking the legal door to opposition to their practice of subjugating and oppressing a people based on race. The Montgomery convention hurriedly organized their provisional government, and then rushed military forces into the field to discourage opposition from the North.

On July 5, 1861, President Lincoln, in his first speech to the members of the Senate and the House of Representatives, reminded them that the new Confederacy had just adopted the current U.S. Constitution as their governing beacon—with what they referred to as a few additional changes. President Lincoln said of those changes:

> Our adversaries have adopted some declarations of independence, in which, unlike the good old one, penned by Jefferson, they omit the words "all men are created equal." Why?

> They have adopted a temporary national constitution, in the preamble of which, unlike our good old one, signed by Washington, they omit "We, the people," and substitute "We, the deputies of the sovereign and independent States." Why?

> Why this deliberate pressing out of view the rights of men and the authority of the people?[445]

Why did they take such drastic action? It was not, as they later claimed, merely to exercise their perceived right to secede. The answer came directly from them in their state secession

---

[445] Speech to the US Congress by Abraham Lincoln, July 5, 1861

convention declarations. Charles B. Dew records, in *Apostles of Disunion*, that the Texas convention stated that with the election of a Republican president the country had fallen under the control of a "great sectional party…proclaiming the *debasing doctrine of the equality of all men, irrespective of race and color…*"[446] The Alabama preamble charged that Lincoln's party, the Republicans, were "avowedly hostile to the *domestic institutions* [slavery] and to the peace and security of the people of Alabama."[447] The Georgia Convention stated, "For twenty years past, the Abolitionists and their allies in the Northern states, have been engaged in constant efforts to subvert our *institutions* [slavery], and to excite insurrection and *servile* war among us." Republican rulers' "avowed purpose is to subject our society, and subject us, not only to the loss of our *property* [slaves] but the destruction of ourselves, our wives, and our children, and the desolation of our homes, our altars, and our firesides."[448]

Mississippi's official statement made no efforts to cloak their true design. It flatly stated, "Our position is thoroughly identified with the *institution of slavery.* There was no choice left us but submission to the mandates of abolition, or a dissolution of the union, whose principles have been subverted to work our ruin."[449] It went on to cite a number of hostile acts against slavery, then charged that a Northern abolitionist majority now "advocates negro equality, socially and politically, and promotes insurrection and incendiarism in our midst. We must either submit to degradation and to the loss of *property* [slaves] worth four billions of money, or we must secede from the Union."[450] And finally, South Carolina's "Declaration of the Immediate Causes Which Induce and Justify Secession" focused primarily

---

[446] *Apostles of Disunion*, Charles W. Dew, p 11
[447] *Apostles of Disunion*, Charles W. Dew, p 11
[448] *Apostles of Disunion*, Charles W. Dew, p 12
[449] *Apostles of Disunion*, Charles W. Dew, p 12
[450] *Apostles of Disunion*, Charles W. Dew, p 13

on the Northern embrace of the antislavery movement and the evil designs of the newly triumphant Republican Party. The Northern states "have encouraged and assisted thousands of our slaves to leave their homes; and those who remain, have been incited by emissaries, books, and pictures to servile insurrection."[451]

Lincoln had always wanted to somehow eradicate slavery; he just didn't know how to do it legally, and such a dramatic move would surely have political and civil repercussions. As a teenager, when he first saw the inhumanity of slavery in New Orleans, he told his friend that if he ever got a chance in his life to address slavery that he would hit it hard. And it was Lincoln's six years of speeches around the country on the immorality of slavery that brought him eventually to the White House. William J. Wolf sheds some light on President Lincoln's challenge with slavery:

> We can better understand Lincoln's final act of emancipation when we realize that for long he was balked by the Constitutional dilemma. He believed that despite the moral wrong of slavery the federal government was prevented by the Constitution from disturbing it in the original states. He said, 'I have here stated my purpose according to my view of *official* duty; and I intend no modification of my oft-expressed *personal* wish that all men everywhere could be free.'[452]

With the soon-to-be-raging Civil War laid in the lap of the new president, he was unexpectedly provided the legal opening for him to act against slavery *within the law* with the constitution-

---

[451] *Apostles of Disunion*, Charles W. Dew, p 33
[452] *The Almost Chosen People*, William J. Wolf, p 21

al powers granted to a president in time of war. He later explained in an open letter to the nation that the laws of war allow for property to be taken when needed in defense of the nation's freedom. The Southern lawmakers had so masterfully labored in the earlier decades to legally define their slaves as mere property, to be owned, worked, bought, and sold like cattle. Lincoln, who would never act contrary to existing law, saw in this time of war the legal window for him to confiscate such "property," free them, and then marshal them in the fight to preserve their newfound freedom and that of the nation. With Lincoln now able to act within the law, his mind was set to the monumental possibility to move forward with the heretofore unthinkable: to free the slaves and do so legally. But timing for such a task was critically important and Lincoln would look to God, not Congress, not his Cabinet, to signal the correct moment. There were Border States that could be easily influenced to leave the Union and join the Confederate cause over the issue of emancipation.

This was another reason for Lincoln's hesitation; he had not as yet received an affirmation from God that the time had come to free the slaves. That affirmation arrived some time in the summer of 1862, more than a year into the war. William J. Wolf describes the events:

> Lincoln was waited upon by two clergymen who presented a memorial from a mass meeting of Chicago Christians of all denominations. He listened to the document, which demanded immediate emancipation, and then replied with a firmness probably stiffened by his distaste for the oversimplification of a very complex issue:
>
> I am approached with the most opposite opinions and advice, and that by religious men,

who are equally certain that they represent the divine will. I am sure that either the one or the other class is mistaken in that belief, and perhaps in some respects both. I hope it will not be irreverent for me to say that if it is probable that God would reveal his will to others, on a point so connected with my duty, it might be supposed *he would reveal it directly to me* (italics added); for, unless I am more deceived in myself that I often am, it is my earnest desire to know the will of Providence in this matter. *And if I can learn what it is, I will do it!*"[453]

Lincoln then analyzed the pros and cons of their proposal and invited a reply. The two clergymen replied point by point in an hour of earnest discussion. The interview ended with the president saying:

Do not misunderstand me, because I have mentioned these objections. They indicate the difficulties that have thus far prevented my action in some such way as you desire. I have not decided against a proclamation of liberty to the slaves, but hold the matter under advisement. And I can assure you that the subject is on my mind, by day and night, more than any other. Whatever shall appear to be God's will I will do. I trust that, in the freedom with which I have canvassed your views, I have not in any respect injured your feelings.[454]

---

[453] *The Almost Chosen People*, William J. Wolf, p 20
[454] *The Almost Chosen People*, William J. Wolf, p 22

William J. Wolf describes the scene in the days that followed this meeting,

> At the end of the week following the visit of the Chicago delegation Lincoln summoned his Cabinet. He was ready to issue a proclamation freeing most of the slaves, but first, heeding Seward's earlier advice, he wanted the announcement to follow a military victory. He did not want the act to be interpreted as the despairing gesture of a sorely pressed government. Also he had been seeking to submit this question to his higher authority, to the God who, he firmly believed, presided over man's history and who acted within that history, even if His will might be difficult for man to understand. By the date of the cabinet session in September 1862, Lincoln was convinced that "God had decided this question in favor of the slave." He was satisfied it was right—was confirmed and strengthened by the vow and its results.[455]

Something had occurred during that week between God and Lincoln that moved Lincoln to take the dramatic action of emancipation. Somehow, Lincoln had received the divine assurance for which he had so desperately hoped: that the time had finally come. Without that assurance he would not have acted.

Wolf describes his announcement to the Cabinet,

> It was September 22, 1862. The President's Cabinet was in session to consider an urgent problem on which Lincoln wanted ad-

---

[455] *The Almost Chosen People*, William J. Wolf, p 19

vice. Secretary of the Treasury Salmon Chase had just asked the President to repeat what he had been saying. Lincoln had described his decision to emancipate the slaves in territories that were then in rebellion against the federal government. Toward the end, the President's voice had become lower and more solemn. Secretary Chase wanted to be certain he had understood Lincoln's words. The President repeated, 'I made a solemn vow before God, that if General Lee was driven back from Pennsylvania, I would crown the result by the declaration of freedom to the slaves.'[456]

There are at least two detailed accounts from the diaries of Cabinet members on this momentous event. This first is the entry of Secretary Chase:

The President then took a graver tone, and said, Gentlemen: I have, as you are aware, thought a great deal about the relation of this war to slavery; and you all remember that, several weeks ago, I read to you an order I had prepared on this subject, which, on account of objections made by some of you, was not issued. Ever since then my mind has been much occupied with this subject, and I have thought, all along, that the time has come now. I wish it were a better time. I wish that we were in a better condition. The action of the army against the rebels has not been quite what I should best like. But they have been driven out of Maryland, and Pennsylvania is not longer a danger of invasion. When the Rebel Army

---

[456] *The Almost Chosen People*, William J. Wolf, p 17

was at Frederick, I determined, as soon as it should be driven out of Maryland, to issue a Proclamation of Emancipation, such as I thought most likely to be useful. I said nothing to anyone, but I made a promise to myself, and (hesitating a little) to my Maker. The Rebel Army is now driven out, and I am going to fulfill that promise.[457]

The second confirmation comes from the diary of Gideon Welles, the secretary of the Navy:

We have a special Cabinet meeting. The subject was the Proclamation concerning emancipating slaves.... There were some differences in the Cabinet, but [Lincoln] had formed his own conclusions, and made his own decisions. He had, he said, made a vow, a covenant, that if God gave us a victory in the approaching battle (which had just been fought) he would consider it his duty to move forward in the cause of emancipation. We might think it strange, he said, but there were times when he felt uncertain how to act; that he had in this way submitted the disposal of matters when the way was not clear to his mind what he should do. God had decided this question in favor of the slave. He was satisfied it was right—was confirmed and strengthened by the vow and its results; his mind was fixed, his decision made; but he wished his paper announcing his course to be as correct in terms as it could be made without any attempt to change his determination. For that was fixed.[458]

---

[457] *The Almost Chosen People*, William J. Wolf, p 18

[458] *The Almost Chosen People*, William J. Wolf, p 19

Lincoln then spoke of a division in a New York delegation and of perplexity in the last Congress, even though the majority was antislavery. He pointedly went on:

> Why, the rebel soldiers are praying with a great deal more earnestness, I fear, than our own troops, and expecting God to favor their side; for one of our soldiers, who had been taken prisoner, told Senator Wilson, a few days since, that he met with nothing so discouraging as the evident sincerity of those he was among in their prayers.[459]

As expected, Lincoln's Emancipation Proclamation in September 1862 caused an avalanche of criticism from the South. And not surprisingly it caused a sizable furor among many in the North especially among the Northern Democrats. The opposition even came from among the soldiers in the Union forces who were willing to fight for the Union but not for the freedom of four million African-American slaves. Correspondents embedded with the Union troops claimed "hardly one soldier in ten approved of emancipation."[460] Democratic papers from New York to Chicago "smeared the proclamation as 'a wicked, atrocious, and revolting deed' which would unleash hordes of 'negro barbarism.'" "It is impudent and insulting to God as to man," cried one Democrat, "for it declares those 'equal' whom God created unequal."[461] The backlash even alarmed many pro-emancipation Republicans in Congress into questioning its propriety at such a time of war. Many, including some of his closest friends, begged Lincoln to change or repeal his Emancipation Proclamation for the sake of the Union, but "Lincoln was as

---

[459] *The Almost Chosen People*, William J. Wolf, p 18
[460] *With Malice Toward None*, Stephen B. Oates, p 339
[461] *With Malice Toward None*, Stephen B. Oates, p 339

immovable as stone."[462] He responded to one importuning friend that "I am a slow walker, but I never walk backwards."[463]

With his emancipation edict in place, he and his secretary of war, Edwin Stanton, initiated the next step by marshalling and arming black soldiers for the Union army. Many whites believed that the experiment would be an utter failure since the "docile and moronic Sambos"[464] would never have the discipline or courage to fight effectively. To avoid utter rebellion within the Union ranks, the War Department placated the white soldiers by paying the blacks less for their military service. Lincoln, on the other hand, "believed that Negroes would make good Union troops."[465] He even went so far as to assert, "the bare sight of fifty thousand armed and drilled black soldiers on the banks of the Mississippi, would end the rebellion at once."[466] Union commanders operating throughout the South began conscripting blacks who had come to them from the plantations, and formed all-Negro units. Within eight months of Lincoln's issuance of the proclamation "some fourteen Negro regiments were in the field from North to South alike..."[467] "In all, some one hundred eighty thousand blacks—a majority of them emancipated slaves—were to fight in Union military forces, adding enormous strength to Lincoln's war machine."[468]

It was the Massachusetts Fifty-fourth "Colored" Infantry, under the command of a young white colonel named Robert Gould Shaw, that was the first to prove categorically that they would fight as hard and courageously as any white regiment when they led the assault on Fort Wagner near Charleston Harbor.

---

[462] *With Malice Toward None*, Stephen B. Oates, p 340
[463] *With Malice Toward None*, Stephen B. Oates, p 340
[464] *With Malice Toward None*, Stephen B. Oates, p 341
[465] *With Malice Toward None*, Stephen B. Oates, p 341
[466] *With Malice Toward None*, Stephen B. Oates, p 341
[467] *With Malice Toward None*, Stephen B. Oates, p 341
[468] *With Malice Toward None*, Stephen B. Oates, p 356

Referring to Lincoln's freeing of the slaves, William J. Wolf explains,

> Lincoln is one of the greatest theologians of America—not in the technical meaning of producing a system of doctrine, certainly not as the defender of some one denomination, but in the sense of seeing the hand of God intimately in the affairs of nations. Just so the prophets of Israel criticized the events of their day from the perspective of the God who is concerned for history and Who reveals His will within it. Lincoln stands among God's greatest latter-day prophets.[469]

---

[469] *The Almost Chosen People*, William J. Wolf, p 24

Chapter Nine

"The Will of God Prevails"

Much has been said of errors of the Southern politicians and slave owners that led up to the Civil War, but it is important to remember, as Lincoln frequently pointed out, that Americans on both sides, North and South, were victims of the terrible war. Reinhold Niebuhr, a leading American theologian, wrote in 1965, "Lincoln's religious convictions were superior in depth and purity to those held by the religious as well as by the political leaders of his day."[470] Niebuhr was struck by Lincoln's ability to resist "the natural temptation" to do what most other politicians did by asserting that God was on the side to which that politician was committed. He said, "Lincoln had a sense of historical meaning so high as to cast doubt on the intentions of both sides."[471] Lincoln would often respond to those from all persuasions who would express their assurance that God was on their side by reminding them that what mattered most to him was that he be always found on God's side. In the years leading up to the war, Lincoln did at times express his belief that his personal battle for right against wrong might have been

---

[470] *The Eloquent President*, p 165
[471] *The Eloquent President*, p 166

deeper than slavery and the division of the Union. He said, "While pretending no indifference to earthly honors, I *do claim* to be actuated in this contest by something higher than an anxiety for office."[472]

Lincoln often expressed his belief that America's wayward ways were an offense to the "Living God" and the culminating events in the 1850s provide a plethora of political and moral deteriorations that could sustain such a notion. Not the least of these was the two and a half centuries of the inhumanity of slavery, which was ironically practiced by the most blessed people on earth, bestowed with freedoms that Lincoln believed were granted by a merciful Creator who expected His "almost chosen people" to treat all others with similar mercy and justice. But that freedom was taken by the fortunate Protestant Anglo-Saxons of America, and they reserved it only for themselves, disregarding the Declaration of Independence's assertion that "all men are created equal." Lincoln referred to slavery as an "unqualified evil"[473] in America. As was noted earlier, he told a friend, just days prior to his election as president:

> I know there is a God and that He hates injustice and slavery. I see the storm coming and I know that His hand is in it. If He has a place and a work for me, and I think He has, I believe I am ready. I am nothing, but truth is everything. I know I am right because I know liberty is right, for Christ teaches it and Christ is God.[474]

When asked to define the compelling difference between the Democratic and Republican Parties, amidst all of the various

---

[472] *Lincoln's Virtues*, p 339
[473] *The Civil War and Reconstruction,* J.G. Randall and David Herbert Donald
[474] *Church in War and Peace*, Stephen L. Richards

planks on their platforms, Lincoln stated emphatically that "the Republicans regard slavery as 'a moral, social, and political wrong,' while the Democrats do *not* consider it a wrong."[475] He went on to say that "the Republican Party hold[s]…that slavery is an unqualified evil to the Negro, to the white man, to the soil, and to the state."[476]

God's wrath may also have been kindled by the widening and debilitating damage caused by the wound in the side of the Constitution, successfully placed there by the proslavery Founding Fathers, who were so insistent that slavery remain unfettered in this land that they succeeded in including the three-fifths clause in its contents. This clause not only allowed for slavery, but also reinforced it by creating an unfair balance of proslavery lawmakers in the halls of Congress for the coming eroding decades.

For these declining decades, the freedoms of speech and of the press that were guaranteed by the Constitution were largely ignored when it came to the expression of opinions against slavery in most Southern states. State governments simply disregarded these guaranteed freedoms and passed legislation that made it unlawful to speak and or to write against slavery in their state. Individuals who did not heed these prohibitions of freedoms were frequently harassed, sometimes driven from their homes or found hanging from a tree. The North was also intolerant of pro-slavery rhetoric. The passage of the Fugitive Slave Law by the U.S. Congress and President Millard Fillmore served to deepen the grip of slaveholders' influence on the nation and reinforced the growing movement to make slavery an accepted American institution. This law made it unlawful for white citizens *not* to participate in the capture and return of runaway slaves.

The Dred Scott Decision, in which the highest court in the land declared that the African-American people were "beings of

---

[475] *Lincoln's Virtues,* p 322
[476] *Lincoln's Virtues,* p 323

an inferior order" and unworthy of the same inalienable rights as Anglo-Americans, thereby legitimized and legalized prejudice, discrimination, bigotry, and racism in the United States.

The passage of the Kansas-Nebraska Bill and the repeal of the Missouri Compromise, which left Lincoln "roused" and "thunderstruck" at its transformation of slavery from a moral issue into an Anglo-Saxon fringe benefit, had tremendous potential to further deaden the conscience of Americans for injustice toward targeted groups. Lincoln was convinced that this nation could not survive "half slave and half free."

The formation of the oath-bound secret society known as the American Party or Know-Nothings came about during the 1850s; they were also known as nativists, and they could freely and without censure express enmity for and discrimination against a targeted class of people or a religion. The precedence of discrimination against an entire class of people was firmly entrenched in the American fabric. While many citizens comfortably reasoned the social and spiritual values of slavery for the whites and for the blacks, the Know-Nothings openly directed their venom toward foreigners and Catholics.

Marauding mobs in Missouri, Ohio and Illinois remained unchallenged during two decades of persecution of the members of the Church of Jesus Christ of Latter-Day Saints or Mormons. This injustice culminated in the murder of their prophet, Joseph Smith and his brother Hyrum, and in three major violent expulsions in which more than 15,000 Mormons were driven from their homes and farms. No one was ever convicted for these crimes even though the Mormons plead for the protection and redress for their losses that they were entitled to by the Constitution from local, state and federal authorities, yet received none.

A blatant disregard for the Constitutional rights of these ethnic and religious groups along with decisions made by the highest court in the land and by the highest legislative and executive branches of this government had legitimized these injustices in America. Under this umbrella, the nativist movement was growing at an alarming pace with the aim to politically single out and discriminate against a religion, foreigners, and "inferior races."

The Southern Confederacy would turn out to be so fundamentally dysfunctional that, in a matter of months, some of the eleven Southern states were clamoring to secede from the Confederacy over differences. Instead of continuing as one strong, moral, and free nation, this continent faced the real possibility of being dotted with independently thinking nation-states, much like Europe, each with their own constitution and set of values, and there would have been no one powerful government, founded on basic inalienable rights, to defend the original Constitution that guaranteed such rights.

One will search in vain for any semblance of Godliness in these political developments, which reflected a deteriorating social morality, propagated by the mounting self-righteous pride and materialism of white Protestant America. Nor can one easily fathom the damaging magnitude of this convergence of political and moral corruptions that were embraced by such a large segment of Christian America. Lincoln's belief that God's wrath was incurred by some, if not all, of the above conditions in this nation and quite possibly for other reasons known only to God, was often and clearly expressed. Referring to the abundant blessings bestowed upon Americans as well as the trials of the devastating civil war, he told America in his Thanksgiving Proclamation:

> They are the gracious gifts of the Most High God, who, while dealing with us in anger for our sins, hath nevertheless remembered mercy.[477]

---

[477] Thanksgiving Proclamation, Abraham Lincoln

Referring to the untold death and misery of the Civil War, Lincoln also reminded America in his second inaugural address, quoting Psalms 19:9, that "The judgments of the Lord are true and righteous altogether." It would take a prophet to accurately surmise just where this nation would be today had President Abraham Lincoln not stood so resolutely against this growing national debacle, as he did in defense of morality, the Union, the Constitution, and the Declaration of Independence. He stood virtually alone, with his God, in defense of right against wrong in America. Anyone can see that the course being taken by mid-1800 America held little to admire and Lincoln's solitary stand must be recognized for its high level of significance. He was a deep and true believer in God, yet he eschewed organized church membership. The nation was full of Christian politicians, congregations, and coalitions who were raising their voices for or against the various national issues. Lincoln stood apart from them before and during his presidency, rather than seeking to establish alliances for the sake of building support for his position. As a Whig, as the Republican national chairman, and as the Republican nominee for president, he spoke little on the various political planks of these parties. Yet he spoke incessantly on his personal mission to turn America from wrong in the sight of God so as to embrace that which was right in the sight of God. Nor did he seek alliances on the political side. Alliance almost always meant compromise, and there could be no compromise in Lincoln's plan to battle for what was right, "As God allows us to see the right,"[478] as he would often humbly qualify. He felt that he could not allow the moral principles for which he stood to be diluted in any degree so he conducted his political cause essentially on his own, placing his greatest trust in his Almighty God.

---

[478] Abraham Lincoln's Second Inaugural Address

As president he could have acquiesced to the intense pressure from the North to just let the Southern states go to form their own separate nation, to let Fort Sumter go and fall into their hands along with all of the other forts, ports, and military installations that the Confederacy had confiscated in the Southern states. He could have made such compromises with significant approval from the North. But he saw what most of pre-Civil War America did not see, that such compromises would only be the continuation of a long string of moral compromises. And more compromises would only lead to further weakening of the nation and the Constitution. Lincoln perceived that this nation was well into a self-destructive course with its newly acquired *popular sovereignty*, the right for new territories to choose or not choose slavery; with the Dred Scott Supreme Court decision and its alarming *legalization* of racial discrimination; and with the Know-Nothings' celebrated movement to discriminate against religion and nationality. It was Abraham Lincoln's resoluteness and the horrific Civil War that put an end to these anti-liberty influences in America.

It is possible that the political and moral decline was so great in America that only God's judgment in the form of the terrible Civil War could break this debilitating cycle and result in the unimaginable transformation and cleansing that followed the war, wherein these colliding political aberrations would be eradicated. But any historian can easily surmise that this convergence of materialism, religious discrimination, prejudice, and racial supremacy in the land of freedoms had no hope of anything more than a dismal future, fraught with strife, uncertainty, and widespread injustice.

Prior to his presidency, Lincoln summarized in his seventh and last debate with Douglas, spoken in the midst of this convergence of racial and religious intolerance, that the "real issue" in this contest, this "eternal struggle," rested between these two principles—right and wrong throughout the world; that right and wrong "have stood face to face from the beginning of time…"[479]

Several times in his six years of debate with Douglas leading up to his presidential election victory over Douglas, Lincoln said that what happened in this political race between him and Douglas was of no consequence—what mattered instead was the triumph of morality in America.

> "Think nothing of me," he said passionately, "but come back to the truths that are in the Declaration of Independence. You may do anything with me you choose, if you will but heed these sacred principles. You may not only defeat me for the Senate, but you may take me and put me to death."[480]

In the fall of 1862, with the war going badly for the North, the off-year gubernatorial and congressional elections reflected what Lincoln already knew; he told his cabinet in September prior to the elections, "I believe that I have not so much of the confidence of the people as I had some time since."[481] The new Republican Party's jubilant rise in the 1860 election was quickly reversed two years later by the disheartening lack of Union progress in the war. Disenchantment over the war had eroded the party's popularity and the Democratic Party candidates retook many state and federal seats from the Republicans, including the president's home state of Illinois where they charged that Lincoln and the Republican Party were trying to Africanize their state. These reversals placed in peril the prospects of an 1864 presidential re-election for Lincoln. David Herbert Donald said, "Most blamed Republican defeats on what Lincoln called the

[479] *Lincoln's Virtues*, p 338
[480] *Lincoln's Virtues*, p 339
[481] *Lincoln*, David H. Donald, p 381

'ill-success of the war.' That failure they attributed to the President."[482] During these months there was no lack of criticism for President Lincoln. A New Yorker charged that Lincoln's "weakness, irresolution, and want of moral courage was to blame for the Republican reversals of 1862."[483] A contingent of Pennsylvania Republicans, smarting from the Republican defeats, traveled to the White House to personally deliver their censure and then instruct the beleaguered president on his mishandling of the war and the government. One told him coldly that "Some Pennsylvania Republican leaders would be glad to hear some morning that you had been found hanging from a post of a lamp at the door of the White House."[484] Through all of this, Lincoln was, as always, meekly absorbed with perfect humility and sadness. In fact he was once referred to as the saddest president ever to serve in the White House. Francis B. Carpenter, the artist who lived in the White House for part of 1864, said of Lincoln, "I have said repeatedly to friends that Mr. Lincoln had the saddest face I ever attempted to paint."[485] "I never saw a sadder face."[486] The alarming death counts and lack of progress in the war, coupled with the death of his beloved Willie, brought unrelenting sorrow to Lincoln's presidential years.

By this time he quietly held to a personal and solitary conviction that as a punishment for the nation's sins, God intended for this war to continue, but as the criticism mounted he was left to bear this mountain of rancor alone, and he did so with a most Godlike of patience as he himself suffered in humble silence for the nation's sorry condition. A few months later, after more crip-

---

[482] *Lincoln*, David H. Donald, p 383
[483] *Lincoln*, David H. Donald, p 383
[484] *The Eloquent President*, p. 384
[485] Internet: Lincoln Research Site
[486] Internet: Lincoln Research Site

pling Union defeats, a caucus of angry senators was held. Lincoln was aware of the caucus and confided with a friend by asking,

> "What do these men want?" Then answering his own question he continued, "They wish to get rid of me, and I am sometimes half disposed to gratify them. We are on the brink of destruction, and it appears to me that the Almighty is against us, and I can hardly see a ray of hope."[487]

By early 1863, many in Lincoln's own party were prepared to pursue a court-martial of the president at the first opportunity. "Battered from all sides, Lincoln grew deeply despondent."[488] One observer noted that "his hand trembled…he looked worn and haggard." Admiral John Dahlgren, a frequent visitor to the White House, recorded that "I observe that the President never tells a joke now." And when asked about his thoughts on a run for a second presidential term Lincoln responded, "Oh…I have ceased to have any personal feeling of expectation in that matter,—I do not say I never had any,—so abused and borne upon as I have been."[489] Lincoln did want to win his bid for reelection. He felt it important to complete the mission into which he had been placed. On this he told a friend, "It is not a good idea to change horses mid stream."[490] While it is possible, there is little evidence that his interest in being reelected was for his own personal ambition, for he said and did little to indicate that he derived personal gratification from the honors accompanying the high office. But he did fear that, as expressed by a close associate in the White House, "If they [the people] go for the Democracy, then Mr. Lincoln

---

[487] *Lincoln,* David H. Donald, p 402
[488] *The Eloquent President,* p 426
[489] *Lincoln,* David H. Donald, p 426
[490] *Lincoln,* David H. Donald, p 493

will not wind up the war [and] a new feeling and spirit will inspire the South."[491]

Sometime during this low point in his life and presidency, Lincoln, for reasons unknown, made a dramatic personal transformation that would change his presidency, the course of the war, and the course of this nation. The weight of the failing war effort coupled with the mounting criticism may have triggered a spiritual awakening for Lincoln, for it was under this cloud of failure and criticism that he had his own presidential rebirth. He had somehow come to the conclusion that he needed to exert a more personal leadership both with the war and with the government. Heretofore, he had labored to listen and respond to the advice and demands of his cabinet and Congress with the hope of forming a unified coalition that would lead to victory. Yet this approach proved to be dismally unsuccessful. From that moment he seemed to look and to see beyond the myriad of angry and impassioned voices in Congress, his cabinet, and the citizenry, as he set out with a renewed confidence to do what he felt in *his* heart and mind to be the right thing to do. The one voice he would not tune out was the voice of inspiration from his Almighty God. From here to the end of his life he would conduct his presidency and the affairs of this country in the way that he believed God would have him conduct it. David Herbert Donald said of Lincoln, "Increasing in self-confident, he relied less and less on the advice of his cabinet officers."[492] And increasingly he relied on his own impressions derived from his personal prayers and meditations to achieve God's will as opposed to the vastly vacillating will of those around him. His cabinet was troubled and even angered by his new resolve as the frequency of cabinet meetings declined, as did his consultations with them. But while his cabinet fumed Lincoln revived. His secretary John Hay observed during this transformation, "The

---

[491] *The Eloquent President*, p 454
[492] *Lincoln*, David H. Donald, p 449

tycoon is in fine whack. I have rarely seen him more serene and busy. He is managing this war, the draft, foreign relations, and planning a reconstruction of the Union, all at once."[493] After two years of trying to execute the presidency as had been expected of him, Lincoln came to the conclusion that the only adviser who could lead him and this nation out of this dark abyss was the Almighty God Himself, and Lincoln had now marshaled the determination to do what he had always wanted to do as president: make God's will paramount in the execution of his office. From this point he led the nation with God as his closest adviser.

John Wesley Hill said of Lincoln, "Perhaps no American, save the prophets only, has put such implicit trust in God as did the Great Emancipator. Out of his personal experiences he testified he was as certain that God acts directly upon human affairs as he was of a fact apparent to the senses, such as that he was in the room where he was then speaking."[494]

Whether merely coincidental or a major influencing factor on his newfound resolve, it was during this spiritual-presidential awakening that Lincoln wrote what has come to be known as his *Meditation on the Divine Will,* privately commending into the hands of God the outcome of the nation's travail. With Lincoln's newfound single-hearted resolve he conducted a number of presidential maneuvers that would, over the coming months, electrify the nation in the North and pull his plummeting popularity out from the despairing depths. It was during this period that he surprised his cabinet with the world-altering decision to issue the Emancipation Proclamation.

Lincoln had a practice of turning ideas over and over in his mind, writing his conclusions and musings on the backs of envelopes and pieces of paper, and then placing them in his tall stovepipe hat or in nooks and drawers in his desk. One such

---

[493] *Lincoln,* David H. Donald p.449
[494] *Abraham Lincoln—Man of God,* John Wesley Hill, p 124

written meditation was neither discovered nor made public until after his death. It is of singular significance in catching a glimpse of Lincoln's faith and conviction that God was the silent architect of the war that was ravaging the country. John Hay, Lincoln's private secretary, discovered this private notation among a number of other such notes and kept it. In 1872, Hay gave it a title: *Meditation on the Divine Will*. He included it in the biography of Lincoln that he and Nicolay published in 1890, with the description "This meditation was not meant to be seen of men."[495]

Meditation on the Divine Will
September 2(?) 1862, sixteen months into the war

> The will of God prevails. In great contests each party claims to act in accordance with the will of God. Both may be, and one must be wrong God cannot be for, and against the same thing at the same time. In the present civil war it is quite possible that God's purpose is something different from the purpose of either party—and yet the human instrumentalities, working just as they do, are of the best adaptation to effect His purpose. I am almost ready to say this is probably true—that God wills this contest, and wills that it shall not end yet. By His mere quiet power, on the minds of the now contestants, He could have either saved or destroyed the Union without a human contest. Yet the contest began. And having begun He could give the final victory to either side any day. Yet the contest proceeds.[496]

This private musing merits a close analysis.

---

[495] *The Eloquent President*, p 154
[496] *The Eloquent President*, p 153

The will of God prevails.

Lincoln had expressed this belief dozens of times and in various ways. There can be no doubt of his sincerity in this solitary expression. He once told a friend:

> That the Almighty does make use of human agencies and directly intervenes in human affairs is one of the plainest statements in the Bible. I've had so many evidences of His direction, so many instances when I have been controlled by some other power than my own will, that I cannot doubt that this power comes from above…All we have to do is trust the Almighty and keep on obeying His orders and executing His will. I frequently see my way clear to a decision when I am conscious that I have not sufficient facts upon which to found it. But I cannot recall one instance in which I have followed my own judgment founded upon such a decision, where the results were unsatisfactory; whereas, in almost every instance where I have yielded to the views of others I have had occasion to regret it.[497]

In this present civil war it is quite possible that God's purpose is something different from the purpose of either party…

This conviction that God was at the helm of the war must have been at least some solace to Lincoln, who suffered greatly in mind and spirit at the massive number of war deaths, nearing two hundred thousand by the time of Lincoln's penning of this meditation, and at the terrible economic strain placed on the nation with the enormous costs of financing the war.

I am almost ready to say this is probably true—that God wills this contest, and wills that it shall not end yet. By His mere quiet power, on the minds of the now contestants, He could have either _saved_ or _destroyed_ the

---

[497] *In War and Peace*, Stephen L. Richards

Union without a human contest. Yet the contest began. And having begun He could give the final victory to either side any day. Yet the contest proceeds.

It is safe to say that few mortals, if any, were closer to God or looked to Him more intently than did Lincoln during this time. The public and the politicians were unaware of Lincoln's solemn *Meditation*; it appears to have been written only as his own contemplation. However, he would reflect these same sentiments in at least two conversations in the following days and in his proclamation that established our time-honored tradition of Thanksgiving a year later.

It was just days following this *Meditation* that Lincoln stunned his cabinet by revealing his vow to God that if the Union army was successful in driving out the Confederates from Maryland, which they did just days earlier at Antietam, he would interpret that as an indication from God that He approved of Lincoln's private and personal decision to free the slaves in the rebelling states by issuing the Emancipation Proclamation. Lincoln said solemnly to his cabinet, "God had decided this question in favor of the slaves."[498]

Three months later in December of that year, Lincoln gave the traditional annual message to Congress in which he reinforced his monumental decision to issue the Emancipation Proclamation. Again, many angry and troubled hearts were softened as he skillfully and humbly presented their nation's dire condition in relation to the world and the future of all mankind by saying, "In giving freedom to the slave, we assure freedom to the free—honorable alike in what we give, and what we preserve. We shall nobly save, or meanly lose, the last best hope of earth."[499]

Lincoln's assessment of this struggle as being the "last best hope of earth" was probably more accurate than even he knew.

---

[498] *The Eloquent President,* p 168
[499] *The Eloquent President,* p 170

The principles emanating from the Declaration of Independence and the Constitution were vital to the continuance of this nation and somehow, as he had at times expressed, for the betterment of the world. And it is a marvel to see that one man moving not by political or military might, but by an unwavering stand upon the principles of righteousness "as God allows us to see the right,"[500] that would strike a decisive blow upon the enormous blight of character that stained the American citizenry and the self-destructive political track on which this nation was coursing in the mid-1800s.

In August 1863, again, Lincoln felt a need to communicate a message to the public, and his old friend James C. Conkling unwittingly presented that opportunity. Conkling invited the president to attend and speak at a rally to be held in Springfield that was projected to be the "largest popular meeting of the war in support of the Union."[501] The Lincolns desperately wanted to attend and return to their beloved hometown and friends but the pressures of the war did not permit it. So again Lincoln wrote and sent his carefully prepared message to Conkling with instructions to "read it very slowly"[502] to those at the rally, knowing again that it would be published in newspapers, North and South. To an astoundingly large crowd, estimated to be between fifty thousand and seventy-five thousand Unionists assembled in Springfield, his message was read. This speech was a firm and steadfast defense of his recent administrative decisions. Beset with calls for compromise with the South abounding in the North, he affirmed that it was the long series of compromises with the Southern aristocracy that had led to this national tragedy. So under his leadership there would be no compromising; there would be nothing short of a complete reunit-

---

[500] Lincoln's Second Inaugural Address
[501] *The Eloquent President*, p 191
[502] *Lincoln*, David H. Donald, p 456

ing of the entire Union, and he made it clear that he was not about to let this divinely endowed opportunity to free the slaves slip away. After thanking his friends for the invitation and offering a tribute to "all those who maintain unconditional devotion to the Union,"[503] he turned his remarks to his detractors.

> There are those who are dissatisfied with me. To such I would say: You desire peace; and you blame me that we do not have it. But how can we attain it?[504]

He answered his own question by masterfully reviewing all possible options, as he habitually did, and then stated the option that he felt to be right "as God allow us to see it." Next he explained why he chose as he did, and then he held all listeners to be accountable for their own positions on these critical matters.

> There are but three conceivable ways. First, to suppress the rebellion by force of arms. This, I am trying to do. Are you for it? If you are, so far we are agreed. If you are not for it, a second way is, to give up the Union. I am against this. Are you for it? If you are, you should say so plainly. If you are not for <u>force,</u> nor yet for <u>dissolution,</u> there remains some imaginable <u>compromise</u>. I do not believe any compromise, embracing the maintenance of the Union is now possible.

> But to be plain, you are dissatisfied with me about the negro. Quite likely there is a difference of opinion between you and my-

---

[503] *The Eloquent President,* p 199
[504] *The Eloquent President,* p 199

self upon that subject. I certainly wish all men could be free, while I suppose you do not...

You dislike the emancipation proclamation; and, perhaps, would have it retracted. You say it is unconstitutional—I think differently. I think the constitution invests its Commander-in-Chief, with the law of war, in time of war.[505]

He went on to explain that among the provisions in the law of war is one that allows for property to be taken when confiscation of such property would aid in the defense the nation. It was the Southern lawmakers' success at legally defining their slaves as mere property, coupled with the war and the accompanying constitutionally granted war powers given to the president, that opened the *legal* door for the abolishment of the "peculiar institution." It was Lincoln's firm although unpopular belief that the blacks would be capable soldiers and that the infusion of tens of thousands of these soldiers would not only turn the tide of the war in the Union's favor; it would hasten the end to the horrific bloodshed. In the letter he again affirmed that there would be no retreating from the emancipation process by saying simply, "Promises being made must be kept."[506] It is a fair question to ask: to what promises was he referring? And it is quite possible that in Lincoln's frame of mind at that time, these "promises made" were as much the promises he personally made to his Maker as any others made to the public.

You say you will not fight to free the negroes. Some of them seem willing to fight for you; but, no matter. Fight you, then exclusively

---

[505] *The Eloquent President,* p 201
[506] *Lincoln,* David H. Donald, p 456

to save the Union. I issued the proclamation on purpose to aid you in saving the Union. Whenever you shall have conquered all resistance to the Union, if I shall urge you to continue fighting, it will be apt time, then, for you to declare you will not fight to free negroes.[507]

Then he reminded them that when peace would eventually be restored:

There will be some black men who can remember that, with silent tongue, and clenched teeth, and steady eye, and well-poised bayonet, they helped mankind on to this great consummation, while, I fear, there will be some white ones, unable to forget that, with malignant heart, and deceitful speech, they have strove to hinder it.[508]

Referring to the war he assured them that "the signs look better" with the recent victory at Vicksburg and the renewed command of the Father of Waters (the Mississippi River). He concluded his message with a heartfelt expression of gratitude for the brave soldiers: "For the great republic—for the principle it lives by, and keeps alive—for man's vast future,—thanks to all."[509]

The large crowd in Springfield enthusiastically received his message, and as expected, every major newspaper covered the letter. Lincoln's friend and colleague Charles Sumner called it "a

---

[507] *The Eloquent President*, p 203
[508] *Lincoln*, David H. Donald, p 456
[509] *Lincoln*, David H. Donald, p 457

true and noble letter, which is an historic document."[510] The *New York Times* praised the once-beleaguered president by characterizing him as a "ruler who is so peculiarly adapted to the needs of the time, as clearheaded, dispassionate, discreet, steadfast, honest Abraham Lincoln."[511] The often-critical *Chicago Tribune* responded to the letter as being "one of those remarkably clear and forcible documents that come only from Mr. Lincoln's pen," ending their editorial with "God bless Old Abe!"[512] His message was reread in a large gathering in New York City, where it "was received with shouts, cheers, thanksgiving, and tears."[513] In the coming weeks Lincoln's popularity soared. The *Chicago Tribune* again could not withhold its praise, saying that Lincoln was "the most popular man in the United States," and that were the election for President to be held tomorrow, Old Abe would, without the special aid of any of his friends, walk over the course, without a competitor to dispute with him the great prize which his masterful ability, no less than his undoubted patriotism and unimpeachable honesty have won.[514]

Later that year, he issued his Thanksgiving Proclamation in which he "[invited] his fellow citizens in every part of the United States…to set apart and observe the last Thursday of November next, as a day of Thanksgiving and Praise to our beneficent Father who dwelleth in the Heavens."[515] He opened the proclamation by specifically outlining the numerous blessings that this nation had received in spite of the war and then declared:

---

[510] *Lincoln*, David H. Donald, p 457
[511] *Lincoln*, David H. Donald, p 457
[512] *Lincoln*, David H. Donald, p 457
[513] *Lincoln*, David H. Donald, p 457
[514] *Lincoln*, David H. Donald, p 458
[515] Thanksgiving Proclamation, Abraham Lincoln, October 3, 1863

No human counsel hath delivered nor hath any mortal hand worked out these things. They are the gracious gifts of the Most High God, who, while *dealing with us in anger for our sins* [italics added], hath nevertheless remembered mercy. And I recommend to them that while offering up the ascriptions justly due to Him for such singular deliverances and blessings, they do also, with *humble penitence for our national perverseness and disobedience* [italics added], commend to his tender care all those who have become widows, orphans, mourners or sufferers in the lamentable civil strife in which we are unavoidably engaged, and fervently implore the interposition of the Almighty Hand to heal the wounds of the nation and to *restore it as soon as may be consistent with Divine purposes* [italics added] to the full enjoyment of peace, harmony, tranquility and Union.[516]

From the beginning of the war and throughout its entirety, the city of Charleston, South Carolina was on the minds of nearly all Americans. Its wartime status was eagerly followed in newspapers throughout the continent. For the Southerners, Charleston became the honored birthplace of secession. It was in Charleston that the first Secession Convention was held and where, with a vote of 169 to 0, the South Carolina delegates, disproportionately selected for their pro-secession opinions, voted to rebel against the United States and to become their own nation. They were also the first to become an enemy to the United States by forcefully seizing the U.S. munitions arsenal stationed in Charleston and the U.S. forts throughout South

---

[516] Thanksgiving Proclamation, Abraham Lincoln, October 3, 1863

Carolina. And it was in Charleston Harbor where the first shots were fired on the government's Fort Sumter. To the citizens in the North, Charleston became the focal point of resentment for having precipitated the terrible war. To the Union military, Charleston and Richmond, Virginia, the capital of the Confederacy, became the focal point of their offensives, knowing that the successful invasion of either would mark a significant turning point in the war. But both cities were heavily fortified and it wasn't until late 1864, four years from the start of the war, that they were successfully vanquished. Had either of these cities fallen earlier in the war, the duration of the war would quite likely have been shortened. The U.S. Navy spent the entire four years of war in unsuccessfully gaining entry to Charleston because it was so heavily and skillfully protected.

In 1863 federal forces succeeded in capturing Morris Island at the mouth of Charleston Harbor, placing them within firing distance of the highly symbolic Fort Sumter and Charleston, both now occupied and heavily fortified by Confederate troops and artillery. The Union forces immediately set to work at building their own batteries with guns trained on the island fort. In July the first Union cannon fired upon Fort Sumter and would mark the beginning of a year-and-a-half siege of continuous shelling of the fort that refused to surrender.

July 1863 also marked the beginning of a nearly two-year artillery siege on the emotional target of Charleston. Deliberate targeting and destruction of an entire city had not been a part of the war efforts by either the North or South until this point, but Charleston was different because of its perceived role in the war. Union army chief of staff General Henry Halleck's letter to General William Tecumseh Sherman on his dramatic and devastating approach to Charleston toward the end of the war in 1864 sums up the feelings of many in the North: "...should you capture Charleston, I hope by some accident that the place be destroyed, and if a little salt should be sown on the site it may prevent the future growth of nullification and secession."[517]

Those whose properties had survived Charleston's highly destructive fire of December 1861 were now terrorized by the constant shelling of the city, the "viper's nest of secession,"[518] which compelled most of them to leave their comfortable homes and businesses. Many of these evacuated homes and businesses would later be occupied by Confederate soldiers stationed there to defend against a ground attack by Union troops. They looted the remaining homes and businesses that were fortunate enough to remain unoccupied by the soldiers. Eighteen-year-old Augustine T. Smythe, son of a minister from Charleston, was one of those Confederate soldiers. He wrote a number of letters to his family who had evacuated to avoid the shelling. These letters chronicle the damage to the city and the status of their family home:

> Our soldiers are doing us more damage than the shells. I would much prefer a shell to go thro' the house than to let them do so. They just roam at will through the whole lower portion of the city. They have done three times the damage to the city that the shells have done. This [is] a shame. The soldiers stole lead pipe, copper kitchen boilers, lead from bathing tubs and pantry, pumps from cisterns, and brass fixtures. This scrap they sold to the ordinance office, getting as much as $1 per pound for bronze from chandeliers.[519]

In another letter he wrote:

---

[517] *Charlston At War*, Jack Thomson, p 5
[518] *Charlston At War*, Jack Thomson, p 5
[519] *Charlston At War*, Jack Thomson, p 168

The Yanks have been shelling all morning throwing the shells well into the City & nearly all of them bursting. They shell now nearly every day...A shell struck the pavement in front of our gate, knocking off a small piece of the wall....The garden is in fine condition. The rose-trees are all budding and will be magnificent if the shells don't spoil it all. *To Mother, 12/20/63*[520]

[Our big dog] Don is still in the yard & is a great protection. All of the solders are afraid of him & none of them will venture to go into the yard. This is fortunate for our pumps & pipes, nearly every yard in our neighborhood has been rifled.[521]

Barker's lot [next door, to the south], is ruined.[522]
John Bennett recorded that a group of soldiers were eating breakfast in a nearby home when

> a Federal shell broke through the house-wall, penetrated the floor and fetched up in the cellar. So familiar were all with the nature of shells and shell fire, bomb-explosion, and the like, that no one left his seat, or left off eating the food before him; as each one knew that if the shell was to explode at all the explosion would be instantaneous; and not a man would have an instant's reprieve from immediate death; that if the shell did not explode at once, the likelihood was that it would not explode at all; in which the best thing to do was just to go

---

[520] *Charlston At War*, Jack Thomson, p 153
[521] *Charlston At War*, Jack Thomson, p 153
[522] *Charlston At War*, Jack Thomson, p 153

on doing what they were busy about, and finish their breakfast.[523]

Two [shells] fell into the street exactly in front of our house, between us & Mr. Roper. One of these I had dug up, & as it is a large one, a 100 pdr., have put it by the small one which came in to the house as mementoes...Tuesday several fell in our yard, one even coming into the house, & into this room. *Aunt Janey, 8/4/64*[524]

The federal artillerymen on Morris Island, some four and one half miles away, would often use the steeple of St. Michael's Church as their aiming point, it being the most visible landmark from that distance. The Confederates also used it as an observation point. In fact young Augustine was assigned frequent duty in the steeple.

My very dear Mother,
I have just been ordered on duty in St. Michaels Steeple. March 28, 1864...Here I am on my lofty perch, behind a big telescope, looking out for any movements of the Yankees...It is quite interesting to watch them, as we have a splendid glass.
My very dear Mother 3/31/64[525]

They struck the Court House steps the other day. Yesterday they aimed at the steeple & the shells flew round here thick and fast. Thir-

---

[523] *Charlston At War*, Jack Thomson, p 155
[524] *Charlston At War*, Jack Thomson, p 162
[525] *Charlston At War*, Jack Thomson, p 162

teen fell between Queen St. & St. Michael's alley...[526]

After months of continued shelling of the mostly deserted
yet near impenetrably defended city, the arrival of Sherman's
army at Savannah, fresh from their razing of Atlanta in February 1865, made it clear that rebel forces would have to end their
gallant defense of their prized city, Charleston. Young Augustine T. Smythe wrote this final note from Charleston: "I am
afraid Charleston is doomed...We are expecting orders to leave
tomorrow, or even tonight. Dear old Charleston. My heart is
very sad." *To Miss Lou, 2/14/65*[527] "Despite the alertness of the
Federals, however, the Confederates slipped away like shadows
on the night of February 17, 1865,"[528] just three months prior
to Lee's surrender to Grant at Appomattox, Virginia.

The following morning, after raising the Stars and Stripes
over Fort Sumter, five federal officers and twenty-two soldiers
cautiously rowed the five miles from their post to the Cooper
River piers and climbed ashore, the first Union soldiers to set
foot in Charleston since the war began four years earlier at this
very place. Charleston had fallen. And the magnitude of its fall
is astounding. After the fire of December of 1861 destroyed
nearly a third of the city, the two years of bombing by federals
and looting by Confederate soldiers had left one of America's
most beautiful cities in a state of ruin and abandonment. The
once-wealthy planters and businessmen were also left in ruin.
Before the war, some twenty banks thrived in the city; all but
one folded. What plantations survived foreclosure for unpaid
debts and the burning, looting, and the freeing of slaves by
General Sherman's army, as well as other advancing Union

---

[526] *Charlston At War,* Jack Thomson, p 162
[527] *Charlston At War,* Jack Thomson
[528] *Charlston At War,* Jack Thomson, p 180

forces from the now-open port in Charleston, had no slaves to work the plantations. Many a once-wealthy aristocratic Southern survivor of the war now had only his own hands to push the plow, while the women, with no slaves to cook, clean, or garden, had to learn to do it for themselves. The two-hundred-fifty-year injustice of eating their bread by the sweat of another man's brow, as Lincoln had so often expressed it, had come to an end in America.

The presence of the Union army, having occupied the once great city of Charleston without firing a shot, dealt a severe blow to the staggering Confederate rebellion. But it was an even more poignant picture to see the once-beautiful streets of Charleston now occupied by hundreds of Union soldiers who were, in fact, African-American Union soldiers. Men who just days and weeks earlier were freed from the generations of bondage—former slaves, now with musket in hand and military authority—walked freely through the city: a dramatic ending to two and a half centuries of slavery in America. And nowhere to be found were the original signers of the secession declaration in their beloved city. Their lives were riddled with grief and despair from lost sons, fathers, brothers, and fortunes. After the Union occupation of Charleston, Union soldiers watched as "hundreds of poor free-men and women" came to the "Invalids Commissary," where "tickets are issued to needy families, two thirds being colored...Many millionaires...are reduced by the war, to want, penury and beggary...The [chief] cashier of the Bank of Charleston comes every day to [the] store, to get his peck of rice or meal."[529] The scene at this time in Charleston was one of the great ironies of the Civil War, with the absence and ruin of the myriad of once-wealthy slave-owning aristocrats and the Fathers of the Secession being replaced by hundreds of

---

[529] *Charlston At War*, Jack Thomson, p 182

former slaves, now free and in Union army uniforms, occupying the streets of their once great and proud city.

Weeks earlier, General William Tecumseh Sherman conquered and burned Atlanta, then Savannah, cutting a sixty-mile-wide swath of destruction on his fearful march. Sherman's awful advance toward Charleston took an unexpected turn to the northwest, and instead of entering the now vanquished and demolished Charleston, Sherman's troops took their machine of destruction to Columbia, South Carolina, the capital of the once-great secession state. Columbia was burned and surrounding plantations similarly destroyed.

Chapter Ten

"The Almighty Has His Own Purposes"

The fall of 1863 brought a lull in the war and Lincoln began to think of another message to the citizens, one that would communicate the vast significance of this war. In November 1863, Lincoln quite surprisingly accepted an invitation to speak, something he had regularly turned down throughout his presidency. The occasion was the dedication of a new Soldiers' National Cemetery on the Gettysburg battlefield. The celebrated orator Edward Everett would be the principal speaker and it was anticipated that he would draw a large crowd. President Lincoln was invited to follow Everett's oration to "set apart these grounds to their sacred use by a few appropriate remarks."[530] One would not be surprised to have a president of the United States turn down an offer to be second billing at this or any highly public event but Lincoln readily accepted the invitation and the terms. He would give "a *few* appropriate remarks," and he would humbly follow the featured speaker, just as they asked. He accepted the invitation because he felt the setting at Gettysburg, which had stunned both North and South with the enormity of the loss of life, to be a suitable setting to restate to the whole of America his resolve to stay the course

---

[530] *Lincoln*, David Herbert Donald, p 460

and win this terrible war for the original purpose of preserving the Union and with the added purpose of freeing the slaves. He also knew that the newspapers throughout the country would eagerly pick up, this isolated message once again. Lincoln was beginning to see that the Union cause might at last be prevailing in the horrific conflict. And even though the Union sustained a staggering 23,049 casualties in that epic Gettysburg battle compared to the Confederacy's losses of 28,063, the Union, with its infusion by that time of some 100,000 freed African-Americans into the Union army and its stronger base of resources, weathered the terrible losses much better than did the Confederacy. The sight of Robert E. Lee in retreat was a rare event in the war, and the Union victory at Gettysburg was in every way a crippling defeat to the Confederacy. Lincoln was exultant with gratitude over the news of the great victory and issued a press release to the nation. As notable as its brief contents was what Lincoln did not say in the message. There were no words assailing the Southern rebellion, nor jubilant words of victory, nor was there political rhetoric to rally support for himself and his upcoming bid for reelection. Instead all he chose to express was his deep gratitude to his God by admonishing God's children to do the same:

> *that on this day, He whose will, not ours, should ever be done, be everywhere remembered and reverenced with profound gratitude.*[531]

The victory at Gettysburg was followed shortly thereafter by news that U. S. Grant's Union forces had prevailed at the highly important Vicksburg campaign, giving the Union full access to the Mississippi River. There, the Union army lost 4,550 men

---

[531] *Lincoln*, David Herbert Donald, p 446

while the Confederacy sustained astonishing losses, at 31,275 killed and captured. The Confederacy's war efforts suffered another damaging blow. Although fierce and costly fighting would continue for still another year, the Union continued to gradually gain the upper hand in the war.

Edward Everett arrived at the Gettysburg speakers' podium thirty minutes late, keeping the president and the crowd, estimated at between fifteen thousand and twenty-five thousand people, waiting while he conducted his personal tour of the battlefield. He spoke for two hours and eight minutes and the standing crowd responded with "polite applause."[532] Lincoln arose to address the somewhat tired and restless audience and, to the surprise of all—including the photographer who failed in his assignment to take a picture of Lincoln at the podium—who were expecting him to speak much longer, was back in his seat three minutes later.

Lincoln opened his address with a Biblical style found in Psalms 90 by using the phrase "Four score and seven years ago" rather than simply saying eighty-seven years ago. "The psalms were a favorite portion of the Bible for Lincoln,"[533] and the book interestingly consists of communications with praises for, and prayers to God. "At noontime in the Executive Mansion, or early in the mornings...multiple observers have left independent reports of Lincoln's love of reading the Bible, especially the psalms."[534] Captain Mix, who was frequently invited to breakfast at the White House, records,

> Many times have I listened to our most eloquent preachers, but never with the same feeling of love and reverence, as when our Christian Pres-

---

[532] *The Eloquent President*, Ronald C. White, Jr., p 242
[533] *The Eloquent President*, Ronald C. White, Jr., p 243
[534] *The Eloquent President*, Ronald C. White, Jr., p 243

ident, his arm around his son, each morning read a
chapter from the Bible.[535]

"At Gettysburg he was not only retrieving biblical words,
but employing a biblical cadence expressed in the rhythms of
the King James Version that he thought appropriate for the
solemnity of the day."[536]

> Four score and seven years ago our fathers
> brought forth on this continent, a new nation,
> conceived in Liberty, and dedicated to the
> proposition that all men are created equal.

Lincoln used his humble Gettysburg address to remind every
American of the critical link they had to the origins and purposes of this nation and its foundation. This link to the Founding
Fathers was something he had expressed dozens of times over
the years as he boldly communicated the need for fundamental
changes in the people and government of the United States to
preserve their original cause. The difference with this speech
was the fact that, at Gettysburg, he was speaking with the authority of the president of the United States and he used this
venue to affirm his presidential resolve to effect these fundamental changes: his was a determined stand to reclaim the broken Union that it might again be whole and strong, and to free
the slaves because "all men were created equal," and because
the addition of the tens of thousands of willing African-
American soldiers was needed to win the war. Because he believed he was doing God's will, he would not bend on these
principles, nor would he let America forget that the Founding
Fathers were far from foolish and erring men for proclaiming

---

[535] *Six Months in the White House*, p. 262
[536] *The Eloquent President*, Ronald C. White, Jr., p 243

that all men were created equal, as many proslavery politicians had propounded.

> Now we are engaged in a great civil war, testing whether this nation, or any nation so conceived and so dedicated, can long endure.

Lincoln saw that the United States was on the brink of dissolution at the ungrateful hands of the very children of God, who were the recipients of these unprecedented freedoms. In the experiment of a new nation governed "of the people, by the people, and for the people," two of the three critical tests that he had expressed in an earlier speech to Congress had been passed: the establishing of such a government and the administering of it; although both were fraught with great difficulties, they had both proven to be successes. The third test of whether or not such a government could be maintained was the battle that Lincoln now superintended against what he referred to as the "formidable internal force to overthrow it."[537] This third test, to determine whether such a government could "long endure," would be by far the costliest of the three.

He then changed directions to express the words for which he was invited to the ceremony. He dedicated the battlefield to the brave men whose lives had ended here and whose blood had been spilt in battles throughout the land. His eloquence and depth of feeling are unmatched.

> We are met on a great battle-field of that war. We have come to dedicate a portion of that field, as a final resting place for those who here gave their lives that that nation might live.

---

[537] *The Eloquent President*, Ronald C. White, Jr., p 245

It is altogether fitting and proper that we should do this.

But, in a larger sense, we cannot dedicate— we can not consecrate—we can not hallow— this ground. The brave men, living and dead, who struggled here, have consecrated it, far above our poor power to add or detract. The world will little note, nor long remember what we say here, but it can never forget what they did here.

Lincoln suffered personally and deeply at the enormity of the loss of life during the war. He was constantly reminded of the depth of pain and grief experienced by families everywhere over the loss of a loved one, especially with the ache in his own heart over the passing of his and Mary's own beloved sons, Eddie and Willie.

Lincoln then turned his remarks to those of admonishment to all in America as to their responsibility to protect and preserve these freedoms that were, at this time, so seriously threatened with extinction. And although nearly all in the Confederate effort would quickly clarify that they had no intention of eliminating these treasured freedoms, Lincoln could clearly see that "the house divided against itself" (another phrase which he garnered from God's Holy Scripture) could not have the strength to withstand "the formidable internal attempt to overthrow it."[538] And he knew that these freedoms hung precariously on the Union's success or failure in the appalling civil conflict.

It is for the living, rather, to be dedicated here to the unfinished work which they who

---

[538] *The Eloquent President*, Ronald C. White, Jr., p 245

fought here have thus far so nobly advanced. It is rather for us to be here dedicated to the great task remaining before us—that from these honored dead we take increased devotion to that cause for which they gave the last full measure of devotion—that we here highly resolve that these dead shall not have died in vain—that this nation, under God, shall have a new birth of freedom—and that government of the people, by the people, for the people, shall not perish from the earth.[539]

Following the speech, Lincoln doubted its effectiveness and said to his aide, Ward Hill Lamon, "Lamon, that speech won't scour! It is a flat failure, and the people are disappointed."[540] Edward Everett and Lincoln's secretary of state, William Seward, agreed that it had missed its mark. All three were mistaken. David Herbert Donald points out that the effectiveness of the speech was revealed in the intensity of the response by the Northern opposition. The New York *World* sharply responded with "This United States was not a product of the Declaration of Independence's claim that all men are created equal, but rather on the Constitution which says nothing about equality."[541] "The ultra-Democratic *Chicago Times* recognized that in invoking the Declaration of Independence Lincoln was announcing a new objective in the war. Calling the Gettysburg Address "a perversion of history…"[542] the paper went on to say, "The officers and men who gave their lives at Gettysburg died 'to uphold this constitution and the Union created by it' not to 'dedi-

---

[539] *The Eloquent President*, Ronald C. White, Jr., p 223

[540] *The Eloquent President*, Ronald C. White, Jr., p 234

[541] *Lincoln*, David Herbert Donald, p 466

[542] *Lincoln*, David Herbert Donald, p 466

cate the nation to the proposition that all men are created equal.'"[543]

Donald, regarding the effects of Lincoln's speech, says, "The bitterness of these protests was evidence that Lincoln had succeeded in broadening the aims of the war from Union to Equality and Union."[544] Armed with his newfound conviction that it was God's will that the slaves be set free, along with his newfound presidential authority to confiscate the slave "property" in time of war, Lincoln was determined to complete the unthinkable and utilize the war itself as the tool to bring about the full eradication of slavery. And as the critics correctly pointed out, he had successfully used his Gettysburg Address to ensure the implantation of equality as a main issue to be dealt with. The favorable response to the speech by the rest of the nation confirmed Lincoln's successful introduction of the precept of racial equality as a new objective in the war.

The arrival of 1864 brought a buzz and anticipation for the November presidential election. Lincoln, in the first two and one half years of his presidency, made no mention in writings or speeches of interest or intent to run for reelection. No president since Andrew Jackson had been reelected, some thirty years earlier. David Herbert Donald said,

> But, for all the burdens of his office, he did desire reelection. As he would remark later, he viewed a second term not as just a personal compliment but as an expression of the people's belief that he could 'better finish a difficult work...than could any one less severely schooled to the task.[545]

---

[543] *Lincoln*, David Herbert Donald, p 466
[544] *Lincoln*, David Herbert Donald, p 466
[545] *Lincoln*, David Herbert Donald, p 474

As the months rolled on, candidates emerged to oppose Lincoln, but, as custom dictated, it was improper for a candidate to openly campaign for office, allowing Lincoln to focus the bulk of his attention on the pressing matters of war and let the election process run its course.

Remarkably, his 1863 speeches and newspaper messages together with some key Union victories reversed the tide of dissatisfaction with him and his presidency. At the Republican National Convention in June 1864, Lincoln was clearly the front-runner but being such was no guarantee that he would win against the Democratic candidate. He worried that defeat would end all that he had hoped to gain. He took advantage of his strong position to press the Republican platform to include the plank of a constitutional amendment to end slavery throughout the entire country—something he would push in his remaining year as president and something that a new president could not overthrow should Lincoln be defeated. He suggested to the party chairman that he urge the convention to "declare for such an amendment of the Constitution as will positively prohibit African slavery in the United States."[546] The proposal was greeted with resounding applause and support, opening the door for Lincoln to begin the process of garnering the needed support for the Thirteenth Amendment to the Constitution. In the first round of voting for the Republican candidate for president, Lincoln won 484 of the possible 506 votes, and the twenty-two votes from Missouri that had gone for Ulysses S. Grant (who was not even a candidate because he refused to run against Lincoln) quickly moved into Lincoln's camp. Lincoln would be the unanimous choice of the Republicans for the 1864 presidential election, to which Lincoln replied, "I will neither conceal my gratification, nor restrain the expression of my gratitude, that the Union people, through the convention…have deemed me

---

[546] *Lincoln*, David Herbert Donald, p 504

not unworthy to remain in my present position."[547] On another occasion he said,

> I confess that I desire to be re-elected. God knows I do not want the labor and responsibility of the office for another four years. But I have the common pride of humanity to wish my past four years Administration endorsed.[548]

"[I want] to finish this job of putting down the rebellion, and restoring peace and prosperity to the country."[549]

As important as his reelection was, he could not and would not devote much of his time to it. "I cannot run the political machine," he said, "I have enough on my hands without *that*. It is the *people's* business."[550] During that year he participated in none of the hundreds of pro-Lincoln campaigns and torchlight processions. He made very few public appearances in 1864 but did exert considerable effort to resolve conflicts between squabbling Republican factions that threatened to damage Republican chances in the upcoming November election. And though he was the resounding choice for the Republican ticket, he faced mounting opposition from the Democrats, who wanted compromise with the South to end the bloodshed with their "Peace at Any Price" campaign.[551] But compromise meant stepping back from freeing the slaves or a less-than-complete reunification of the states, neither of which Lincoln would do. Stephen B. Oates wrote that Horace Greeley "begged Lincoln to negotiate for peace, arguing that the people wanted the war

---

[547] *Lincoln,* David Herbert Donald, p 504
[548] *Lincoln,* David Herbert Donald, p 540
[549] *Lincoln,* David Herbert Donald, p 540
[550] *Lincoln,* David Herbert Donald, p 537
[551] *Abraham Lincoln, Man of God,* John Wesley Hill, p 299

to end."[552] Lincoln did nothing to encourage partisan newspapers that took upon themselves to discredit the Democratic ticket, nor did he make any public refutations of Democratic accusations against him and his administration. The Democrats seized upon Lincoln's expression that "it was not best to swap horses"[553] while crossing a stream to mount a "TIME TO SWAP HORSES" campaign. Democratic banners and pamphlets were distributed with this phrase. Others called Lincoln "Abraham Africanus the First," with the first of the president's own Ten Commandments reading, "Thou shalt have no other God but the negro."[554] The race had the appearance of a close one but Lincoln refused to bow to pressure by Republicans to rush the admittance process of the proposed new states of Colorado and Nebraska, and to readmit the two partially reconstructed states, Louisiana and Tennessee—all of which would have brought him additional electoral votes. Nor would he be moved by conservative Republicans who were certain that the Emancipation Proclamation had to be dropped in order to win reelection. He was not about to remove the critically important black Union soldiers from the battlefields, saying, "I would be damned in time and eternity"[555] if he backed away from freeing the slaves. If he was to win, he would do it fairly. He stated emphatically, "Except it be to give protection against violence, I decline to intervene in any way with any presidential election."[556]

Lincoln's Democratic opponent was George McClellan, his former leading general of the Union forces. McClellan thought Lincoln to be an imbecile and stated so often. McClellan, while

---

[552] *With Malice Toward None*, Stephen B. Oates, p 395

[553] *Lincoln*, David Herbert Donald, p 537

[554] *Lincoln*, David Herbert Donald, p 537

[555] *With Malice Toward None*, Stephen B. Oates, p 395

[556] *Lincoln*, David Herbert Donald, p 540

commanding the Union forces, did so much complaining and so little fighting that Lincoln was forced to replace him. One night during the early years of the war, Lincoln and Seward called upon General McClellan at his headquarters to discuss a pressing military matter. He was not in at the time but was expected shortly. When he arrived he nodded curtly to his distinguished visitors and went directly up the stairs to his bedroom. After some time, the visitors inquired as to the delay, and were told that the general had retired to his bed and would see them on the morrow. Seward was incensed at McClellan's insolence, but Lincoln quietly left and said not another word about it.

As 1864 pressed on, Lincoln—weary of the war's length and unthinkable casualties—pushed hard for victory. He had finally found some generals who would fight in Grant, Phil Sheridan, and William T. Sherman; but with the increased victories came additional defeats. It seemed that his efforts were stymied on nearly every side. "At times he even despaired," observed David H. Donald, "and increasingly he came to feel that the outcome of the war, and of his administration, was in the hands of a Higher Power."[557] The final year of Lincoln's term brought some of the heaviest fighting of the war. Intense fighting during a six-week period that summer caused nearly one hundred thousand killed and wounded Union soldiers alone. Lincoln continued to suffer for the expansive death and destruction that would not seem to end. During this especially difficult time, his friend Isaac N. Arnold recorded that Lincoln was "grave and anxious, and he looked like one who had lost the dearest member of his own family."[558] One evening, while riding with Arnold, as they passed a long line of ambulances carrying wounded and dying soldiers, Lincoln in deep sadness lamented, "Look

---

[557] *Lincoln,* David Herbert Donald, p 493
[558] *Lincoln,* David Herbert Donald, p 513

yonder at those poor fellows. I cannot bear it. This suffering, this loss of life is dreadful."[559]

To another friend, Representative Daniel Voorhees of Indiana, he said,

> Doesn't it seem strange to you that I should be here? Doesn't it strike you as queer that I, who couldn't cut the head off of a chicken, and who was sick at the sight of blood, should be cast into the middle of a great war, with blood flowing all about me?[560]

David Herbert Donald observed that "all [Lincoln's] exertions could not erase the knowledge that in the final analysis he was responsible for all the suffering."[561] Donald continues: "...with the burden of a never-ending war weighing ever more heavily upon his shoulders, he reverted to [the Bible] more and more frequently."[562] Lincoln sought for solace and found it in prayer and in reading the Bible. He told General Daniel Sickles, "I talk to God because my mind is relieved when I do." He added, "When I could not see any other resort, I would place my whole reliance in God, knowing that all would be well, and that He would decide for the right."[563]

The Reverend Dr. Newell Dwight Hill recorded:

> I have a woman in my congregation who is the daughter of the Presbyterian minister in whose church Mr. Lincoln worshipped during the war. She says: Mr. Lincoln frequently came to

---

[559] *Lincoln*, David Herbert Donald, p 513

[560] *Lincoln*, David Herbert Donald, p 513

[561] *Lincoln*, David Herbert Donald, p 513

[562] *Lincoln*, David Herbert Donald, p 514

[563] *Abraham Lincoln's Daily Treasures*, Thomas Freiling, p 11

our house in the evening, stopped at the door, and said to my father, Doctor, you must pray to-night. One night he called at half-past one, called my father up and said, Doctor you must come down and go to my room with me. I need you. My father went and found Mr. Lincoln's room strewn with maps, where he was marking out the movements of the troops. He said to my father, 'There is your room. You go in there and pray, and I will stay here and watch.' My father heard him repeatedly praying for the Army. Three times he came to my father's room and fell down on his face on the floor by his side and prayed mightily to God to bless the boys about to die for the Republic, and to save the Republic.[564]

On a night during the war's dreadful 1864 summer, Lincoln was seeking such solace in the Bible when his old friend from Springfield, Joshua Speed, came to visit and said, "I'm glad to see you are so profitable engaged," referring to Lincoln's worn and well-used Bible in his hand.

"Yes," said the president, "I am profitably engaged."

"Well," commented the visitor, "if you have recovered from your skepticism, I am sorry to say that I have not."

Looking intently at his friend, Lincoln replied, "You are wrong Speed, take all of this book upon reason that you can, and the balance on faith, and you will live and die a happier and better man."[565] This comment reflected a similar sentiment expressed to a delegation of African-Americans from Baltimore who had presented him with a beautifully bound Bible, as an expression of their gratitude for the Emancipation Proclama-

---

[564] *Abraham Lincoln, Man of God*, John Wesley Hill, p 299
[565] *Lincoln*, David Herbert Donald, p 514

tion and his determination to hold to it. He said to them, "This Great Book...is the best gift God has given to man."[566]

When asked by another friend and newspaper editor why he had diverted from his inaugural pledge of noninterference with slavery, Lincoln explained, "I claim not to have controlled events, but confess plainly that events have controlled me." He continued, "Now at the end of three years struggle the nation's condition is not what either party, or any man devised, or expected. God alone can claim it."[567] David Herbert Donald notes, "again and again he reverted to the idea that behind all the struggles and losses of the war a Divine purpose was at work."[568] Lincoln eloquently expressed this conviction in a letter he wrote in September 1864 to Mrs. Eliza P. Gurney, who extended the sympathy and prayers of the Society of Friends:

> The purposes of the Almighty are perfect and must prevail, though we erring mortals may fail to accurately perceive them in advance. We hoped for a happy termination of this terrible war long before this; but God knows best, and has ruled otherwise...we must work earnestly in the best light He gives us, trusting that so working still conduces to the great ends He ordains. Surely He intends some great good to follow this mighty convulsion, which no mortal could make, and no mortal could stay.[569]

September 1864 brought electrifying news. Atlanta had fallen to Sherman and Sheridan was victorious at Shenandoah; the

---

[566] *Lincoln*, David Herbert Donald, p 514

[567] *Lincoln*, David Herbert Donald, p 514

[568] *Lincoln*, David Herbert Donald, p 514

[569] *Lincoln*, David Herbert Donald, p 514

two victories landed crippling blows to the rebel cause. Lincoln was so encouraged and grateful for the victories that he pronounced them "a gift of God" and proclaimed the following Sunday a day of national thanksgiving.

Pressure continued from North and South for Lincoln to negotiate with and make concessions to the rebels. But Lincoln said that even though such negotiations would certainly "end the struggle," they would also mean that the horrendous loss of life by Union soldiers would be in vain. And returning slaves to their masters in the South would be catastrophic to the Union cause, removing them from the Union military ranks. Perhaps Lincoln also recognized that once the slaves were returned, nothing could stop the South from changing the uniforms of the one hundred eighty thousand black soldiers to gray and turning them on the North. No, Lincoln remained firm; he was not about to let these divine endowments slip away. He told his detractors to keep his policies "and you can save the Union. Throw it away, and the Union goes with it."[570] On this, Stephen B. Oates said, "So long as he was in office, he would not violate his promise of freedom to black people. He would accept no measure that would re-enslave them." "It can *not* be," Lincoln resounded.[571]

Riding this wave of popularity and support augmented by the September military victories, Lincoln turned his efforts to the preparation of the hearts and minds of the Northern citizens for his addressing of what he called "the greatest question ever presented to practical statesmanship."[572] How would he safely and peacefully reintroduce the Southern states back into the Union at the war's conclusion? Lincoln had no interest in domination of their recalcitrant Southern brothers; he wanted inclusion and he wanted forgiveness. He wanted the South's

---

[570] *With Malice Toward None*, Stephen B. Oates, p 395
[571] *With Malice Toward None*, Stephen B. Oates, p 395
[572] *Lincoln*, David Herbert Donald, p 467

elected representatives back in their rightful seats in Congress and on the judicial benches; but just how the now-bitter enemies could suddenly become collaborating fellow-citizens once again was a task of immense proportions, and one that no man on earth except one—the backwoods American president, Abraham Lincoln—had any hope of accomplishing. By this time, most in America knew that if any man could lead them through such a daunting task it would be their now-revered, wise, and kindly president.

As widely varying plans and strategies of reunification floated about Washington, Lincoln's cabinet member Montgomery Blair flatly said that the "safe and healing policy of the President" was the proper way to restore the Union.[573] Through 1864, as Union victory appeared more imminent, there were voices from all sides and all approaches to the matter. Many viewed the situation "through a glass, darkly," demanding revenge, justice, trials, confiscation of properties, incarceration, and hangings for those in the South who led the rebellion.[574] Lincoln, once again, saw it differently. In his eyes and expansive perspective, those in the North were still desperately in need of redemption for their own transgressions and were in no position in the sight of God to demand retribution. Lincoln saw that it would again take the intervention of God to enact such a formidable reunification, and the key to the Almighty's mediation would be forgiveness on the part of all. In both the North and South, the people needed to forgive each other's trespasses so that they might be finally forgiven, by the mercy and grace of God, for their own. And both sides, especially those in the South who had suffered untold judgments for their transgressions, had certainly been made to feel the indignation and chastening hand of an Almighty God. Lincoln saw that the time was approaching for peace, forgiveness, and inclusion. Lincoln be-

---

[573] *Lincoln*, David Herbert Donald, p 470
[574] I Corinthians 13:12

lieved that this would be this erring nation's best hope for meriting God's merciful intervention to bring reconciliation and reunion.

Lincoln used his January 1864 address to Congress, with more than a year of bitter fighting still ahead, to announce a proclamation of amnesty and reconstruction for the returning South. He told them that "there is no greater task before us," then he declared a "full pardon...with restoration of all rights of property, except as to slaves," to all rebels.[575] The great task" before them, once reunited, was how to prevent the rebel majority in the Southern states from "outvoting and overwhelming the loyalist minority and thus restoring the old Southern ruling class to power."[576] Lincoln wrote his reconstruction plan to "virtually outlaw the old Southern rulers, so that loyal Unionists—the former Whigs and antisecessionists—could become the new leaders in Dixie."[577] High-ranking members of the Confederate government and military would have to swear an oath of loyalty to the Union and the Constitution, with a pledge to obey acts of Congress and presidential proclamations relating to slavery. David Herbert Donald explained,

> The requirement that rebels must swear to uphold the legislation and proclamations ending slavery was necessary to prevent any attempt at reenslavement of the newly freed blacks, which would be 'a cruel and astounding breach of faith,' and [Lincoln] went on to pledge, buoyed by his assurance that God was in this great deliverance, 'While I remain in my present position I shall not attempt to retract or modify the emancipation proclamation; nor

---

[575] *Lincoln*, David Herbert Donald, p 470
[576] *With Malice Toward None*, Stephen B. Oates, p 370
[577] *With Malice Toward None*, Stephen B. Oates, p 371

> shall I return to slavery any person who is free
> by the terms of that proclamation.'[578]

Lincoln left no doubt as to the firmness of his resolve to retain the divinely endowed gift found in the demise of slavery in this land of promise.

Even though he could see that the war's end was still at some distance away, he wanted the citizens of the United States to clearly understand the position of their now-beloved and respected leader. He knew that this concept of extending the hand of forgiveness, acceptance, and love for neighbor and enemy alike, of which so many Americans read and claimed to believe in their own Bibles, would need some time to work in the minds and hearts of the people, both North and South. And he hoped that in time, they would come to accept that the principles of mercy and compassion, rather than more iniquity in the form of revenge and retribution, would be the only possible implements capable of inviting the approbation and intervention of the Almighty God in the colossal task of reconstruction and unification. And with that same faith of our Founding Fathers, Lincoln fully believed that no such reunification could be hoped for without the merciful hand of his Lord and Redeemer.

The effect of this message, again read by a clerk to members of Congress, was, in the words of John Hay, "something wonderful."[579] He reported that "men acted as if the millennium had come."[580] Lincoln had managed to satisfy each of the fractious three groups in Washington: the conservative Republicans, the Radical Republicans, and by and large the Democrats. Most importantly, he had sown the seed of hope for the tired and beleaguered Southerners that a Union victory would be accompanied by charity and an absence of malice. Horace Greeley's

---

[578] *Lincoln*, David Herbert Donald, p 472
[579] *Lincoln*, David Herbert Donald, p 473
[580] *With Malice Toward None*, Stephen B. Oates, p 372

radical *New York Tribune* "declared that no presidential message since George Washington's had 'given such general satisfaction.'"[581]

Later that year in April, Lincoln wrote what he referred to as a "Little Speech" for Albert G. Hodges, editor of the *Frankfort Commonwealth*; one of the prominent newspapers in Kentucky. Again, Lincoln knew that this message would be printed in newspapers throughout the country. Lincoln had become proficient in drafting public letters for the sake of influencing the minds and hearts of Americans. Hodges had traveled to Washington with the governor of Kentucky to express their consternation over the Union army's recruitment of black troops in their state. Lincoln granted them a long interview and at the end asked them if he could make "a little speech" to clearly state his position.

> I am naturally anti-slavery. If slavery is not wrong, nothing is wrong. I can not remember when I did not so think and feel. And yet I have never understood that the Presidency conferred upon me an unrestricted right to act officially upon this judgment and feeling.

> I claim not to have controlled events, but confess that events have controlled me. Now, at the end of three years struggle the nation's condition is not what either party, or any man devised, or expected. God alone can claim it...If God now wills the removal of a great wrong, and wills also that we of the North as well as you of the South, shall pay fairly for our complicity in that wrong, impartial history will find

---

[581] *Lincoln*, David Herbert Donald, p 473

therein new cause to attest and revere the justice
and goodness of God.[582]

Present in this message, as in nearly all other messages he
gave to the country, was his conviction that God was the silent
architect of the war, and what was taking place in America at
that time was just and righteous. Ronald C. White states, "A
close reading of the paragraph reveals that Lincoln is intent on
pointing beyond himself and his activity to God's activity in
history."[583]

Election day, November 8, 1864, finally arrived with the Republicans garnering a decidedly strong victory carrying every
state but New Jersey, Delaware, and Kentucky, the latter being
the birth state of both Lincoln and Mary. Abraham Lincoln was
reelected to serve four more years as president of the United
States with a resounding margin of 221 electoral votes to 21 for
George McClellan. Lincoln was particularly pleased with the
margin of votes by the soldiers in the field: 116,887 for Lincoln
and 33,748 for former General McClellan. He strategically selected as vice president the "cranky" Andrew Johnson, who was
the Unionist, antislavery Democratic governor of Tennessee, a
Southern border state. As Stephen B. Oates put it, his reelection
demonstrated to his critics that

> the American people approved of his war
> policies, approved of his decision to fight the
> rebels with everything the Union could muster,
> approved of emancipation, Negro troops, and
> presidential reconstruction. A change of admin-
> istrations, Lincoln confided in Noah Brooks,
> would be 'virtually voting him a failure.'[584]

---

[582] *The Eloquent President*, Ronald C. White, Jr., p 260
[583] *The Eloquent President*, Ronald C. White, Jr., p 275
[584] *With Malice Toward None*, Stephen B. Oates, p 380-

He seemed happier that the election went off without violence in the midst of the instability caused by the war than he was for his own victory.

On election night, a friend exultantly told Lincoln that two of his most vehement Radical Republican critics were defeated as well. Lincoln responded: "You have more of that feeling of personal resentment than I. Perhaps I have too little of it, but I never thought it paid."[585] David Herbert Donald said, "He had no intention of using his impressive mandate to settle old quarrels with his Republican critics," saying instead, "I am in favor of a short statute of limitations in politics." "Nor did he gloat over the defeat of the Democrats."[586] That night after Lincoln retired to his room, Ward Hill Lamon quietly arrived outside the president's door with blankets, pistols, and bowie knives, and there he slept in mounting fear that many, more than ever, sought to take Lincoln's life.

On November 10, when serenaders came to the north portico of the White House to celebrate Lincoln's victory, he appeared in a second-floor window to make a brief response. Instead of trumpeting the Republican triumph, he used the occasion to seek reconciliation with his political foes, asking, "Now that the election is over, may not all...reunite in a common effort, to save our common country?" "For my own part," he continued, "I have striven and shall strive to avoid placing any obstacle in the way. So long as I have been here I have not willingly planted a thorn in any man's bosom."[587]

Yet even with victory, Lincoln revived but little from his burdensome load. Mary observed that he continued to seem "so broken hearted, so completely worn out."[588] Of this last volatile

---

[585] *Lincoln*, David Herbert Donald, p 546
[586] *Lincoln*, David Herbert Donald, p 546
[587] *Lincoln*, David Herbert Donald, p 546
[588] *With Malice Toward None*, Stephen B. Oates, p 401

campaign leading to his reelection, Lincoln commented to his young secretary, John Hay, that while he had never been a vindictive man, "almost all his elections were marked with 'great rancor' and bitterness."[589] A supporter came to Lincoln with news that Winter Davis, a fierce opponent to Lincoln's reelection, had gone down to his own political defeat in Maryland. "It served him right," said the friend. Lincoln's predictable response was, yes, Davis had been "very malicious against me" but he went on to inform the friend that he held no ill will toward Davis. In truth, said Stephen B. Oates, "Lincoln tried not to carry personal resentments." Quoting Lincoln, "A man has not time to spend half his life in quarrels."[590]

Even though as a young man Lincoln had always wanted to see the end of slavery, as president, he found that dream overshadowed by the more pressing issue of saving the Union. His momentous Emancipation Proclamation by his own admission was done as a "fit and necessary military measure" to shore up the weakening Union military with the infusion of the capable black soldiers.[591] But he couldn't have been more hopeful with this unexpected opportunity that had presented itself to end the "peculiar institution." And even then, his initial proclamation ended slavery only in the Southern rebelling states. He took it no further at the time because of the volatility of the issue and because he did not want to create even more division across the nation. Lincoln, while thrilled with the Emancipation Proclamation, still harbored fears that the courts or future administrations might overturn it. So he set to work in earnest on the constitutional amendment to abolish slavery completely. When 1865 arrived, after nearly four years of bitter war, Lincoln was blessed to see the first fruits emerge from the great chastise-

---

[589] *With Malice Toward None*, Stephen B. Oates, p 400
[590] *With Malice Toward None*, Stephen B. Oates, p 401
[591] *The Eloquent President*, Ronald C. White, Jr., p 365

ment in an unexpected yet monumental development for this humbled nation. He worked tirelessly and skillfully with the opposing Democrats in Congress for the ratification of the Thirteenth Amendment to the United States Constitution that would officially abolish and prohibit slavery. The amendment read simply:

> **Section 1.** Neither slavery nor involuntary servitude, except as punishment for crime whereof the party shall have been duly convicted, shall exist in the United States, or any place subject to its jurisdiction.

> **Section 2.** Congress shall have power to enforce this article by appropriate legislation.

This amendment would slam shut the door that the Constitution's destructive three-fifths ruling had propped open for the expansion of slavery in America for some "four score and seven years" after its creation. Lincoln had longed for its legal removal, and now the war provided the unexpected opportunity. On January 31, 1865, amid "a storm of cheers," Lincoln had the great satisfaction to observe as the Thirty-eighth Congress, under his guidance, with a vote of 119 to 58, proposed to the legislatures of the several states that the Thirteenth Amendment be ratified.[592] And then with guarded elation, Lincoln would observe over the period from February to

---

[592] *With Malice Toward None*, Stephen B. Oates, p 405

his assassination in April how one by one, beginning with his own home state of Illinois, twenty-seven of the thirty-six states—the needed three-fourths majority—ratified the new amendment to end slavery forever in this nation. All other states would eventually ratify the amendment, with the last state doing so quite recently: Mississippi ratified the amendment in March 1995. At the news of the amendment's passing, African-Americans assembled in large groups where they clapped and sang, "Sound the loud timbrel o'er Egypt's dark sea, Jehovah has triumphed, His people are free."[593]

The Thirteenth Amendment would be the first fruit to emerge from the great national cleansing. There would be more highly significant harvests yielded through the Almighty's refining and the resulting softened hearts of the now disciplined American people, as demonstrated with the votes of their representatives in Congress to end slavery forever in the United States, something that was unthinkable before the war. From the White House Lincoln pronounced the amendment "a great moral victory."[594] Then pointing toward the Potomac River and his brothers in the South he said, "If the people over the river had behaved themselves, I could not have done what I did."[595]

Indeed the war was the catalyst for a series of dramatic national transformations. The Thirteenth Amendment would be a crowning and lasting achievement in any president's legacy, but there were several more "great moral victories" just on the horizon that the Almighty God and His "humble instrument" would complete—a horizon that Lincoln would not live to see.

As inauguration day approached, a friend said Lincoln "looked badly and felt badly." To his long-time friend Joshua

---

[593] *With Malice Toward None*, Stephen B. Oates, p 405

[594] *With Malice Toward None*, Stephen B. Oates, p 405

[595] *With Malice Toward None*, Stephen B. Oates, p 405

Speed, he admitted, "I am very unwell, my feet and hands are always cold—I suppose I ought to be in bed."[596]

Still, on March 4, Lincoln climbed into the carriage that would take him on the traditional ride on Pennsylvania Avenue, lined with waving crowds and playing bands, to the Capitol where he would give his inaugural address and be sworn in for four more years. There having been rain in the days prior, Washington was awash with mud that was particularly troublesome to the women and their fine dresses. Noah Brooks observed that these women were in a "most wretched, wretched plight" with the mud. Inauguration day was again wet, cold, windy, and gray as Lincoln stood under the recently completed Capitol dome that had been years in the building, delayed by the war. This new dome towering over the tired president was a fitting symbol of the now near completion of the grand and harrowing process of nation-building, started four score and nine years earlier. The process had been sabotaged by the powers of darkness but would finally be set in motion as it was originally intended, with the inalienable rights of all men, all of whom are created equal, guaranteed by the United States Constitution and protected by a strong and righteous central government of *United* States. As Lincoln stood before the Washington crowd, he stood at the threshold of completion of the most critical test of this great governmental experiment started by the faith and courage of the Founding Fathers: whether such a government can be maintained or "long endure." The cleansing that was now concluding would insure that this "government of the people, by the people, and for the people shall not perish from the earth,"[597] as it so nearly did.

There may have been another highly significant manifestation that morning. The moment Lincoln took the podium the clouds parted and the brilliant sunlight shone on him and the

---

[596] *With Malice Toward None*, Stephen B. Oates, p 409

[597] *Gettysburg Address*, Abraham Lincoln

large crowd for a brief moment. After the short yet powerful address Lincoln asked his trusted friend Noah Brooks, "Did you notice that sunburst? It made my heart jump."[598] The sunburst was either a fortuitous coincidence or Lincoln just may have perceived the hand of God, confirming His humble and unwavering servant who had only forty-two days remaining in this earthly realm.

In the days preceding the second inauguration an unusual mix of people streamed into Washington to observe the historic event. At this inauguration most of the estimated forty to forty-five thousand present that day carried the heartache for lost or seriously wounded loved ones on the battlefields. There were many more black faces in the crowd than at any other inauguration: African-Americans who wanted to hear the words of "Father Abraham" their deliverer, and who, though now free, were beginning to experience a new resentment from whites for having won such a prize as their freedom at such a high cost. There were thousands of soldiers present as well, most from the some forty hospitals in the Washington area, and many of these soldiers were sad and pain-ridden amputees, having received the common war-injury medical treatment of the war. Others bore the disfigurement of the facial and head injuries from bullet or shrapnel that would be theirs to endure for the rest of their lives. There were those who carried a heightened hope, as signs were now strong that the Confederate military was rapidly collapsing and the war was near its end. Still others bore a boiling hatred and resentment for the North and especially for Abraham Lincoln for the terrible injustice that, in their minds, he had inflicted on the South. One such stood in the crowd some thirty-five feet behind and above Lincoln as he gave the greatest sermon of his presidency. John Wilkes Booth looked down intently on Lincoln as his mind conjured up his delusional plans

---

[598] *With Malice Toward None*, Stephen B. Oates, p 411

to accomplish what so many had failed to do. And, as at the first inauguration, there were sharpshooters on the tops of buildings and police and military at the ready to ward off what all knew was a heightened reality: that there were many now who sought to take the life of Lincoln.

His address consisted of only 703 words, the second-shortest inaugural address to be given. George Washington's was the shortest when no tradition was yet in place for newly elected presidents. Lincoln's message would be but four paragraphs in which Lincoln referred to God fourteen times, quoted the Bible four times, and invoked prayer three times. Nothing would be said of his astounding accomplishments of the past four years. As was his pattern, he spoke little of politics, preferring to speak of the greatness of the Almighty whom he so faithfully served and so deeply loved.

In his book *The Eloquent President*, Ronald C. White, Jr., makes a compelling comparison of Lincoln's address to that of four previous presidents who would deliver a second inaugural address: Presidents Jefferson, Madison, Monroe, and Jackson. Each of them made reference at the beginning to the "confidence" of the people expressed in their election. Of the four, White observes, "One cannot miss, however, the self-referential quality that was advanced by many different personal pronouns in each of their opening words. There was a steady staccato of 'I' in all of these addresses."[599] However, Lincoln's makes a distinctive divergence from those distinguished men who served before him.

> The opening words in his Second Inaugural are all the more remarkable when heard against the backdrop of the four previous second inaugural addresses. He nowhere speaks of the

---

[599] *The Eloquent President*, Ronald C. White, Jr., p 286

'confidence' or 'approbation' of the electorate. He uses personal pronouns only twice, *I* and *myself*, in the first paragraph, and never again. Because we approach the Second Inaugural through the larger lens of his previous speeches, we should not be surprised. He never spoke of himself, did not use one personal pronoun in the Gettysburg Address. All of his rhetoric, from the outset of the address, is directed away from himself.[600]

Lincoln did not speak of himself and his great victory, or revile the guilty in the South and the vociferous detractors in the North, which would have been met with resounding approbation by the crowd; his intent and delivery is quite apart from traditional political rhetoric. He used this occasion not to speak for himself, but to speak for God by declaring to the nation and to the world the great national deliverance from sure destruction and chaos, which was now culminating. His purpose was to instruct the people of America that this dramatic deliverance was not done by him or by the superiority of the Union military, but by the "Living God." He also meant to clearly declare that the horrific castigation of the Civil War, which was finally coming to a close, was the just and disserved chastening of the Almighty God for the sins of a highly blessed people gone astray.

Unlike so many political speeches that are organized and reviewed by a team of speechwriters, Lincoln's speech was developed alone, and no one can doubt that it was done with open Bible and fervent prayer, asking his trusted God for guidance and for His approbation of its contents. Lincoln began his address with an introduction and a very brief overview of the past

---

[600] *The Eloquent President*, Ronald C. White, Jr., p 286

four years' events. In his second paragraph he moves toward the heart of his message by meekly declaring:

> On the occasion corresponding to this four years ago, all thoughts were anxiously directed to an impending civil war. All dreaded it—all sought to avert it. While the inaugural address was being delivered from this place, devoted altogether to <u>saving</u> the Union without war, insurgent agents were in the city seeking to <u>destroy</u> it without war—seeking to dissolve the Union, and divide effects, by negotiation. Both parties deprecated war; but one of them would make war rather than let the nation survive; and the other would <u>accept</u> war rather than let it perish. And the war came.[601]

In his book *Lincoln's Virtues,* William Lee Miller observes,

> [Lincoln] would not stoke the fires of national self-righteousness. His interpretation of America's role in the world...would stand as something of a corrective to blatant national egoism and self-deception. President Lincoln would not insist, as President Polk had insisted [with the War with Mexico], that the other side in his war was altogether and absolutely to blame for the war's beginning and for its continuance—even though some might say that President Lincoln would have far more justification for doing so than had President Polk. Lincoln would not reiterate the South's guilt;

---

[601] *The Eloquent President,* Ronald C. White, Jr., p 289

he would recommend amnesty toward the Confederate leaders and generosity to the Southern people; he would say that neither side wanted war, and would describe the beginning impersonally: "And the war came."[602]

"The people who begin a war," says Ronald C. White, Jr., "almost always do so with the sense that they are in charge. Lincoln, looking back with the hindsight of four years, is suggesting that the generals, the soldiers, and the commander-in-chief were not completely in control of the war."[603]

In paragraph three Lincoln would "situate slavery as an inclusive problem that was the responsibility of the whole nation."[604]

One eighth of the whole population were colored slaves, not distributed generally over the Union, but localized generally in the Southern part of it. These slaves constituted a peculiar and powerful interest. All knew that this interest was somehow the cause of the war. To strengthen, to perpetuate, and extend this interest was the object for which the insurgents would rend the Union, even by war; while the government claimed no right to do more than to restrict the territorial enlargement of it. Neither party expected for the war, the magnitude, or the duration, which it has already attained. Neither anticipated that the <u>cause</u> of the conflict might cease with, or even before, the conflict itself should cease. Each

---

602 *Lincoln's Virtues*, William Lee Miller, p 191
603 *The Eloquent President*, Ronald C. White, Jr., p 289
604 *The Eloquent President*, Ronald C. White, Jr., p 289

looked for an easier triumph, and a result less fundamental and astounding.[605]

Ronald C. White, Jr., said, "No one knew it, but Lincoln was preparing his audience to hear about God's purposes by rehearsing the finitude of human purposes."[606]

Lincoln continued:

> Both read the same Bible, and pray to the same God; and each invokes His aid against the other. It may seem strange that any man should dare to ask a just God's assistance in wringing their bread from the sweat of other men's faces; but let us judge not that we be not judged. The prayers of both could not be answered; that of neither has been answered fully.[607]

Again, Mr. White notes of Lincoln,

> Speaking to an audience so ready to judge, Lincoln invoked the authority of Jesus in the New Testament to restrain an all too human impulse.
>
> The audience does not know it yet, but in this transitional section Lincoln is about to connect human purposes, with their tendency toward pretentiousness, to what will emerge as

---

[605] *The Eloquent President*, Ronald C. White, Jr., p 289
[606] *The Eloquent President*, Ronald C. White, Jr., p 290
[607] *The Eloquent President*, Ronald C. White, Jr., p 290

the central theme in this address, the purposes of God.[608]

William Lee Miller said,

> President Lincoln, with the strongest of motives to do so, would not claim that God has marked out a superior role for...his side in the war. In the Second Inaugural he would say that, 'the Almighty has His purposes,' meaning exactly that [God's] purposes were larger than those of either side, including his own.[609]

Lincoln continued:

> The Almighty has His own purposes. "Woe unto the world because of offenses! For it must needs be that offenses come; but woe to that man by whom the offense cometh!" If we shall suppose that American Slavery is one of those offences which, in the providence of God, must needs come, but which, having continued through His appointed time, He now wills to remove, and that He gives to both North and South, this terrible war, as the woe due to those by whom the offense came, shall we discern therein any departure from those divine attributes which the believers in a Living God always ascribe to Him?[610]

White explains, "Lincoln arrived at the architectural center of his address. After chronicling a variety of purposes and intentions,

---

608 *The Eloquent President*, Ronald C. White, Jr., p 293
609 *Lincoln's Virtues*, William Lee Miller, p 191
610 *The Eloquent President*, Ronald C. White, Jr., p 293

Lincoln presented his own meaning of the war, to be found in the purposes of God."[611] To describe these purposes, he again wisely chooses the words of Jesus Christ himself, found in Matthew 18:7, to remind his listeners that since the beginning of time, the Great Jehovah has allowed woe to come to the rebellious and impenitent as a fitting process of redemption. The terrible woe endured at this time is no departure from His eternal ways. Lincoln's reference to "American Slavery" rather than Southern slavery is significant. While it was the slave-owning insurgents in the South who triggered the Civil War, for many decades earlier the slave *trade* (the capturing, shipping, and selling of Africans) was centered in New England. The trading of slaves, though abolished earlier in the nineteenth century, was very much a part of the two and one half centuries of the "peculiar institution" that had become a long overdue debt that had come due for those in the North.

Having plainly communicated his primary message that the protracted war was expressly God's justice and cleansing, he was now, unexpectedly to everyone, ready to close. And he would do it as was his pattern by expressing words of kindness and reconciliation, but they would include the reality and righteousness of God's judgments, that this war would end only when God felt that the "uttermost farthing" had been paid to fulfill the demands of justice. Lincoln would use words from his beloved Psalms, the nineteenth chapter and ninth verse, to proclaim as he so often had before that the works of God and His judgments could never be abrogated in the centuries preceding, nor in the present, by mortal man.

> Fondly do we hope—fervently do we pray—that this mighty scourge of war may speedily pass away. Yet, if God wills that it continue, until all the wealth piled by the bond-

---

[611] *The Eloquent President*, Ronald C. White, Jr., p 293

man's two hundred and fifty years of unrequited toil shall be sunk, and until every drop of blood drawn with the lash, shall be paid by another drawn by the sword, as was said three-thousand years ago, so still it must be said, "the judgments of the Lord, are true and righteous altogether."[612]

Jesus said, "For out the abundance of the heart, the mouth speaketh."[613] Lincoln had just spoken from his guileless heart, and would now close with another expression of the abundance of quite possibly the purest heart of any mortal man or woman, with these enduring words:

> With malice toward none; with charity for all; with firmness in the right, as God gives us to see the right, let us strive on to finish the work we are in; to bind up the nation's wounds, to care for him who shall have borne the battle, and for his widow, and the orphan—to do all which may achieve and cherish a just, and a lasting peace, among ourselves, and with all nations.[614]

In seven minutes, even as people were still arriving, it was over. He bowed solemnly to the applauding crowd, and turned to his former cabinet member Salmon P. Chase to be sworn in as president for four more years. Lincoln had appointed Chase a few months earlier as chief justice of the Supreme Court, replacing Roger B. Taney, author of the lamentable Dred Scott decision. Lincoln told the new justice that he hoped he would

---

[612] *The Eloquent President*, Ronald C. White, Jr., p 298
[613] Matthew 12:34
[614] *The Eloquent President*, Ronald C. White, Jr., p 301

understand that "the function of courts is to decide *cases*—not *principles.*"[615] Chase was the same who opposed Lincoln in his second run for the Republican nomination and who was involved during that election in questionable tactics against Lincoln. But again, there was no room for resentment or retribution in Lincoln's heart, as it was filled only and always with tolerance and forgiveness. And he knew that Chase, in spite of his disloyal ambition, was the most capable defender of law and order and the best choice for such a critical office. Placing his hand on a Bible, this time opened to the fifth chapter of Isaiah, Lincoln took the solemn oath of office ending with an emphatic "so help me God," and then reverently bowed again and kissed the Holy Book. Chase noted that he kissed the scriptures near to verses 25 and 26.

> *Verse 25*
> *Therefore is the anger of the Lord kindled against his people, and he hath stretched forth his hand against them, and hath smitten them: and the hills did tremble and their carcasses were torn in the midst of the streets. For all this his anger is not turned away, but his hand is stretched out still.*

> *Verse 26*
> *And he will lift up an ensign to the nations from far, and will hiss unto them from the ends of the earth, and behold they shall come with speed swiftly.*

The address was to the people whom he had so humbly and diligently served. The oath taken with his hand over the compelling words of the prophet Isaiah, and the kiss on chapter

---

[615] *Lincoln*, David Herbert Donald, p 551

five, seemed to be his personal yet public oblation to his beloved God and Redeemer.

A few days later, Lincoln responded to a congratulatory letter from a friend, New York politician Thurlow Weed, and said of the address, "I expect the latter to wear well—perhaps better than anything I have produced."[616] Of course, millions for nearly a century have read and will continue to read the words of this address emblazoned on the wall of the inspiring Lincoln Memorial in Washington, DC; this message has, indeed, worn well. He continued in the letter to his friend:

> I believe it [the address] is not immediately popular. Men are not flattered by being shown that there has been a difference of purpose between the Almighty and them. To deny it, however, in this case, is to deny that there is a God governing the world. It is a truth that I thought needed to be told.[617]

In fact the speech was only interrupted a couple of times with mild applause. It was far from the expected and traditional political speech. What could have been one of the most rousing victory speeches in history had in fact no words of jubilation, conquest, or political rhetoric. Lincoln had no interest in instilling triumphant elation in the hearts of the large crowd or in the nation overall. His aim was quite the opposite: he hoped to instill contrition and penitence, knowing that in such a condition, "the better angels" of their natures, become so much more easily inclined to their merciful Heavenly Father in humble repentance and adoration.[618] The eloquent and defiant voice of black America, Fredrick Douglass, now a respected friend of the pres-

---

[616] *The Eloquent President*, Ronald C. White, Jr., p 303

[617] *The Eloquent President*, Ronald C. White, Jr., p 303

[618] Abraham Lincoln's First Inaugural Address (EP 62)

ident, noted in his diary, "The whole proceeding was wonderfully quiet, earnest, and solemn. The address sounded more like a sermon than a state paper."[619] Indeed, the president of the United States did not address his audience as a politician; this president rarely did. Instead, he addressed them as a mouthpiece of, using his term, the "Living God."

---

[619] *The Eloquent President*, Ronald C. White, Jr., p 301

Chapter Eleven

"I Think We Are Near the End at Last"

On Christmas Day, 1864, Lincoln received a telegram from General William Tecumseh Sherman: "I beg to present you as a Christmas gift, the city of Savannah."[620] From Savannah, and in twenty days of rain, Sherman and his so-called avenging angels made an unexpected turn westward, bypassing Charleston, which was already abandoned and occupied by white and black Union forces, and marched for Columbia, the capital of South Carolina. Sherman, regarding the men he led, remarked that, "The whole army is burning with an insatiable desire to wreak vengeance upon South Carolina. I almost tremble at her fate, but...she deserves all that seems in store for her."[621] Sherman's march of destruction was a 425-mile-long and 60-mile-wide swath of terror. Little of what stood in their path escaped destruction. They slaughtered livestock they couldn't eat; plundered silver, jewelry and anything else of value; terrorized women and old men; and burned homes, shops, entire villages, plantations, and libraries.

---

[620] *With Malice Toward None*, Stephen B. Oates, p 404
[621] *April 1865, The Month that Saved America*, Jay Winik, p 308

Mary Chesnut recorded the horror felt by all in the South: "Since Atlanta I have felt as if all were dead within me, forever. We are going to be wiped off the face of the earth."[622] But Sherman stopped at nothing to punish the state that had spawned the rebellion, saying, "We are not fighting hostile armies, but a hostile people, and must make old and young, rich and poor, feel the hard hand of war."[623] Indeed, Sherman and his march of destruction sucked out any remaining fight from the heart of the Confederacy. In addition to burning and destroying everything in their path, they were now targeting the railroad lines that had been the lifeline to the great General Lee and his army in Virginia. The noose was tightening on the neck of the once feared Confederate fighting force. With supply lines cut off, Lee's army would now be forced to choose starvation or come to out from their formidable entrenchments near Richmond and fight.

Mary Chesnut recorded the following entries in her diary:

> February 23, 1865
> Letter from my husband—he is in Charlotte. He came near being taken prisoner in Columbia, for he was asleep the morning of the 17th, when the Yankees blew up the RR depot. That woke him, of course. He found everybody had left Columbia and the town surrendered by the mayor, Colonel Goodwyn. [General] Hampton and his command had been gone several hours. Isaac Haynes came away with General Chesnut [her husband]. There was no fire in the town when they came away. They overtook Hampton's command at Meeks Mill. That night, from the hills where they encamped they saw the fire and knew the

---

[622] *April 1865, The Month that Saved America*, Jay Winik, p 307
[623] *April 1865, The Month that Saved America*, Jay Winik, p 307

Yankees were burning the town—as we had every right to expect they would.[624]

Then I sat down and wrote my husband—so much worse than anything I can put in this book—and as I wrote I was blinded by tears of rage. Indeed, I nearly wept myself away.[625]

February 26, 1865

[The book of] Job is my comforter now.

And yet I would be so thankful to know it never would be any worse with me. I am bodily comfortable, if somewhat dingily lodged, and I daily part with my raiment for food. We find no one who will exchange eatables for Confederate money. So we are devouring our clothes. Ellen is a maid...and if I do a little work it is quite enough to show me how dreadful it would be without her *if I should have to do it all.*

My faith fails me. It is too late. No help for us now—in God or man.[626]

March 5, 1865

Is the sea drying up? Is it going up into mist and coming down on us in this waterspout? The rain—it raineth every day, and the weather represents our tearful despair on a large scale.

---

[624] *Mary Chesnut's Civil War*, Mary Chesnut, p 725
[625] *Mary Chesnut's Civil War*, Mary Chesnut, p 725
[626] *Mary Chesnut's Civil War*, Mary Chesnut, p 733

It is also Lent—quite convenient, for we have nothing to eat. So we fast and pray. And go draggling to church like drowned rats, to be preached at.

News at last [from Columbia]. Sherman's men had burned the convent. Mrs. Munro had pinned her faith to Sherman because he is Catholic—and now! Columbia is but dust and ashes—burned to the ground. Men, women, and children left there, houseless, homeless, without one particle of food—picking up the corn left by Sherman's horses in their picket ground and parching it to stay their hunger.[627]

Letter from Quentin Washington to Mary Chesnut:
"I have given up," he writes. "The bitterness is over." But then he adds, "I will write to you no more—I have not the heart."

General Manigault told Miss Middleton that Sherman burnt out all families whose heads had signed the secession ordinance. Members of legislature's houses were burned.

Jack Middleton writes from Richmond: "The wolf is at the door here. We dread starvation far more than we do Grant or Sherman. Famine—that is the word now."[628]

Dr. Brumby has been at last coaxed into selling me some leather to make me a pair of

---

[627] *Mary Chesnut's Civil War*, Mary Chesnut, p 744
[628] *Mary Chesnut's Civil War*, Mary Chesnut, p 747

shoes— else I should have to give up walking.[629]

As the four-year war neared its close, there remained few reminders of the aristocratic days in the South. Jay Winik describes the unimaginable scene:

> Where proud antebellum homes and mansions once stood, there was rotting wood and cracked paint and weed-choked grass; where Southerners once took evening promenade walks down hundred-foot-wide boulevards and through acres of rich green parks, there is the stench of urine and feces and decaying animal carcasses; and where there was once the clamor of commerce and exchange, there are now ghost towns and equally ghostly urban pockets. And of course, there are the ubiquitous chimney stacks, themselves charred and lonely reminders of once thriving cities and bustling plantations.[630]

The Confederate government sent three emissaries with whom Lincoln reluctantly agreed to meet at Hampton Roads, Virginia. They pressed for compromise but Lincoln again rebuffed this final and desperate attempt. Lincoln's thoughts were on the arduous task of transforming mortal enemies into friends and fellow citizens again and he wanted nothing to do with the same conditions that lead to the war. His terms were fixed; he told them that there would be no end of the fighting until the South formally recognized the supremacy of the national government, and that the abolition of slavery had to be completely and permanently accepted. After hedging and vacillating, the

---

[629] *Mary Chesnut's Civil War*, Mary Chesnut, p 749
[630] *April 1865, The Month that Saved America*, Jay Winik, p 307

emissaries returned empty handed. Reflecting his sense of fairness and the absence of enmity for his enemies, Lincoln had long wanted compensation to the slave owners for their freed slaves. He pressed for this again but his cabinet was unanimous against it, saying that Congress would have no stomach for such compassion. Lincoln dropped the idea, knowing that they were right about the mood in Congress.

In the days following his second inaugural address he continued to feel weak and ill. That week's cabinet meeting had to be held in his bedroom with him in his bed and his cabinet huddled around him. But he would revive somewhat when an unexpected invitation arrived from General Uysses Grant and his wife, for the president and Mary to visit them in Virginia. Lincoln jumped at the chance to escape the incessant press of office-seekers and the rigors of Washington. He, Mary, and their son Tad boarded the *River Queen* for a two-day riverboat ride to City Point, where they were graciously met by the Grants. The next morning Lincoln followed Tad up a bluff to take in the beautiful sight around them. Below, the river was teeming with Union troop transports, gunboats, and supply vessels all engaged in the business of war. Later he wandered among the busy Union forces and saw some Confederate prisoners and lamented their "sad condition." On the ground were dead soldiers, both Union and Confederate, and the wounded from that morning's skirmishes were being attended to. During this visit, Generals Sherman and Sheridan met with Lincoln and Grant to confer on their closing efforts on the war.

On March 29, as Lincoln approached the final two weeks of his life, Grant made his planned assault on the formidable Confederate entrenchments at Petersburg as Lincoln paced nervously on the *River Queen*, anxiously awaiting news of the outcome. Lincoln could hear the booming guns and see the flashes of light in the night sky from his perch on the riverboat. On April 3, Grant unleashed a thunderous barrage on Petersburg and the Confederate troops, forcing them from their strongholds. And this time, as Lee retreated, Lincoln's new set of generals did what he had always unsuccessfully pressed the earlier ones to do: they pursued the retreating forces. Grant pursued Lee's forces while Generals Meade and Sheridan rushed to cut off their retreat. At the news, Lincoln fearlessly rushed to the now-demolished and smoldering town of Petersburg to "pump Grant's hand for this glorious victory."[631]

Later that day, news arrived that Jefferson Davis and the entire Confederate government were on the run from their nearby rebel capital of Richmond, and that much of Richmond had been reduced to smoldering rubble. It was too much for Lincoln to simply stay at City Point when he was so close to these significant events, and he wired his secretary of war, Edwin Stanton, and informed him that he and twelve-year-old Tad were going to Richmond to take a look. So president and son, with two bodyguards and a dozen armed sailors, boarded a gunboat on the James River for Richmond. The smoke rising from the ruined city could be seen for some time before they reached their destination. As Lincoln entered Richmond, which was now being patrolled by Union troops, many of whom were black, another irony of ironies came to view: the leading officials of the Southern rebellion, the same aristocratic insurgents who started this rebellion for the sake of expanding the scourge of slavery, were now homeless and on the run while armed African-American former slaves occupied their homes and seat of government.

Lincoln was immediately recognized by them and other black workers, who flocked around him, some calling his name, others shouting "Glory, Glory, Glory!" and "God bless you," with still others addressing him as their "Redeemer" and "Sav-

---

[631] *With Malice Toward None*, Stephen B. Oates, p 420

ior."[632] The lead man of a black work party, on seeing Lincoln, dropped to his knees and exclaimed, "Bless the Lord, there is the great Messiah! Glory Hallelujah!"[633] Some of the workers fell in turn to their knees and tried to kiss Lincoln's feet, to which Lincoln said, "Don't kneel to me. That is not right. You must kneel to God only, and thank him for the liberty you will hereafter enjoy."[634] "I am but God's humble instrument but you may rest assured, that as long as I live, you shall have all the rights which God has given to every free citizen of the Republic."[635]

The more fortunate white residents, whose homes had escaped the fires and destruction, remained nervously inside, troubled by the bewildering irony of the Confederate capital now occupied and controlled by uniformed and armed former slaves. They could be seen staring through their windows at the added startling spectacle of the president of the United States and his son solemnly walking hand in hand down the streets of burned-out Richmond with a column of jubilant Negroes trailing behind. One of the bodyguards recorded, "But it was a silent crowd. There was something oppressive in those thousands of watchers without a sound, either of welcome or hatred."[636] Stephen B. Oates writes,

> He stepped along through the business section now, surrounded by burned-out buildings. Before evacuating the city, the rebels had set the bridges and warehouses afire, but a high wind whipped the flames into downtown

---

[632] *With Malice Toward None*, Stephen B. Oates, p. 420, *The Wit and Wisdom of Abraham Lincoln*, p 72

[633] *Lincoln*, David Herbert Donald, p 576

[634] *Lincoln*, David Herbert Donald, p 576

[635] *The Wit and Wisdom of Abraham Lincoln*, p 72

[636] *With Malice Toward None*, Stephen B. Oates, p 421

Richmond, and some structures were still blazing. A cavalry escort came and took him to the rebel executive mansion, now Union military headquarters. Inside, Lincoln looked around the deserted rooms. He seemed "pale and utterly worn out" said one witness, as he asked for a glass of water. In the executive office, Lincoln sat down in Jefferson Davis's chair, and the Union troops broke into cheers.[637]

He boarded a carriage and was driven to the capitol where the Confederate congress had convened for the prior four years. He solemnly roamed about the empty and ransacked rooms. Before he left Richmond, a meeting was arranged with the Confederate assistant secretary of war, in which Lincoln dictated terms of complete and unconditional surrender. "He did not promise amnesty to rebels, but did say he had the power to pardon them and 'would save any repenting sinner from hanging.'"[638] He then gave tentative authorization for the Virginia state legislature to convene for the purpose of officially discharging all Virginia troops and sending them home.

Back at City Point, Lincoln pored over dispatches describing the Union's advance. Sheridan had seized the Danville Railroad, ending Lee's hope of escape into North Carolina. Although sporadic fighting would continue for a few more weeks, the final decisive battle was held on April 6, in which Union forces smashed half of Lee's beleaguered army at Appomattox. Then Lincoln read a telegram that Sheridan sent to Grant: "If the thing be pressed I think that Lee will surrender." Lincoln telegraphed Grant: "Let the *thing* be pressed."[639] Shortly after this, word came from Washington that Lincoln's secretary of state,

---

[637] *With Malice Toward None*, Stephen B. Oates, p 421
[638] *With Malice Toward None*, Stephen B. Oates, p 421
[639] *With Malice Toward None*, Stephen B. Oates, p 421

William Seward, had been seriously injured in a carriage accident, and Lincoln concluded that he must return to Washington. But before he did, he visited the Union hospitals and camps in the area, shaking hands with some seven thousand wounded soldiers, sensing that "he would probably never see them again and he wanted them to know how much he appreciated what they had done for the Union."[640] This dramatic expression, and later Lincoln's reading of Duncan's assassination in *Macbeth* on the return home, seemed to have reflected a foreboding that his own end was near. And it was.

On April 8, six days before his assassination, he began his two-day return to Washington, where, upon arrival late on Palm Sunday, he visited his ailing friend William Seward, who had broken both arms and his jaw in the carriage accident. "I think we are near the end at last," he solemnly told Seward; then, ever mindful of their dependence on the Almighty, he discussed plans for a national day of thanksgiving.[641] That night he learned that Generals Grant and Lee had their poignant and historical meeting at Appomattox, in which Lee accepted Grant's gracious terms of surrender—terms that reflected Lincoln's heartfelt desire for compassion, healing and reconciliation. Jay Winik writes,

> Lee's reluctant yet dignified surrender to Grant at Appomattox, accompanied by Grant's equally dignified, and largely unprecedented, handling of his fallen foe, was a masterful act that set the tone for the rest of the war and the peace to come.[642]

---

[640] *With Malice Toward None*, Stephen B. Oates, p 421
[641] *April 1865, The Month that Saved America*, Jay Winik, p 203
[642] *April 1865, The Month that Saved America*, Jay Winik, p xxi

The next morning, April 10, Washington was greeted with five hundred cannon blasts heralding the surrender of General Lee at Appomattox. Jubilant crowds reveled in the streets and surrounded the White House, calling for words of victory from Lincoln. That night he appeared in a second-story window of the White House—with son Tad holding the light—before a cheering jubilant crowd, but again the excited crowd would be disappointed to hear nothing of victorious jubilation from their president. In this, his final presidential message, he was again brief, and as in the other messages, he directed the listeners' attention away from him and his momentous victories, telling them instead, "He from Whom all blessings flow, must not be forgotten…no part of the honor…is mine."[643] He also gave them a solemn reminder of the tasks that still lay ahead. He said that he hoped the recent victories would "give hope of a righteous and speedy peace."[644] He promised a national day of thanksgiving to God and expressed his gratitude to "Gen. Grant, his skilled officers, and the brave men."[645] He reminded them that "re-inauguration of the national authority was now paramount and would be 'fraught with great difficulty.'"[646]

But even as the war crescendoed to a close, there remained the most significant question of all—one that had consumed Abraham Lincoln, haunted him, kept him awake at night, and etched lines of worry deep in his face: It was not simply how to subjugate the Confederacy by force of arms, but, more importantly, how to reunite two separate political, social, and cultural entities that had been bitter military enemies just days before. There is "no greater [task] before us," Lincoln bluntly told his cabinet, or for that matter before "any future Cabinet." In

---

[643] *Manhunt,* James Swanson, Prologue, p 5

[644] *Lincoln,* David Herbert Donald, p 582

[645] *Lincoln,* David Herbert Donald, p 582

[646] *Lincoln,* David Herbert Donald, p 582

truth, this was the foremost challenge of April 1865. "This accomplishment—two nations becoming one—perhaps among the most momentous of all time, make the story of April 1865 not just a tale of the war's denouement but, in countless ways, the story of the making of our nation."[647]

Jay Winik said,

> ...no period was more harrowing, or had so great an impact upon this country, as the days that followed Lee's surrender. Within six days Abraham Lincoln was dead, the first-ever assassination of an American President. Never before or since in the life of this nation has the country been so tested as in this week alone.

> For historians, it is axiomatic that there are dates on which history turns, and that themselves become packed with meaning. For Americans, one magic number is, of course, 1492, the year marking the discovery of America—which is to say its Europeanization—or 1776, the American Declaration of Independence. But April 1865 is another such pivotal date.

> It was not inevitable that the American Civil War would end as it did, or for that matter, that it would end at all well. Indeed, what emerges from the panorama of April of 1865 is that the whole of our national history could have been altered but for a few decisions, a quirk of fate, a sudden shift in luck. Through out this period,

---

[647] *April 1865,* Intro., p xii

there were critical turning points, each of which
could have shattered a fragile, war-torn America, thrusting the new nation back into a renewed war, or even worse, into a protracted, ug-
ly, low-level North-South conflict, or toward a
far harsher, more violent, and volatile peace,
with unpredictable results. Time and again,
things might have gone altogether differently.[648]

With the end of the war all but secure, new calls rose up for
the rounding up of Confederate leaders for trial and hanging.
But Lincoln again sought other measures. He had no interest in
hunting down and capturing them. In his final meeting with his
cabinet, he told them again, as he had been pressing for almost
a year, his plan for reconciliation. "He hoped there would be no
persecution, no bloody work, after the war was over. None
need expect he would take any part in hanging or killing those
men, even the worst of them."[649] Days earlier at City Point,
General Sherman asked Lincoln what he intended to do with
Jefferson Davis and the other rebel leaders and he responded
that he hoped that they would "escape the country."[650] There
was also a strong move by Northern leaders to completely reor-
ganize the Southern states—another approach in which Lincoln
had no interest because he saw it would detract from his mission for "a righteous peace." In his mind, such plans would further strain those friends of the Union residing in the South on
whom he was placing great hope. For Lincoln, forgiveness, inclusion, and mutual respect would be the implements for peace.

In that disappointed audience on the night of Lincoln's last
speech from the White House window stood a seething John
Wilkes Booth. Born and raised in a Maryland slaveholding

---

[648] *April 1865, The Month that Saved America,* Jay Winik, p xii
[649] *Lincoln,* David Herbert Donald, p 582
[650] *Lincoln,* David Herbert Donald, p 583

community, Booth considered himself one of the few Northerners who understood the injustice inflicted upon the South. A
self-absorbed yet popular and passionate actor, he was especially appreciated by the Southern audiences who had enjoyed
Booth's performances in the theater at Richmond. On the issue
of slavery, Booth said it was "one of the greatest blessings (both
to themselves and us) that God ever bestowed upon a favored
nation." And he believed, as did many other Americans, that
"the country was formed for the white, not for the black
man."[651] He made no attempt to conceal his hatred for the
"false president," as he referred to President Lincoln, and his
sympathy for the Confederate cause. Following Lincoln's
reelection, secret meetings between Booth and Confederate
agents in Canada, Boston, and Maryland took place in which
Booth presented his plan to kidnap the president and hold him
hostage for the release of Southern prisoners languishing in
Northern prisons. He spent the winter of 1864 recruiting a mot-
ley group of fellow conspirators and studying maps, roads, and
waterways with which he would hatch his plan.

He developed a melodramatic and implausible plan to kidnap the president while attending Ford's Theater on January 18,
binding him and lowering him to the stage below. However,
Lincoln changed his plans and decided not to attend the theater
on that stormy night. Booth and his group planned another ab-
duction of the president on March 17, near the Soldiers' Home
where the Lincolns would often reside; but again Lincoln's
plans changed and he did not pass by the point where Booth
and his conspirators laid in wait.

Booth supposed that removing Lincoln from office would
bring him great fame, that he would be a modern-day William
Tell or Brutus who murdered Caesar. But by early March,
Booth's thoughts began turning from kidnapping to assassina-

---

[651] *Lincoln*, David Herbert Donald, p 586

tion and by this time he was working entirely on his own with his plans. Such thoughts were in his mind as he stood with his fiancée above and behind the president, as he gave his second inaugural address, and when Booth stood outside the White House window during Lincoln's final speech, during which Lincoln revealed his desire that blacks be allowed to vote. To which Booth muttered, "That means nigger citizenship." He then vowed, "That will be the last speech he will ever make."[652] The string of setbacks for the Confederacy in April caused Booth to conclude that "something decisive and great must be done."[653]

On Good Friday, April 14, Lincoln began his final day in mortality with breakfast in company of Mary and their oldest son, Captain Robert Todd Lincoln, who had just arrived from his military service as an aide for General Grant at Appomattox. The Lincolns were joyful to see their son again, and were deeply relieved that he had escaped harm in the conflict. Robert was able to inform his father on many details of Lee's surrender, since Robert spent that momentous day on the porch of the Appomattox farmhouse in which Grant and Lee met. They also had a pleasant discussion in which the loving father advised his son regarding the future plans in Robert's career. Their trusted and beloved White House resident and Mary's official dressmaker, Elizabeth Keckley, observed, "His [Lincoln's] face was more cheerful than [she] had seen it for a long while."[654] Lincoln was in high spirits; this Good Friday was certainly one of the happiest days of Lincoln's presidency, and possibly his life.

Later that morning his final cabinet meeting was convened, to which General Grant had been invited to report on the surrender at Appomattox. Lincoln's friend Joshua Speed remarked that he did not recall ever before seeing Lincoln so vibrant and

[652] *Lincoln*, David Herbert Donald, p 588
[653] *Lincoln*, David Herbert Donald, p 596
[654] *Team of Rivals*, Doris Kearns Goodwin, p 731

alive. Lincoln's secretary of war, Edwin Stanton, said Lincoln that day was "grander, graver, more thoroughly up to the occasion than he had ever seen him."[655] He also said that Lincoln "spoke very kindly of General Lee and others of the Confederacy," exhibiting "in marked degree the kindness and humanity of his disposition, and the tender and forgiving spirit that so eminently distinguished him."[656] Then, adding to Lincoln's contentment, this cabinet meeting was devoid of the despairing bad war-news that had been ever-present in the past four years. Fredrick W. Seward, who was attending in place of his injured father, recorded that all members present expressed "kindly feelings toward the vanquished, and [a] hearty desire to restore peace and safety at the South, with as little harm as possible to the feelings or property of the inhabitants."[657] Such sentiments for their former enemies by his cabinet reflected that Lincoln's approach of forgiveness and charity, so consistent with the principles Lincoln had repeatedly read of the Savior in the New Testament, was taking hold.

He told them that he considered it "providential that this great rebellion was crushed just as Congress had adjourned," allowing him and his cabinet to move ahead with their reunification campaign based on the foundation of "malice toward none and charity for all."[658] "We could do more without them than with them,"[659] he said, and then added, "There were men in Congress who, if their motives were good, were nevertheless impracticable, and who possessed feelings of hate and vindictiveness in which he did not sympathize and could not participate."[660] Such feelings of hate and vindictiveness would certain-

---

[655] *Lincoln*, David Herbert Donald, p 591

[656] *Team of Rivals*, Doris Kearns Goodwin, p 732

[657] *Team of Rivals*, Doris Kearns Goodwin, p 731

[658] *Team of Rivals*, Doris Kearns Goodwin, p 732

[659] *Lincoln*, David Herbert Donald, p 592

[660] *Team of Rivals*, Doris Kearns Goodwin, p 732

ly have hampered the reconstruction effort had Congress been in session; another coincidental advantage or maybe divine design.

In this final cabinet meeting Lincoln expressed his hope that Grant would have news of Confederate general Joc Johnston's surrender to General Sherman in the South. Grant regretfully informed the president that such news had not arrived, to which Lincoln calmly expressed his certainty that it would soon come "for he had last night the usual dream which he had preceding nearly every great and important event of the War."[661] Secretary of the Navy Gideon Welles then asked Lincoln to describe the dream. Turning to Welles he said that it involved the navy's

> element, the water—that he seemed to be
> in some singular, indescribable vessel, and that
> he was moving with great rapidity towards an
> indefinite shore; that he had this dream pre-
> ceding Sumter, Bull Run, Antietam, Gettys
> burg, Stone River, Vicksburg, Willington,
> etc.[662]

Grant responded by saying that not all of those battles resulted in Union victories, to which Lincoln explained that good news always followed this dream and he was confident that Johnston would surrender (which he did a few days after).

By now his cabinet was accustomed to hearing Lincoln express sentiments and make decisions based on his dreams and his spiritual impressions of divine guidance that followed his prayers of supplication to "the living God." In light of this firmly held belief, we must consider the condition of Lincoln's mind and of his spirit in these the last hours of his life. For four years

---

[661] *Team of Rivals*, Doris Kearns Goodwin, p 732
[662] *Team of Rivals*, Doris Kearns Goodwin, p 731

he had "talked to God" regarding the nation's crisis, and he had yearned for God to reveal His will to him throughout the war, and for years Lincoln felt that God had, in various ways, guided his decisions and actions. It can be safely propounded that few men on earth had drawn closer to God during that time than had Lincoln. It is undeniable that Lincoln made a number of key presidential decisions during this nation's greatest crisis, based on his belief that God—not Congress, nor his cabinet, nor public opinion—had guided him to such conclusions and actions. These dreams of the high-speed aquatic journey toward the shore could certainly be coincidental and meaningless happenings. But it is clear that Lincoln did not see them as such; on the contrary, he placed a high degree of confidence in their reliability as personal affirmations that God's hand was guiding this great national transformation. But if they were communications from the Lord to His humble instrument, as God had historically done with his chosen servants many times before, why had this dream occurred with defeats as well as victories? We may never know the answer, but Lincoln often expressed his belief that God had his own purposes in the war and that such purposes might be beyond preserving the Union and freeing the slaves. One such additional purpose, again as declared by Lincoln, was the humbling and punishment of the wayward people of the United States, in which case each bloody battle, whether won by the Union or not, certainly contributed to a chastening contrition, the rising of the "better angels" of their natures, on the part of white Christian America that resided on that "indefinite shore."[663] This state of contrition, which was now pervasive throughout America, would pave the way for the people's humbled acceptance of the greatest social and moral transformation in this nation's history that followed the war and Lincoln's assassination.

---

[663] *Team of Rivals*, Doris Kearns Goodwin, p 731

The troubled Mary Lincoln, who at times had been masterful as First Lady and at other times an embarrassment, was a full beneficiary of Lincoln's cheerful final day. She told Francis Carpenter, "She had never seen him so cheerful" and that "his manner was even playful." She said,

> At three o'clock, in the afternoon, he drove out with me in the open carriage, in starting, I asked him, if any one, should accompany us, he immediately replied—"No—I prefer to ride by ourselves today." During the drive he was so gay, that I said to him, laughingly, "Dear Husband, you almost startle me by your great cheerfulness," he replied, "and well I may feel so, Mary, I consider *this* day the war, has come to a close"—and then added, "We must *both*, be more cheerful in the future—between the war & the loss of our darling Willie—we have both, been very miserable."[664]

On this their last afternoon together, Lincoln was in a rare contemplative mood, speaking of their happy and sad days in Springfield, "and recollections of his early days, his little brown cottage, the law office, the court room, the green bag for his briefs and law papers, his adventures when riding the circuit."[665] He and Mary made plans for the end of the next term to travel to Europe, to the Holy Land, over the Rocky Mountains to California and then back to Springfield to live out their final days. As the carriage was nearing their return to the White House, Lincoln saw that a group of old friends, who had come to the White House to visit, were now leaving. He called out to them to return and he spent the late afternoon with these treasured

---

[664] *Team of Rivals*, Doris Kearns Goodwin, p 733
[665] *Team of Rivals*, Doris Kearns Goodwin, p 733

friends. Soon he was called to an early dinner to allow for their eight o'clock arrival to Ford's Theatre to see the celebrated actress Laura Keene in *Our American Cousin*. Again one of these last visitors recorded that Lincoln had never seemed "more hopeful and buoyant concerning the condition of the country. He was full of fun and anecdotes, feeling especially jubilant at the prospects before us."[666]

After dinner, Lincoln, accompanied by Detective Crook, made one last walk across the street to the War Department office for any telegraphed news of surrender by Johnston. There was none. But unbeknownst to Lincoln, Generals Sherman and Johnston had, on that same Good Friday, held their first of several meetings for a negotiated surrender that would be completed a few days later. Sherman, who had been influenced by Lincoln's interest in forgiveness and reconciliation that he communicated in his visit just two weeks earlier at City Point, and by Grant's Lincoln-influenced magnanimously merciful terms of surrender with General Lee, offered similar terms to Johnston. Lincoln's oft-seen dream of the night before had again portended the good fortune for which he had hoped and prayed. As they walked back to the waiting carriage, Detective Crook "almost begged" Lincoln to change his plans to attend the theater and remain safely in the White House.[667] But Lincoln was determined to go. At which point Crook asked to stay on as an extra guard. "No," Lincoln replied. "You've had a long hard day's work, and must go home." "They parted at the portico of the White House, Lincoln calling out good-bye as he started up the steps."[668] Crook was left feeling uneasy at the seeming finality inflected in Lincoln's farewell.

Lincoln's marshal and protector, Ward Hill Lamon, had been sent days earlier on an assignment to Virginia, but before

---

[666] *Team of Rivals*, Doris Kearns Goodwin, p 734
[667] *With Malice Toward None*, Stephen B. Oates, p 429
[668] *With Malice Toward None*, Stephen B. Oates, p 429

leaving, he begged the president, "Promise me you will not go out at night while I am gone, particularly to the theater."[669] Despite all the concern, Lincoln rarely appeared to be preoccupied with his own safety.

John Wilkes Booth began Good Friday, April 14, quite the opposite of Lincoln as he awoke hung-over and despondent. The past eleven days had been one piece of bad news after another. They started with the April 3 announcement that, with Grant closing in, Richmond, the Confederate capital, had been abandoned to the Union and destroyed by fires set by the fleeing Confederates. The next day Lincoln visited his captive prize and had the audacity to sit behind the desk occupied by the first and last president of the Confederate States of America, Jefferson Davis. Then on April 9, at Appomattox Court House, Robert E. Lee and his glorious Army of Northern Virginia surrendered. Two days later Lincoln made a speech proposing to give blacks the right to vote, and last night, April 13, all of Washington celebrated with a grand illumination of the city. And today, in Charleston Harbor, the Union planned to stage a gala celebration to mark the retaking of Fort Sumter, where the war began four years ago. "These past eleven days had been the worst of Booth's life."[670] When Booth awoke that Good Friday morning he had no idea that, that night, he would consummate his scheme and end the life of Abraham Lincoln.

After breakfast that morning in the dining room of the National Hotel where he was staying, Booth walked over to Ford's Theatre to collect his mail. It was customary for theaters to be the receptacles of mail belonging to their itinerate actors. The morning edition of the *National Republican* carried the announcement that the Lincolns would be attending tonight's play with General and Mrs. Grant but Booth had neither read the

---

[669] *Lincoln*, David Herbert Donald, p 594

[670] *Manhunt*, James Swanson, p 1

paper nor heard the news. A messenger from the White House had arrived earlier at Ford's Theatre to confirm that the Lincolns and Grants would be in attendance, and preparations were being made by the excited theater owners and crew to prepare the presidential box for their most distinguished guests. The president's attendance was always good for business; they could now expect a full house tonight.

Booth had received a letter, and as he sat outside on the front steps of the theater to read it he overheard the news that startled him. James L. Swanson, in *Manhunt*, describes the world-changing moment.

> Of all places, Lincoln was coming here. Booth knew the layout of Ford's intimately: the exact spot on Tenth Street where Lincoln would step out of his carriage; the place the president sat every time he came to the theatre, the route through the theatre that Lincoln would walk and the staircase he would ascend to the box; the dark, subterranean passageway beneath the stage; the narrow hallway behind the stage that led to the back door that opened to Baptist Alley; and how the president's box hung directly above the stage.[671]

> And Booth also knew *Our American Cousin*—its duration, its scenes, its players, and, most important, as it would turn out, the number of actors onstage at any given moment during the performance. It was perfect. He would not have to hunt Lincoln. The president was coming to him. But was there enough time

---

[671] *Manhunt*, James Swanson, p 14

to make all the arrangements? The checklist was substantial: Horses; weapons; supplies; alerting his fellow conspirators; casing the theatre; so many other things. He had only eight hours. But it was possible.[672]

One thing was certain for Booth: nothing could be better than to perform his heroic and glorious deed in front of an audience. Fame was in his grasp. Later that day, as he was making his preparations, he urged a friend to attend the theater as "There is going to be some splendid acting tonight."[673]

When the Lincolns would arrive with their guests, young Clara Harris and her fiancé Major Henry Rathbone, who were invited to replace the Grants who had unexpectedly decided not to attend, John Wilkes Booth and three of his accomplices would be just one block away reviewing details of a much-expanded plan from Booth's early afternoon design. He had decided to include the assassination of the vice president, Andrew Johnson, and of Lincoln's close friend and secretary of state, the powerful politician William Seward. He was certain that such a blow to the North would immortalize him in all of history. The triple assassination was set for ten fifteen p.m. David Herold was to lead Lewis Powell to Seward's house and wait outside while Powell was to enter the home and kill him. George Atzerodt was assigned to assassinate the vice president in his rented room at the Kirkwood Hotel. Booth would be completely free to enter and move about the theater, being known by the management and stage crew, and at the appointed time he would simply walk to the presidential box and assassinate the president from behind.

---

[672] *Manhunt*, James Swanson, p 14
[673] *Manhunt*, James Swanson, p 17

Good Friday had been the best day for the severely injured William Seward since the carriage accident; his daughter noted in her journal that it was the first day that he had been able to take solid food. The spacious three-story house was filled with people that night; in addition to the six Sewards, there were six household servants and two soldiers assigned to guard the secretary of state when a knock came at the door. Lewis Powell, tall, strong, and well dressed, told the servant that he had some medicine for Secretary Seward and was instructed by Seward's physician to deliver it to him personally. The servant told Powell that he could not go up to Seward's room and that he would take it to Seward. But Powell insisted and, intimidating the young servant, started up the stairs, which drew the attention of Seward's son Fred—who had attended that day's cabinet meeting for his injured father—at the landing at the top of the stairs. Fred stepped in front of Powell and said that his father was asleep and that he would deliver the medicine to his father. Powell paused, then turned and started down the stairs when "suddenly turning again, he sprang up and forward, having drawn a Navy revolver, which he leveled, with a muttered oath, at [Fred's] head, and pulled the trigger."[674] Fred would have no other memory of the horrible night that was unfolding. The gun misfired, but Powell struck Fred several times on the head with it so forcefully that Fred's skull was crushed in two places, exposing his brain and leaving him bleeding and unconscious. At the commotion Private Robinson rushed from Seward's bedside and right into Powell's large knife, which slashed his forehead. Powell continued into Seward's room. His daughter Fanny begged him to not harm her father but to no avail, as instantly the knife slashed William Seward's cheek, leaving it dangling and the knife sunk into his neck. Fortunately the crude metal devise that been holding Seward's broken jaw in place deflected

---

[674] *Team of Rivals*, Doris Kearns Goodwin, p 736

the knife enough to render the neck wound superficial. Seward's other son Gus rushed to the room as Powell moved toward Seward, who had by now fallen from the bed. Gus and the bloodied Robinson managed to pull Powell away, but not before he struck Robinson a few more times with the knife and slashed Gus also on the forehead and right hand. Gus ran for his pistol at which point Powell ran for the stairs, and before exiting the house he stabbed young Emerick Hansell, a State Department messenger, in the back and fled into the dark night. Servants ran for Dr. Verdi, who arrived to find the house awash in blood as one victim after another required his attention. Remarkably, all would survive the horrendous attack.

"I enlisted to abduct the President of the United States, not to kill," said the surprised George Atzerodt at hearing the dramatically changed plan to assassinate the president, vice president, and secretary of state.[675] But after curses and threats from Booth, he reluctantly agreed to his part to kill vice president Andrew Johnson. When the conspirators parted he went to the Kirkwood Hotel where Johnson was staying and rented a room, there to wait until the ten fifteen attack time. He was to merely knock on the unguarded door of the vice president, force his way into the room, and shoot or stab him. Seated alone at the bar, Atzerodt had too much time to consider the gravity and danger of the plot, and talked himself out of it. At ten o'clock p.m. he left the hotel and did not return. Vice President Johnson was spared and would find himself only hours away from the presidency of the still-divided nation.

Curtain time at Ford's was eight o'clock but it was after eight when the Lincolns left the White House, where Lincoln said to his friend Schuyler Colfax words that resounded beyond the short carriage ride to the theater, toward the approaching end of his unequaled mortal life: "I suppose it is time to go, though I

---

[675] *Team of Rivals*, Doris Kearns Goodwin, p 738

would rather stay."[676] After picking up their guests, the Lincoln carriage drove down Tenth Street, which was still illuminated in celebration of the Union victory, to Ford's Theatre. By the time they arrived, the play was well into the first act, and anxious spectators kept looking expectantly up to the president's box for their arrival. The moment they entered the theater, a signal was given at which the actors paused and the orchestra broke into a resounding "Hail to the Chief." The audience rose to their feet in loud applause and cheering for their president. One spectator remembered, "The President stepped to the box rail and acknowledged the applause with dignified bows and never-to-be-forgotten smiles."[677] Sitting in a rocking chair, which had thoughtfully been provided by an admirer, Lincoln sat by his wife Mary for over an hour, where they were entertained by the performance and clearly enjoyed each other's company.

> When actors scored hits, Mary applauded, but her husband simply laughed heartily. A man in the orchestra observed that Mrs. Lincoln often called the president's attention to actions on the stage and "seemed to take great pleasure in witnessing his enjoyment." Seated so close to her husband that she nestled against him, she whispered: "what will Miss. Harris think of my hanging on to you so?" With a smile he replied: "She won't think any thing about it."[678]

Booth entered the theater around nine o'clock p.m., listening from the foyer to the play that he knew by heart to determine

---

[676] *Team of Rivals,* Doris Kearns Goodwin, p 734
[677] *Lincoln,* David Herbert Donald, p 595
[678] *Lincoln,* David Herbert Donald, p 595

that it was playing on schedule, then left to saddle his rented horse in the stable behind the theater. He then led the horse to the rear-alley entrance to the theater and left it with a stagehand with instructions to hold it for ten to fifteen minutes. There was time for one more drink, so, walking in the passageway under the stage and listening to the players acting overhead, he crossed to the front of the theater to the Star Saloon next door, and at around ten o'clock p.m. he ordered a whiskey and drank it alone. Slapping some coins on the table, he left the saloon and turned right to the Ford's Theatre entrance just a few feet away. He still had a few minutes so he tarried in the lobby and listened to determine the play's progress. Soon he ascended the curving staircase.

The guard who was stationed with the footman at the presidential box entrance momentarily left his post, leaving the footman alone to guard the entrance. At about 10:12, the impeccably dressed John Wilkes Booth walked up to the footman, presented him his card, and chatted briefly with him. In a moment the footman allowed the well-known actor entrance to the box. Once inside, Booth waited unseen in the vestibule for two of the actors to exit, leaving the stage with only one actor; he wanted as much of the stage as possible for himself. Booth knew that the lone actor's upcoming line would bring a wave of laughter. Just as the audience burst into an arousing laugh, Booth raised his pistol and, at a distance of about two feet from the president, fired a single bullet that entered the back and left of Lincoln's skull.

President Abraham Lincoln's head fell forward; bleeding and unconscious he remained in the chair as if he were asleep. The young Major Rathbone seated at the side of the Lincolns lunged toward the assassin, but Booth was prepared with his sharpened hunting knife and cut a long and deep wound from Rathbone's elbow to nearly his shoulder, leaving him bleeding profusely. Booth pushed him aside and then vaulted over the rail of the box to the stage. The audience was confused; were they being treated to an unscripted surprise? The shot was muffled by the heavy laughter, and the familiar sight of John Wilkes Booth leaping to the stage was not unexpected, as dramatic leaping entrances from heights of ten to twelve feet had been one of Booth's signature renditions in earlier plays. But with Booth's melodramatic shout from the stage of "S*ic semper tyrannis* ['Thus always to tyrants'—the motto of the state of Virginia]! The South is avenged!" with his bloody dagger raised in the air, Mary Lincoln's scream "They have shot the president! They have shot the president!", and the blue-gray smoke from the gunshot rising from the presidential box, the audience quickly realized that their mirthful evening had just become the most singularly tragic moment of this nation's history.[679] Booth's relished leap in front of the startled audience did not turn out as he planned, as his spur caught on one of the draped flags over the box railing and possibly contributed to his breaking his left leg near the ankle with the awkward landing some twelve feet below. Booth hobbled to the alley and his waiting horse and galloped undetected out of the city. Powell and Atzerodt were soon captured and later hanged along with the rest of Booth's accomplices, and the would-be hero John Wilkes Booth was hunted down and unceremoniously shot and killed twelve days later while hiding in a barn. Booth would live long enough to realize that the well-informed in the South did not regard his assassination of President Lincoln as a welcomed or heroic occurrence, but rather quite the opposite; the Confederacy's defeat was so completely devastating, and the North's rising clamor for vengeance so widespread, that Southern leaders saw Lincoln's compassion and magnanimity as the one great source of safety to which they could cling. John Wilkes Booth would become a hero to virtually no one.

---

[679] *Manhunt*, James Swanson, p 19

A young army surgeon from the audience, Dr. Charles A. Leale, was the first doctor to reach the dying Lincoln in the presidential box. He found a faint pulse and light respiration on the unconscious president but could find no wound, so he quickly removed Lincoln's coat and shirt in the search. Finding no wound on his body, the doctor began passing his hands around Lincoln's head and discovered the hole in the skull left by the bullet behind his left ear. Later his friends would comment on their surprise at the muscular arms and shoulders of the president, a product of the many days of chopping wood and hard labor as a young man. Just days before, the president surprised Union soldiers with some vigorous wood-chopping, and then the fifty-six-year-old president playfully extended the ax out parallel to the ground and held it steady just as he was able to do as a young man. The young soldiers tried in vain to imitate the feat of strength as they marveled at the vigor and strength of their president.

Soon the young doctor announced that such wounds left no chance for survival. The next thought was that Lincoln needed to be moved so as to die in a more dignified place than the theater. With near pandemonium throughout the theater and into the street, Lincoln was hastily carried out of the theater through the thronging and angry crowd, and across the street to the Peterson House where he was laid on a bed. There he would labor with strained and uneven breathing until the next morning, April 15, at 7:22 a.m., at which time the doctors pronounced him dead by saying, "It is all over! The President is no more!"[680] Edwin Stanton, the secretary of war and close friend of the president, had arrived at the Peterson House before midnight and set up operations to organize a hunt for Booth and his co-conspirators, to establish protection for other government leaders should the killing continue, and to prepare for a now-suspected Confederate assault on Washington that he feared

---

[680] *Lincoln*, David Herbert Donald, p 599

might have been organized in concert with the chaos caused by that night's attacks.

Upon hearing the doctor's pronouncement, all stood still and quiet with the exception of Lincoln's son Robert, who began weeping, until Stanton asked a minister and close friend of Lincoln's, Dr. Gurley, to pray. Then, standing at the foot of Lincoln's bed, with tears streaming down his cheeks, Edwin Stanton—the same Stanton who had called Lincoln a long-armed ape years before paid a solemn salute to the first president to be assassinated in office: "with a slow and measured movement, his right arm fully extended as if in a salute, raised his hat and placed it for an instant on his head and then in the same deliberate manner removed it." Then he tearfully declared, "Now he belongs to the ages."[681]

---

[681] *Lincoln*, David Herbert Donald, p 599

Chapter Twelve

"Some Great Good to Follow"

Stephen B. Oates describes the shocking impact of President Lincoln's assassination on the country:

> Never had the nation mourned so over a fallen leader. Not only Lincoln's friends, but his legion of critics—those who'd denounced him in life, castigated him as a dictator, ridiculed him as a baboon, damned him as stupid and incompetent—now lamented his death and grieved for their country. As if civil war had not been atonement enough, for the first time in the history of the Republic a President had been assassinated, and the haunting echo of Booth's derringer troubled Americans in all corners of the Union.[682]

Lincoln's funeral was held on Wednesday, April 19; his body lay on a catafalque in the East Room surrounded by subdued soldiers and mourners, very much like in a dream he had some

---

[682] *With Malice Toward None*, Stephen B. Oates, p 434

three weeks earlier. Mary was so inconsolable that she could not attend the funeral service. A weeping General Grant stood at the foot of the coffin, later saying that this was the saddest day of his life. After the service, in which four ministers spoke, his coffin was carried to the funeral carriage, with church bells tolling throughout the city and bands playing dirges for the dead. The funeral procession carried Lincoln's body on the same route he had taken in his two previous inaugural days to the Capitol. Symbolic of the "new birth of freedom" that Lincoln promised in his Gettysburg Address, a detachment of black troops led the slow-moving and solemn procession, a sight no one could have imagined four years earlier and one that signified the end of slavery and the dawning of African-Americans' remaining arduous social struggle for respect and equality. His funeral carriage was next, followed by a riderless horse. Then came a throng of mourners, including thousands of wounded soldiers bandaged and hobbling on crutches from the nearby hospitals. And finally some four thousand additional African-Americans, walked hand in hand, in orderly rows with high silk hats and white gloves.

Lincoln's body was laid in state in the Capitol rotunda under the newly completed Capitol dome symbolizing the long-awaited completion of the founding of this nation that Lincoln's martyrdom would now solidify. For the next day and a half, tens of thousands of mourners would pass through the rotunda to pay their respects to their beloved president. On April 21, Lincoln's coffin was placed on a nine-car funeral train decorated with Union flags to set out on a winding sixteen-hundred-mile journey back to Springfield for his burial. Earlier, the coffin containing the remains of his deceased son Willie was exhumed and placed on the same train to be reburied with his father in Springfield. All along the way people lined the railway to catch a brief glimpse of the passing train, or attended funeral corteges in major cities. In New York, some eighty-five thousand were in attendance. In the Albany statehouse, people solemnly passed by his coffin all through the night. Some one hundred fifty thousand mourners from Ohio, Michigan, and Pennsylvania gathered in Cleveland to catch a glimpse of Lincoln as his coffin rested on a pagoda in Monument Park. On the night run to Indianapolis, bonfires lined the route, and silent crowds stood in the rain as the train rolled slowly by. Hundreds of thousands assembled in Chicago to pay their last respects to Illinois's favorite son, and finally to his beloved Springfield where his remains are entombed today.

Four years earlier, when Lincoln assumed the presidency, he had no doubt as to how to approach the great division of this nation that had so recently occurred in the four months preceding his taking office. From his perspective, the Southern rebellion was much more than a political option that the Southern states were exercising; it was a dangerous threat to world democracy or as he put it, "the last best hope of earth."[683] Lincoln's vision was so expansive that he perceived that the brewing American convulsion would affect the prospects for freedom and peace far beyond the borders of the United States.

As a young man he once said, "Many free countries have lost their liberty and ours may lose hers—but if she shall, be it my proudest pleasure not that I was the last to desert her but that I never deserted her."[684] Lincoln carried this same resounding resolve with him to the White House. To the New Jersey state senate, just days before taking the oath of office, Lincoln's expressed sentiments that reflected his unparalleled foresight as referred to the Founding Fathers:

> I recollect thinking then, boy even though I
> was, that there must have been something
> more than common that those men struggled

---

683 Annual Message to Congress, December 1, 1862
684 Lincoln's Lyceum Speech, January 27, 1838, Springfield, Illinois

for. I am exceedingly anxious that that thing
which they struggled for; that something even
more than National Independence; that something that held out great promise to all the
people of the world to all time to come; I am
exceedingly anxious that this Union, the Constitution, and the liberties of the people shall
be perpetuated in accordance with the original
idea for which the struggle was made, and I
shall most happy indeed if I shall be an humble
instrument in the hands of the Almighty, and
of this , His almost chosen people, for perpetuating the object of that great struggle.[685]

The vehicle for such freedom and peace, as he so clearly saw
it, lay in the Constitution, the Declaration of Independence, and
a strong unified nation to defend and protect them. He, along
with the Founding Fathers, believed that these two expansive
documents were divinely endowed.

For years the Southern rebels (and many Northerners) derided the Declaration of Independence for its claim that all men
are created equal, and they prostituted the Constitution with its
window of allowance for slavery. Lincoln could see that these
two great documents were on the brink of extinction with the
Confederacy's intent to mothball the Declaration of Independence and to rewrite their own constitution. Lincoln's clarity of
vision regarding the long-term effect of the unfolding rebellion,
America's widespread racism, its religious and racial bigotry, and
its tolerance for injustice is what fueled his astounding resolve
to oppose it. And this strength of purpose was challenged on
his first day in office when he found himself surrounded by

---

[685] Eloquent President Ronald C. White, Jr. p326

advisers who urged him to let Fort Sumter be surrendered to the aggression of the Charleston, South Carolina Fire-Eaters. It was on that first day in office that his advisers became witnesses to Lincoln's unmatched perspective and immovable moral courage. To be sure, Lincoln saw these threats six years earlier, which spawned his dramatic one-man offensive that launched the unknown, unrenowned country lawyer to the most powerful office on earth at the modern world's most critical juncture. God, through Lincoln would ensure that this government "of the people, by the people and for the people" would not "perish from the earth."[686]

Just what Lincoln saw and how he came to see it, only he and God know. But long before his improbable assent to the White House he expressed his conviction of some divine mission ordained by God himself. Just days before Lincoln's surprising election as president, Mr. Newton Bateman, the Illinois Superintendent of Public Instruction and a close friend of Lincoln, recorded Lincoln revealing with the clarity of a revelation his sense that God had a work for him to perform:

> Mr. Lincoln paused for long minutes, his features surcharged with emotion. Then he rose and walked up and down the reception room, in an effort to retain or regain his self-possession. Stopping at last, he said, with a trembling voice and his cheeks wet with tears, "I know there is a God, and that he hates injustice and slavery. I see the storm coming, and I know that His hand is in it. If He has a place in this work for me, and I think He has, I believe I am ready. I am nothing, but truth is everything! I know I am

---

[686] Lincoln's *Gettysburg Address*

right, because I know that liberty is right: for Christ teaches it, and Christ is God.

"I have told them that a house divided against itself cannot stand, (Mark 3:25) and Christ and reason say the same thing. [Stephen A.] Douglas does not care whether slavery is voted up or down. But God cares, and humanity cares, and I care. And with God's help, I will not fail. I may not see the end, but it will come and I shall be vindicated; and those men will see that they have not read their Bibles right! Does it not appear strange that men can ignore the moral aspects of this contest? A revelation could not make it plainer to me that slavery, or the government must be destroyed. The future would be something awful, as I look at it, but for this ROCK on which I stand (alluding to the Gospel book he still held in his hand). It seems as if God had borne with slavery until the very teachers of religion had come to defend it from the Bible, and to claim for it a Divine character and sanction. And now the cup of iniquity is full, and the vials of wrath will be poured out."[687]

In his first presidential message to the congressional leaders of the nation, he said,

Our popular government has often been called an experiment. Two points in it, our people have already settled—the successful es-

---

[687] *50 Years in the "Church" of Rome*, Charles Chiniquy, p 304

tablishing, and the successful administering of it. One still remains—its successful maintenance against a formidable internal attempt to overthrow it.[688]

The Founding Fathers were haunted with the historical reality that few republics flourished and most attempts to build such a government ended in failure. The United Netherlands had collapsed in 1787, as did Santo Domingo's attempt in 1791. The British endeavored to build a representative government with their far-off colonies, which also disintegrated. And France's attempt also resulted in its own nightmare of civil war. There was little in history that offered hope of success for the Founding Fathers' "experiment." Of this fact, Jay Winik, the author of *April 1865, The Month that Saved America*, states,

> For the Founders, the destiny of republics was...that they inevitably rise and fall, withering through fragmentation, failing through conquest, dying through despotism.[689]

> So ingrained was this view that nowhere did the Constitution promise perpetuity for the United States as a country. It still does not today. George Washington, as fervent a patriot as ever lived, and a good Federalist, agreed. In his first inaugural, he spoke of the "Republican model of government" as an experiment.[690] Washington, like most of the other Founding Fathers, like most of the country, and like most

---

[688] *The Eloquent President*, Ronald C. White, Jr., p 245
[689] *April 1865, The Month That Saved America*, Jay Winik, p 372
[690] *April 1865, The Month That Saved America*, Jay Winik, p 372

of the world, was not sure that the United States would work.[691]

So why did these great men undertake such a formidable task? For one, the four years that followed their independence from England were a nightmare of self-centered, bickering, and feuding independent states that was growing worse with time and held no hope of resolution. Something dramatic had to be done to avoid complete collapse, and from that desperate convention in 1787 emerged the blessed United States Constitution; flawed as it was with its allowance for slavery, it possessed enough strength to push the states toward their intended composition, as *United* States. Decades later Abraham Lincoln would complete the unifying process. It may also be for a reason that is not often acknowledged—the fact that George Washington and most of the Founding Fathers moved forward with the "experiment" because they hoped. They carried in their hearts an oft-expressed hope and faith that for some unknown reason the hand of Providence, the Living God Himself, as Lincoln at times referred to Him, would have a particular interest in the successful development of this nation. And many of them believed, and frequently expressed, that God wanted them to pursue their independence from England and that He wanted them to formulate this government of unprecedented freedoms. And these great men had the courage to act on that faith.

For reasons unknown to the Founding Fathers, they somehow believed that God would uphold the fragile nation, once founded. They also believed, as did Lincoln, that without His guiding hand it had but little hope of survival. Benjamin Franklin addressed the 1787 Constitutional Convention at a critical juncture by saying:

---

[691] *April 1865, The Month That Saved America,* Jay Winik, p 372

We have been assured, sir, in the sacred writings, that "Except the Lord build the house, they labour in vain that build it." I firmly believe this; and I also believe that, without his concurring aid, we shall succeed in this political building no better than the builders of Babel.[692]

Today, Americans celebrate the Founding Fathers' 1776 declaration of freedom on each July 4, with few fully realizing that the miraculous success of this democratic experiment did not fully materialize until some "four score and seven years" after its founding under the overseeing eye of Abraham Lincoln. In fact, the eight decades that followed the formation of the Constitution brought a widening erosion of the very principles that guaranteed such freedoms. Almost unthinkable today, by 1861 the Declaration of Independence and the Constitution had lost their once-revered status among many, if not most, Americans. The third and completing step to the governmental "experiment," the proof that it could be "maintained" as Lincoln correctly assessed, was not fully realized until all was nearly lost in the mid 1800s. President Lincoln perceived that the coming years would either prove that such a democracy can indeed "long endure"[693] (his phrase in the Gettysburg Address) or he and the American people would witness its demise and the rejection and dissolution of "the last best hope of earth"[694] (a phrase from his first presidential speech to Congress) by the hands of its very benefactors.

Lincoln's belief that he was a "humble instrument in the hands of God" to preserve these divinely endowed documents

---

[692] *Documentary History of the Constitution of the United States,* 3:235-37

[693] Lincoln's *Gettysburg Address*

[694] Annual Message to Congress, December 1, 1862

and the freedoms that they proffered fueled his remarkable resolve to oppose the growing threat to destroy them.[695] To Lincoln, disunion of the states meant the eventual death of these precious documents. In 1861, the Southern rebels' pursuit of the expansion of slavery and the majority of the nation's embracing of racism, religious bigotry, injustice, and mobocracy had unwittingly set the stage for the astonishing display of God's wrath and His judgments. Again, as Lincoln said, "And now the cup of iniquity is full, and the vials of wrath will be poured out."[696] This divine judgment of America would be presided over by a prayerful, meek, yet astoundingly resolute self-educated lawyer as he stepped into the highest office in the land. On this general disregard for the rights of others Lincoln said,

> I mean the increasing disregard for law which pervades the country—the growing disposition to substitute the wild and furious passions in lieu of the sober judgments of the courts, and the worse than savage mobs for the executive ministers of justice…By operation of this mobocratic spirit, which all must admit [is] now abroad in the land, the strongest bulwark of any government, and particularly of those constituted like ours, may effectually be broken down and destroyed.[697]

In a letter to Eliza P. Gurney he confessed,

> We hoped for a happy termination of this terrible war long before this; but God knows

---

[695] *The Eloquent President*, Ronald C. White, Jr., p 326
[696] *50 Years in the "Church" of Rome*, Charles Chiniquy, p 304
[697] *The Wit and Wisdom of Abraham Lincoln* , p 29

best, and has ruled otherwise…we must work earnestly in the best light He gives us, trusting that so working still conduces to the great ends He ordains. *Surely He intends some great good to follow this mighty convulsion* [italics added], which no mortal could make, and no mortal could stay.[698]

Perhaps the most significant utterance in Lincoln's Gettysburg Address was his reference to "a new birth of freedom" for this nation. We don't know if Lincoln knew of the extraordinary national transformation that would follow the war, but in this letter to Mrs. Gurney, Lincoln expressed at least his hope and quite possibly his foreknowledge that some "great good" would follow the Refiner's fire of civil war. Although he did not elaborate on the theme, he touched on it again a few weeks later in a message to Congress when he said, "under the sharp discipline of civil war, the nation is beginning a new life."[699]

Was there "a new birth of freedom" for this nation after the war? Was there "a new life" that emerged from the chaos of mid-nineteenth-century America? And if so, what was it to which America's God-fearing president referred? It is an awe-inspiring fact that some of the most dramatic moral corrections in the history of this nation took place during this period. Jay Winik, author of *April 1865, the Month that Saved America*, had this to say on this subject:

> Even today, what followed in the remaining days of the Civil War seems almost miraculous. April 1865 is a month that could have unraveled the American nation. Instead it saved it. It is a month as dramatic and as devastating as any ever faced in American history—and it

---

[698] *Lincoln*, DHD, p 515
[699] *The Eloquent President*, Ronald C. White, Jr., p 471

proved to be perhaps the most moving and decisive month not simply of the Civil War, but indeed, quite likely, in the life of the United States. [700]

Why did this costly war extend for those four long years, this war that Lincoln believed could have ended at any moment by the hand of the Almighty? Why did "this mighty convulsion, which no mortal could make, and no mortal could stay" (as Lincoln described it), not end in the few weeks that most all expected it would?[701] Lincoln said, "War is most terrible and this of ours in its magnitude and duration is one of the most terrible the world has ever known."[702] As we ponder the severity of the war and Lincoln's conviction that God had His own purpose for it, the following questions beg consideration: Had the war merely lasted a year with some one hundred thousand deaths, would the people of America have given up their destructive states' rights zeal? Had it extended to two years with some two hundred thousand casualties, would this people have accepted the wiping away of the reprehensible beliefs and practices of white superiority, legitimized in the Supreme Court's Dred Scott decision and the United States Congress's Kansas-Nebraska Act that turned slavery into a choice for white Americans rather than the moral wrong that Lincoln declared it to be?

Was it the hardened hearts of the American people themselves, reflected in their widespread acceptance of the above corruptions, in addition to their abhorrence for and persecution of the Mormons, the Catholics, the Irish, the Italians, and who knows who else would follow; was it this "I am free but you are not" ardor that required such a severe degree of chastisement delivered in the horrors of the four-year war? Was it the Ameri-

---

[700] *April 1865, The Month That Saved America,* Jay Winik, Introduction, p X
[701] *Lincoln,* David Herbert Donald, p 515
[702] *The Wit and Wisdom of Abraham Lincoln,* p 46

can people themselves who required the sacrificing of six hundred twenty-three thousand men and boys to bring them to finally accept the emancipation of the slaves? Or would Congress have passed, and would the states have ratified, the Thirteenth Amendment without the living hell of the war's devastation? Consider again Lincoln's own words:

> We hoped for a happy termination of this terrible war long before this; but God knows best, and has ruled otherwise...we must work earnestly in the best light He gives us, trusting that so working still conduces to the great ends He ordains. *Surely He intends some great good to follow this mighty convulsion* [italics added], which no mortal could make, and no mortal could stay.[703]

For God to work his healing transformation, for the people to have purged from their beings the above stated moral aberrations, is it possible that such a national cleansing required the intense severity of the extended death and destruction delivered by the war? For their hearts to finally soften to that point of healing contrition that would allow for the release of these destructive perceptions that had been legitimized by this nation's judges, lawmakers and presidents? Did wayward America itself require God to protract the horrible war to complete the refining? Lincoln would have found precedence for such God-led transformations in the Bible with the ancient Israelites' release from Egypt. What amount of chastening was required for the beleaguered pharaoh Ramses and the Egyptians to release their slaves, to "let my people go" when the two and one half million Israelites were finally and miraculously set free as God worked

---

[703] *Lincoln*, David Herbert Donald, p 515

through His prophet Moses? Then, once freed, it became the Israelites' turn for sanctification with their hearts not yet fully prepared for their Promised Land. For them, it required forty years of wandering in the desert for the cleansing to take. In this same light, how much chastening was required for Americans to finally and forever set the four million African-Americans free from the disgraceful practice of slavery, and for white America's legalized and celebrated racism and prejudice to be imploded?

About a year and a half into his presidency, Lincoln came to the solitary and personal conclusion that the war was a chastening measure used by the Almighty God for the wayward American people, and that it was a punishment for their national sins. And as such, Lincoln believed that "some great good," a "new birth of freedom," a "new life" would be the result of the cleansing baptism.

Who can know the mind of God but a prophet as we ponder these conditions? But what is certain is that these political and social blights in the American fabric and character were, in fact, swept away by the severity of the Civil War. As presidents, George Washington and Abraham Lincoln would embrace the belief that this nation would not be a nation of strength and security without a strong and *righteous* central government.

The United States would eventually emerge from the Civil War, *finally* as *United* States, just as the inspired Founding Fathers hoped and prayed they would. Following the prompting from his Almighty God, Abraham Lincoln would use the war powers to legally declare the slaves free, and the power of war would create a humbling submissiveness; the emergence of "the better angels" of the peoples' nature would *finally*, once and for all, accept it. With emancipation came the heretofore-unthinkable Thirteenth Amendment to the Constitution *finally* removing forever the three-fifths clause in the Constitution and the slave states' unbalanced domination in the halls of

Congress. William Lee Miller sums up this remarkable transformation:

> And when American slavery would finally
> be ended, it would be done altogether within
> the Constitution and the law, by the Thirteenth
> Amendment to the Constitution, recommend-
> ed to the Republican Convention of 1864 by
> President Lincoln, finally passed by the Thirty
> eighth Congress under the urging and through
> the political maneuvering of President Lincoln,
> joyfully signed by President Lincoln after con-
> gress passed it (although Presidents don't need
> to sign amendments), ratified by three-fourths
> of the states after he was dead, and thus made
> a part of the Constitution, ending slavery for-
> ever—*constitutionally* ended, under the law, with
> the Union intact.[704]

Because of the war, this government was now able to
emerge, as originally intended, into one that would no longer
tolerate and legalize racism, prejudice or religious persecution;
instead it would *finally* revert back to its original moorings to
protect the inalienable rights of all men and women, regardless
of race, religion, or national origin. *Finally* there would be freedom of speech and of the press. And *finally*, immigrants from
around the world would be accepted into this nation's borders
with the same inalienable rights that the nineteenth-century
Americans and their ancestors enjoyed. *Finally*, all races would
be respected and protected as equal by the strong and upright
central government.

---

[704] *William Lee Miller*, LV, p 237

The war's devastation went far beyond the six hundred twenty-three thousand young lives that were snuffed out on America's battlefields, far beyond the millions of mourning loved ones back home, and far beyond the economic ruin to which many of the surviving and war-beaten soldiers returned upon the war's close. Few of the wealthy aristocracy in the South escaped financial desolation. During the war, many exhibited their loyalty to the Confederate cause by contributing much of their wealth to the war effort that all hoped would end in a matter of weeks. But over the course of the war years, those resources were depleted and were not replenished because the now slaveless plantations were rendered inoperable through the emancipation, which Lincoln had credited to God, making the powerful yet meek declaration to his cabinet that "God has decided in favor of the slave." As the North's economy was significantly damaged, the Southern economy was brought to its knees when the former slave owners no longer called on the banks to take out their customary bank loans, and when they no longer purchased more property or implements of production, and when the women of the aristocracy no longer purchased their opulent home furnishings and clothing, all of which had fueled the Southern economy years earlier.

Those plantations that were fortunate enough to survive the burning and pillaging of the occupying Union armies became sad, empty reminders of the pride and arrogance that precipitated God's wrath, which He expressed in the war, which the rebels caused and He allowed. And it was the people's chastened contrition at war's end that became the required ingredient that fostered the dramatic moral transformation for which Lincoln fought so courageously in the six years leading to his election and his four years as president. Gone with their wealth was the collective strength of their states' rights and proslavery resolve, as the former Southern aristocracy had neither energy nor will to continue their mischief. They were left to invest all of their energies

348

into their own survival in their broken Southern economy. Although many went to their eventual graves still embracing these same political views, the devastation of the Civil War had dramatically doused these two collective political flames. The once proud Fire-Eaters of the prewar years had been humbled into submission and political oblivion. Not only was their will depleted, but also Lincoln's Thirteenth Amendment would remove the unfair political advantage in congress crafted into the Constitution by the proslavery Founding Fathers.

The Civil War's baptism had extinguished their fires, never to become again, to this day, a threat to the national government. Today it would be a strange sound indeed to hear one of our fifty states clamor for secession from the United States, and today any talk of reintroducing slavery would be met with universal derision. They are gone. They are dead in America. There is no place for them in the hearts and minds of Americans today. Along with them, sanctioned religious persecution was also subdued, as well as the nativist zeal against foreigners. This is the legacy of the American Civil War. Lincoln taught America that not he, but God, defeated the "formidable internal attempt" to overthrow this government that was founded to protect the freedoms guaranteed by the sacred Constitution and Declaration of Independence.

The newfound allegiance to this national republic was most certainly a "new birth of freedom," a "new life," "a great good to follow." The Pledge of Allegiance that can be recited by nearly every American today would never have been tolerated by many, if not most, in America prior to the Civil War. Their allegiance was to their state, not to the republic. Many were like Robert E. Lee, who referred to his home state of Virginia as his country. The blessings of liberty and of justice were not meant for all, but only for white Anglo-Saxons whose Christian religion did not differ from the mainstream. It would likely have moved Lincoln deeply had he lived to hear Americans recite the pledge that was composed by two educators in 1892, and revised four additional times until its final revision in 1954, when President Dwight D. Eisenhower added the words "under God," just as Lincoln inserted these same two words extemporaneously into his Gettysburg Address during its delivery.

I pledge allegiance to the Flag of the United States of America, and **to the Republic** *for which it stands:* **one Nation under God, indivisible, With Liberty and Justice for all.**

William J. Wolf sees significance in the juxtaposition of the phrases "under God" and "new birth of freedom" in Lincoln's Gettysburg Address when Lincoln said "that this nation, under God, shall have a new birth of freedom."[705] Wolf sees the theme of the rite of baptism throughout the address to the American people. On Wolf's baptismal observation, William E. Barton says,

> The New Testament describes baptism as a dying to sin, with Christ in his death as a rising to newness of life in the power of the resurrection. Lincoln conflates the themes of the life of man in birth, baptismal dedication, and spiritual rebirth with the experience of the nation in its eighty-seven year history.[706]

Who could have hoped for such a dramatic moral transformation in the wayward thinking and practices of this Christian nation? Had Lincoln lived to see this reformation, he would have clearly recognized, and openly declared, that only the refining fire of the Almighty God and His immersing baptism of

---

[705] Lincoln's *Gettysburg Address*
[706] *The Soul of Abraham Lincoln*, William E. Barton, p xxxv

sinning America could have accomplished the ending of the old life that had erroneously evolved and the emergence from the cleansing baptismal waters with a "new life."

As the visionary Lincoln hoped for "some great good to follow," the Civil War would secure a number of "new birth[s] of freedom," all of which would give this nation a "new life" that followed its baptism of fire.[707] No longer would there be a choice for slavery in the new territories as formally granted by the Kansas-Nebraska Act. The Thirteenth Amendment to the Constitution guaranteed that there would be no slaves, period, from border to border and from coast to coast. And as Lincoln had correctly predicted regarding slavery, this nation would become either all of one or all of the other. Fortunately for mankind, Americans would no longer "wring their bread from the sweat of another men's faces" and would become a nation, all of which would eventually come to abhor slavery.[708]

The refining fire of war produced another birth of new freedom by cleansing America of the shameful blemish expressed and ratified by the Supreme Court's Dred Scott decision, in which whites were proclaimed to be superior to blacks, so that the African-Americans would be viewed and treated by whites as an inferior race, unworthy of the freedoms guaranteed to all men in the Declaration of Independence. This Supreme Court decision granted all white Americans the right to practice open discrimination and racism under the protection of the law as a political perk. But thanks be to God, the governmental recognition and protection of this notion was drowned in the baptism of the Civil War. And even though racial discrimination in varying degrees continues to this day (the Ku Klux Klan was organized in the year following the end of the war), gone are the days of segregation and seats at the backs of buses for African-Americans. Today

---

[707] Lincoln's *Gettysburg Address*
[708] Abraham Lincoln's Second Inaugural Address

black men and women are educated where white people are educated; they excel in business, education, government, and the arts, as do men and women from all races and all origins. The casting away of the character-decaying Dred Scott decision was ratified by the undeniable courage and strength of the African-Americans in Union uniforms who fought ably for their freedom, ensuring "freedom for the free" and dispelling the commonly held fancy that the Negro would be incapable as a soldier.

There was yet another "great good" to follow that contributed to "new life" for this nation. Lincoln had always been "a man without prejudice in a day when discrimination against race, religion, and foreign birth was widespread."[709] The highly popular prewar movement by the Know-Nothings to openly discriminate against Irish Catholics in America also lost its accepted station in American society by war's end. In 1844, Democrats blamed Lincoln's Whig Party for fostering hate and violence toward foreigners and Catholics. Lincoln responded to the charges in a public meeting by proposing that the following resolution be passed:

> That the guarantee of rights of conscience, as found in our Constitution, is most sacred and inviolable, and one that belongs no less to the Catholic, than to the Protestant; and that all attempts to abridge or interfere with these rights, either Catholic or Protestant, directly or indirectly...shall ever have our most effective opposition.[710]

Not only had the principle of all men being created equal finally been enthroned in America, but the widely held notion

---

[709] *The Wit and Wisdom of Abraham Lincoln,* p 3
[710] *Lincoln,* Carl Sanburg, p 81

that white Anglo-Saxon Protestants were better, were superior, were more favored by God, than people of other races and religions began its gradual erasure as an acceptable tenet in the free land of America. It also meant that the original freedoms of religious expression would no longer be disregarded, but were now to be respected and protected by the nation—a nation that would, once again, be united and strong enough to protect the right to worship. This meant that no longer was any religion to be targeted for opposition as was the Catholic religion by the Know-Nothings, and the Mormon religion or members of the Church of Jesus Christ of Latter-day Saints by the New York, Ohio, Missouri, and Illinois persecutors prior to the cleansing Civil War.

All of the above elements of the "new birth of freedom," the "new life," the "great good to follow" now afforded to all Americans were the very moral elements for which Lincoln had so gallantly asserted himself from the day he proclaimed from the staircase in the Springfield state-house that he would commence his relentless challenge to America's moral decadence by dogging the most powerful politician, Stephen A. Douglas, and his political victories in congress that were poised to deny such freedoms. Abraham Lincoln, arguably America's most remarkable citizen, would single-handedly take on the moral bankruptcy that was reflected in the practice of slavery, the mobocracy, the discrimination toward the Catholics and Irish, the brutal persecutions of the Mormons, and the frequent intimidations and fraud at the polls, that permeated the American fabric, and in which few Americans confessed any wrong. In fact, as Lincoln observed, many Christians heard frequent Sunday sermons regarding God's gift to them of slavery. And many a sermon carried impassioned encouragement for censorship of the press and persecution of Mormons, Catholics, and members of other denominations divergent from the mainstream sects. Lincoln, however, was looking beyond them all and could see that the very existence of this nation and government of the people, by the people, and for the people was hanging by a thread, so dangerously close to dissolution. And he saw that the dissolution of this Union would mark the end of what Lincoln declared to be the "last best hope of earth."[711]

Inspired by the passing of this great final test of the democratic experiment, nation after nation throughout the world would go on to adopt their own individual forms of democracy, complete with freedoms to assemble, to vote, to worship, and to speak, and featuring respect for people of other races and social circumstances. One shudders to consider the condition of this nation and the world had Abraham Lincoln not stood so resolutely in following not the tenets of the Whig, Republican or Democratic Parties; not Congress, his cabinet, or of the Supreme Court; not his own personal political ambitions; but by following what he firmly believed to be the will of the Almighty God to preserve the Union, end slavery and prejudice, and transform the American soul with the emergence of the "better angel" of its nature into the tolerant, peace-loving people that God and the Founding Fathers intended for all of us to be.

Today Lincoln continues to be revered as the Great Emancipator, the Great Communicator, and the Redeemer of the Union, and rightfully so. He is not so well known, and maybe should be, as America's Prophet-President, coincidentally in place during its most harrowing trial, or raised up and placed there by the hand of the Eternal God Himself, as was the Prophet Moses over the Israelites, to guide "an almost chosen people" through their respective refining fires. Perhaps nothing speaks to the role of modern-day prophet more than his eleven proclamations of days of thanksgiving, fasting, repentance, and prayer that he

---

[711] Lincoln's first address to Congress

issued to the American people in his four years as their president. Excerpts of each follow:

Proclamation of a National Fast Day
August 12, 1861

> And whereas it is fit and becoming in all people at all times, to acknowledge and revere the supreme government of God, to bow in humble submission to his chastisements, to confess and deplore their sins and transgressions, in the full conviction that the fear of the Lord is the beginning of wisdom...Therefore, I, Abraham Lincoln, President of the United States, do appoint the last Thursday in September next, as a day of humiliation, prayer, and fasting for all people of the nation.[712]
>
> Abraham Lincoln

Proclamation Recommending Thanksgiving
for Victories
April 10, 1862

> It has pleased Almighty God to vouchsafe signal victories to the land and naval forces engaged in suppressing an internal rebellion, and at the same time avert from our country the dangers of foreign intervention and invasion.
>
> It is therefore recommended to the people of the United States that at

---

[712] *Life and Works of Abraham Lincoln*, Edited by Marion Mills Miller, Litt. D., p 153

their next weekly assemblages in their accustomed places of public worship which shall occur after notice of this proclamation shall have been received, they especially acknowledge and render thanks to our Heavenly Father for these inestimable blessings....And that they reverently invoke the divine guidance for our national counsels, to the end that they may speedily result in the restoration of peace...[713]

Abraham
Lincoln

Proclamation of a National Fast Day
March 30, 1863

And whereas it is the duty of nations as well as of men to own their dependence upon the overruling power of God; to confess their sins and transgressions in humble sorrow, yet with assured hope that genuine repentance will lead to mercy and pardon; and to recognize the sublime truth, announced in the Holy scriptures and proven by all history, that those nations only are blessed whose God is the Lord.

And inasmuch as we know that by his divine law nations, like individuals, are subjected to punishments and chastisements in this world, may we not justly fear that the awful ca-

---

[713] *Life and Works of Abraham Lincoln*, Edited by Marion Mills Miller, Litt. D., p 153

lamity of civil war which now desolates the land may be but a punishment inflicted upon us for our presumptuous sins, to the needful end of our national reformation as a whole people? We have been the recipients of the choicest bounties of Heaven...but we have forgotten God.

It behooves us then, to humble ourselves before the offended Power, to confess our national sins, and to pray for clemency and forgiveness:

I do by this my proclamation designate and set apart Thursday, the 30th day of April, 1863, as a day of national humiliation, fasting , and prayer.[714]

Abraham Lincoln

Announcement of News From Gettysburg
Washington, July 4, 10:30 a.m.

The President announces to the country that news from the Army of the Potomac...is such as to cover that army with the highest honor, to promise a great success to the cause of the Union, [the victory at the battle of Gettysburg] and to claim the condolence of all for the many gallant fallen; and that for this he especially desires that on this day He whose will, not ours, should ever be done be everywhere

---

[714] *Life and Works of Abraham Lincoln*, Edited by Marion Mills Miller, Litt. D., p. 156

remembered and reverenced with profoundest gratitude.[715]

A.
Lincoln

Proclamation for Thanksgiving
July 15, 1863

It has pleased Almighty God to hearken to the supplications and prayers of an afflicted people, and to vouchsafe to the army and the navy of the United States victories on land and on sea…but these victories have been accorded not without sacrifices of life, limb, health, and liberty, incurred by brave, loyal, and patriotic citizens. It is meet and right to recognize and confess the presence of the Almighty Father, and the power of his hand equally in these triumphs and in these sorrows.

Now therefore, be it known that I do set apart Thursday, the 6th of August next, to be observed as a day for national thanksgiving, praise and prayer…[to] render the homage due to the Divine Majesty for the wonderful things he has done in the nation's behalf, and invoke the influence of his Holy Spirit to subdue the anger which has produced and so long sus-

---

[715] *Life and Works of Abraham Lincoln,* Edited by Marion Mills Miller, Litt. D., p. 158

tained a needless and cruel rebellion…[716]
                    Abraham Lincoln

Proclamation for Thanksgiving
October 1863

The year that is drawing toward its close has been filled with the blessings of fruitful fields and healthful skies. To these bounties, which are so constantly enjoyed that we are prone to forget the source from which they come, others have been added…

No human counsel hath devised, nor hath any mortal hand worked out these great things. They are the gracious gifts of the most high God, who, while dealing with us in anger for our sins, hath nevertheless remembered mercy.

It has seemed to me fit and proper that they should be solemnly, reverently, and gratefully acknowledged as with one heart and one voice by the whole American People. I do, therefore, invite my fellow-citizens in every part of the United States…to set apart and observe the last Thursday of November next as a day of thanksgiving and praise to our beneficent Father who dwelleth in the heavens. And I recommend to them that…they do also, with humble penitence for our national perverseness and disobedience, commend to his tender care all those who have become widows, or-

[716] *Life and Works of Abraham Lincoln*, Edited by Marion Mills Miller, Litt. D., p. 158

phans, mourners, or sufferers in the lamentable civil strife in which we are unavoidably engaged...[717]

A. Lincoln

Recommendation of Thanksgiving for Union Success in East Tennessee
December 7, 1863

Reliable information being received that the insurgent force is retreating from East Tennessee, under circumstances rendering it probable that the Union forces cannot hereafter be dislodged from that important position, and esteeming this to be of high national consequence, I recommend that all loyal people do, on receipt of this information, assemble at their places of worship and render special homage and gratitude to Almighty God for this great advancement of the national cause.[718]

A. Lincoln

Recommendation of Thanksgiving
May 9, 1864

To the friends of Union and Liberty: Enough is known of army operations within the last five days to claim an especial gratitude to God, while what remains undone requires our most

---

[717] *Life and Works of Abraham Lincoln*, Edited by Marion Mills Miller, Litt. D., p 159-161

[718] *Life and Works of Abraham Lincoln*, Edited by Marion Mills Miller, Litt. D., p 161

sincere prayers to, and reliance upon, him without whom all human effort is vain. I recommend that all patriots, at their homes, in their places of public worship, and wherever they may be, unite in common thanksgiving and prayer to almighty God.[719]

Abraham Lincoln

Proclamation for a Day of Prayer
July 7, 1864
BY THE PRESIDENT OF THE UNITED
STATES OF AMERICA

A Proclamation
...I, Abraham Lincoln, President of the United States, cordially concurring with the Congress of the United States in the penitential and pious sentiments expressed...do hereby appoint the first Thursday of August next to be observed by the people of the United States as a day of national humiliation and prayer.

I do hereby further invite and request the heads of the executive departments of this government, together with all legislators, all judges and magistrates, and all other persons exercising authority in the land...to assemble in their preferred places of public worship on that day, and there and then to render to the

---

[719] *Life and Works of Abraham Lincoln*, Edited by Marion Mills Miller, Litt. D., p162

Almighty and merciful Ruler of the universe such homages and such confessions, and to offer to him such supplications, as the Congress of the United States have, in their aforesaid resolution, so solemnly, so earnestly, and so reverently recommended.[720]

Proclamation of Thanksgiving
September 3, 1864

The signal success that divine Providence has recently vouchsafed to the operations of the United States fleet and army in the harbor of Mobile, and the reduction of Fort Powell, Fort Gaines, and Fort Morgan, and the glorious achievements of the army under Major-General Sherman in the State of Georgia, resulting in the capture of the city of Atlanta, call for devout acknowledgement to the Supreme Being in whose hands are the destinies of nations. It is therefore requested that on next Sunday, in all places of worship in the United States, thanksgiving be offered to him for his mercy...[721]

Proclamation of Thanksgiving
October 20, 1864

It has pleased almighty God to prolong our national life another year...He has largely

---

[720] *Life and Works of Abraham Lincoln*, Edited by Marion Mills Miller, Litt. D., p 163
[721] *Life and Works of Abraham Lincoln*, Edited by Marion Mills Miller, Litt. D., p 164

augmented our free population by emancipation and by immigration, while he has opened to us new sources of wealth…

Now, therefore, I Abraham Lincoln, President of the United States, do hereby appoint and set apart the last Thursday of November next as a day which I desire to be observed by all my fellow-citizens…as a day of thanksgiving and praise to almighty God, the beneficent Creator and Ruler of the universe And I do further recommend to my fellow-citizens aforesaid, that on that occasion they do reverently humble themselves in the dust, and from thence offer up penitent and fervent prayers and supplications to the great Disposer of events for a return of the inestimable blessings of peace, union, and harmony throughout the land which it has pleased him to assign as a dwelling-place for ourselves and for our posterity throughout all generations.[722]

In testimony, etc.

Abraham Lincoln

Stephen A. Douglas said in one of their debates that Lincoln was "a poor hand to quote Scripture."[723] Lincoln responded by saying,

I will try it again, however. It is said in one of the admonitions of the Lord, "As your Father in Heaven is perfect, be ye also perfect."

---

[722] *Life and Works of Abraham Lincoln*, Edited by Marion Mills Miller, Litt. D., p 165

[723] *The Collected Works of Abraham Lincoln*, Roy P. Basler, p 501

The Savior, I suppose, did not expect that any human creature could be perfect as the Father in Heaven; but He said, "As your Father in Heaven is perfect, be ye also perfect." He set up that standard, and he [Jesus] who did most toward reaching that standard, attained the highest degree of moral perfection.[724]

Few will argue with Lincoln's assessment of Jesus' attainment of moral perfection. And most who study the life of Abraham Lincoln cannot help but conclude that among mortals, few ever came closer to Jesus' height of moral perfection than did Abraham Lincoln, God's humble instrument.

---

[724] *The Collected Works of Abraham Lincoln*, Roy P. Basler, p 501

Bibliography

Fell, Jesse W., Abraham Lincoln, Autobiography 1858-1860, Chester County (Pa.) Times, February 11, 1860.

Altemus, Henry, The Story Life of Young Abraham Lincoln, Philadelphia, 1915

Ashe, Samuel A., A Southern View of the Invasion of the Southern States and War of 1861-65, Raleigh, North Carolina, The Ruffin Flag Company, 1938

Atkinson, Elenor, The Boyhood of Lincoln, New York, McClure and Co. 1908

Basler, Roy P. Collected Works of Abraham Lincoln, New Brunswick, N.J.: Rutgers University Press, 1953

Bibb, Henry, The Life and Adventrues of Henry Bibb, Wisconsin, University of Wisconsin, 2000

Carpenter, F.B., Carpenter's Six Months at the White House. The Atlantic Monthly, vol. 18, issue 109 (November 1866).

Civil War Website West Virginia,
http://www.wvcivilwar.com/

Dew, Charles, B., <u>Apostles of Disunion,</u> Charlottesville and London, University Press of Virginia, 2001

Donald, David Herbert, <u>Lincoln</u>, New York, A Touchstone Book Published by Simon & Schuster, 1995

Freiling, Thomas, <u>Abraham Lincoln's Daily Treasure</u>, Grand Rapids, Michigan, Fleming H. Revell, A Division of Baker Book House Co., 2002

Goodwin, Doris, Kearns, <u>Team of Rivals,</u> New York, Simon & Schuster, 2005

Gross, Anthony, Editor, <u>The Wit and Wisdom of Abraham Lincoln</u>, New York, Barnes & Noble Books, 1994

Guelzo, Allen C., <u>Abraham Lincoln, the Redeemer President, Wm. B. Eerdmans Publishing</u>, 2002

Hapgood, Norman, <u>Abraham Lincoln, The Man of the People</u>, New York, THE MACMILLAN COMPANY, 1899

Hill, John Wesley, D.D., LL.D <u>Abraham Lincoln—Man of God</u>, New York and London, G.P. Putnam's Sons, the Knickerbocker Press, 1920

<u>The Holy Bible</u>

Humes, James C, <u>The Wit and Wisdom of Abraham Lincoln,</u> New York, Gramercy Books, 1996

Kunhardt, Philip B. Jr and Philip B. Kunhardt, III, Peter W. Kunhardt, <u>Lincoln: An Illustrated Biography</u>, New York, Alfred A. Knopf, 1992

Lamon, Ward Hill, <u>Recollections of Abraham Lincoln,</u> Chicago, A.C. McClurg and Company, 1895

Mansch, Larry D., <u>Abraham Lincoln, President Elect,</u> Jefferson, North Carolina, McFarland, 2005

Miller, William Lee, <u>Lincoln's Virtues</u>, New York, Vintage Books, 2002

Oates, Stephen B., <u>Abraham Lincoln, the Man Behind the Myths,</u> New York, HarperCollins Publishers, 1984

Oates, Stephen B., <u>With Malice Toward None, A Life of Abraham Lincoln</u>, New York, Harper & Row Publishers, 1977

Ostendendorf, Lloyd, <u>Abraham Lincoln the Boy the Man,</u> Springfield, Hy Steirman, 1968

Phillips, Donald T., <u>Lincoln on Leadership,</u> New York, NY, Warner Books, Inc., 1992

Sandburg, Carl, <u>Abraham Lincoln The Prairie Years</u>, New York, <u>Harcourt, Brace & World</u>, 1926

Swanson, James, L., <u>Manhunt,</u> USA, Harper Collins Publishers, 2002

Thomas Benjamin P. <u>Abraham Lincoln,</u> New York, <u>Alfred Knopf</u>, 1952

Thomas Benjamin P. <u>Lincoln's New Salem,</u> Carbondale, Illinois, Southern Illinois University Press, 1954

Thomson, Jack, <u>Charleston at War,</u> Gettysburg, PA, Thomas Publications, 2000

Ward, Geoffrey C., Ric Burns, Ken Burns, <u>The Civil War, an Illustrated History,</u> New York, Geographica, Inc., 2007

Whipple, Wayne, <u>The Story Life of Abraham Lincoln</u>, Philadelphia, The John C. Winston Company, 1908

White, Charles, T., <u>Lincoln the Comforter,</u> Hancock, NY, Privately printed, 1916

White, Ronald C., <u>The Eloquent President</u>, New York, Random House, 2005

William E. Barton, <u>The Soul of Lincoln,</u> Urbana and Chicago, University of Illinois Press, 1920

Wilcox, Arthur and Warren Ripley, <u>The Civil War at Charleston</u>, South Carolina, The Post and Courier, 1966

Winik, Jay, <u>April 1865, The Month that Saved America,</u> New York, Harper Collins Publishers, 2001

Wolf, William J., <u>The Almost Chosen People</u> Garden City, New York, Doubleday & Company, Inc., 1959

Woodward, C., Vann, <u>Mary Chesnut's Civil War,</u> New Haven and London, Yale University Press, 1981

About the Author

Having spent more than two decades guiding thousands of individuals and organizations in the process of reaching their highest potential, Ron L. Andersen is an operations officer for a global organization and has shared his expertise throughout the United States and Latin America.

Ron holds a bachelor's degree in psychology and a master's of education degree in guidance and counseling. He has conducted extensive research on the admirable life and character traits of Abraham Lincoln and founded the Lincoln Leadership Society. This organization is dedicated to perpetuating Lincoln's remarkable principles of conduct by highlighting values still relevant to us today that will benefit our families, our careers and our communities.

He is a member of the Foundation for the National Archives, The Illinois Historic Preservation Agency, the Abraham Lincoln Bicentennial Commission of Utah, the Abraham Lincoln Association, and the Abraham Lincoln Presidential Library Foundation.